NO HARD FEELINGS

Mike M3 Mcneill

NO HARD FEELINGS

CONTENTS

CHAPTER ONE

I learned at a very young age how alcohol can destroy a person and a family…you see this is exactly what it did to my father and our family. I remember clearly the day the police came and arrested him for domestic violence. We never really bounced back from that. I took it very hard but my sister, Bernice, did not let it get to her the same way as she was not his biological daughter. Either way, our family dynamic was forever altered.

We were staying on Groveland Street in Mattapan back in those days. I guess you could say we were considered to be "middle class" but the reality was we were just getting by. Once my mom finally put my father out, things got pretty tight for a little while. Fortunately, Polaroid was a large and growing company that was hiring minorities around this time. A lot of folks wanted these jobs because it meant hopefully having employment until you retired. My mom was lucky enough to be hired so things got a little easier at the house even with my pops gone.

I did miss my dad but it was good to see my mom being independent and making her own money. It was also nice not having to witness my pop's drunken rants and abuse; things at home were stable now. My mom was meeting a lot of new friends along with working with my Aunt Jean whom I loved dearly. My Aunt Jean was a thick-handed woman with a very strong personality but a good heart. I could tell she filled a motherly void that my mom was missing since the passing of my grandmother, who died from domestic violence herself. It was evident that my Aunt Jean loved me and my sister Bernice like we were her own kids by the things she did for us, and although my mom is my mom we still respected my Aunt Jean's word the same.

Bernice graduated from high school and my mother, though she wasn't divorced, started dating again. I was entering seventh grade and hyped up on the small reputation I had for getting girls and being down with a neighborhood gang up the street. By this time, I had plenty of home boys but there were two that stood out as my main friends, Gerard Twitty and Vidal Clark, whom was also known as vee. Vidal lived under different circumstances than Gerard and me. He lived in the projects and had an older brother and younger sister and quite a few cousins that lived in the bricks as well, they would come to be known as originally from the bricks. Since Jay and I came up differently we felt like we had to earn some type of acceptance. As far as I could see there weren't many drug dealers in the neighborhood at that time, or rather any that stood out besides Kenny Tee and Poopie. While walking up to the bricks to hang out with Vidal, me and Poopie became familiar with one another, then sort of instantly became friends. Me and Kenny's relationship was different. Kenny's younger brother was a friend of mine that I hung out with often, and seeing how he, as well as everybody else in the neighborhood looked up to Kenny it was easy for me to follow suit. Everything about Kenny impressed me, his dress style, his demeanor, and most of all how people spoke his name with respect despite him being a short dude without a muscular frame. Me being a small person myself I sort of started to mimic his ways in hopes of gaining that type of status.

My eighth grade school year was a pivotal one for me. I was no longer just getting girls' numbers; I was officially having sex. And on top of that, I had one of those fights where I could tell that I earned respect from my crew and was definitely being noticed.

At this time, my cousin Monica had enlisted in the Army. She spent her first tour in Korea and was over there for my July 10th birthday. She sent me a couple belts and hip pouches to start the school year off. To be honest, I didn't like them at first, though I was highly appreciative that she thought about me enough to send a gift. Up until this year, my mom would usually take me school shopping for some Lee jeans and corduroys. But this year was different since my cousin, Tony, told me to have my mother give me the money and he would take me. She was planning on spending $200 so she gave me that and we went to spend it. Tee drove a blue Audi and always wore the most up to date clothes. I wasn't dumb and knew he sold drugs but he kept that away from me and did not discuss it. He loved me like a little brother and wanted to protect me. We went shopping at stores I never knew existed and by the time we finished I had $200 worth of sneakers and more than $300 worth of clothes. Tee even gave me money for my pocket. That was a day I could never forget and would end up speaking on it for many years to come.

DAG, Dominating All Grounds, was the first name that we came up with for our crew of about seven but after we started to hang further down the street that changed to JC, Junior Corbett. A name that came from Boston's most violent street gang at that time, Corbett Street. I never asked but I believe my friend Bum came up with the name seeing that he lived and grew up off of Corbett and was the one that the original Corbett crew was familiar with the most. However, it didn't matter. I was just glad to be down and I knew I had to go even harder now to keep up with the little recognition I had earned while being in the bricks with Vidal.

My cousin Tony had started to let me hang out with him a lot more at this time. He hung at Four Corners in Dorchester, which was where I first met local rappers Ray Dog of RSO and B Chuck from the Body Rock and last but not least Tony McDonald. I was hyped off meeting Big Chuck and Ray Dog because of the music and some street stories. However, it was something about Tee McDonald that instantly stood out to me; he was short and was slim as I was, and he was always talking about something serious and I noticed that people took him seriously. Tony McDonald along with Derek Twitty, who I had met previously at my aunt's house were my cousin Tony's best friends. Neither of them rapped, nor did they identify themselves as being from a street gang, but I would often hear Tony McDonald and Derek say they were dope boys.

My first day of school came and I was hyped a Junior Corbett. I had a new style of dressing, I was now familiar to the older Corbett dudes, plus I knew Ray Dog and the rest of the people my cousin Tony introduced me to in Four Corners; shit, you couldn't tell me nothing, I was gassed. While in class I happened to pull out one of the pouches that my cousin Monica sent me from Korea, took a pencil out then laid it on the floor next to my book bag after my teacher finished explaining the day's assignment. She walked over, picked it up and analyzed it, then put it on my desk saying, "This is nice and I'm sure your parents would appreciate you just laying it on the floor after what they must have paid for it."

I said "thanks" and just continued my work. By the end of the day another teacher had mentioned my pouch, and then another, with the last one saying, "You're very fortunate, kid, for your parents to buy you Louis Vuitton."

Again, I just said thank you, not knowing what fortunate meant nor who or what Louis Vuitton was, but the compliments kept coming from teachers, letting me know this was rare for a kid from a broken family to have this, and I instantly fell in love with it, to the point where brown became my favorite color. I wanted everything to match my pouch and belts.

Roller-skating was in style at the time and Chez Vous was the place to be; I was a decent skater but mostly we would go to see girls and represent JC with the rest of the crew. JC had expanded; we went from seven of us to seventeen. Dre Davis, Rat Neck, Bam and Terrence Jones were the main ones to stand out from the extended crew. It was all love and we all respected each other the same. Within a month we had to have jumped or stabbed over 20 people; everyone was doing violent acts in order to gain rank within the crew. That's just how it was and still is, the more work you put in the more recognition you got. My name stood out not only because it sounded white, but from how people said my name. Michael McNeill did this, Michael McNeill did that. Even when dudes started to accumulate nicknames, I'd still be called Michael McNeill, always expressed by my first and last name and at the time I loved it.

Over the next few months the Vous became less about girls and more about meeting there to see whatever person you and your crew may have had a problem with. Fights started to happen more often than not; even though guns weren't big yet, two kids our age got shot after leaving the Vous one night. Castlegate and Grove Hall were one of the first places in Boston to sell crack. They had crack back when it was sold in crack vials. It was no secret to me that they were making money. Every time I saw little Greg, little Adrienne and Dexter at Chez Vous I had to take a sec to check out what they were wearing because it was always usually something exclusive like that Louis Vuitton stuff my cousin Monica sent me from Korea.

One night me and Vee arrived at the skating rink a little later than the rest of Junior Corbett and stopped at that corner store across the street to get gum before we went in. I came out first and before my feet left the doorway of the store vee tapped me on my shoulder and said look to your right. I looked and saw a group of dudes heading our way walking looking upset. Once they approached me saying, "What's up now?" I just started swinging. The Jamaican owner of the store pulled Vee in and locked his door to prevent them from coming in an tearing up his store. Granted, the jumping didn't last long, I wound up getting stabbed three times in the back and once in the forehead, by the time the police and ambulance came people from the skating rink had got word and started to come out to see who got stabbed along with a couple of females screaming and crying. I could hear one of the older dudes from Corbett Spider D yelling, "He's a dog, he going to be all right, he's a dog this nigger over here said he saw it and that Mike was going for his like a dog."

By the time my mom was notified and arrived at the hospital several people from the skating rink came to the hospital to check on me. The stab wounds were small, nothing that a few stitches would not heal but the mental part of it all was a big part of me becoming who I was soon to become.

After a few days I was cleared to leave and go on my way from the hospital. The nurse on staff that night asked me if I was some sort of celebrity or something. I said, "No, why you ask that?"

She said, "Because I've never seen that many people in the lobby at one time for one person."

Not knowing what to say, I just smiled.

She said in farewell, "Be careful and take care of yourself."

My cousin Tony came to the hospital but didn't say much; but it was all in his face that he was upset. During the first hour of me being home, Tony, Derek and Tony McDonald came to the crib to see me. My cousin Tony was basically asking me what happened and who did it while Tony McDonald lifted his shirt and showed me his pistol and said, "Someone need to go for that, lil man."

I was still feeling self-conscious about my scars; thinking that it was about to be hard for me to get pussy with this on my forehead. It did feel good to know that Spider from Corbett was out here calling me a dog and that my cousin Tee and his boys were ready to ride for me. Shortly after the incident

Me and McDonald started getting close. I would go by his house just to hear him talk. I took his words like lessons on how to be a gangster. I noticed the difference on how niggas around Morton did shit from how a dope boy did it. Corbett was about maintaining respect and reputation while tony an them was about money and correcting anyone that disrespected them. I knew who stabbed me and why but I still didn't tell my cousin or his friends because I felt this was my personal issue that I wanted to handle on my own one day, and I had the scar on my face to reassure that no matter how long it took, at that moment I was just focused on the growth that came along with the situation; I could feel my time coming! Seeing that me and Tony McDonald were about the same size, every time I left his house he would let me take something out of his clothes closet to keep: hundred dollar bike shirts, all types of Adidas sneakers, Jamaican style clocks, polo rugbies. If it was in there I had it. He started treating me like my cousin Tony did. I definitely felt the love.

One day I called McDonald and asked if I could come over. He said, "Yeah, yeah, hurry up. I want to speak with you anyway."

Curious what he wanted to talk about, I caught a cab to his house with $20 of the same money he gave me a few days ago. Once I got there I could easily see he wasn't himself, but I respected him too much to speak on it so I just asked, "was good."

He replied, "Some paper. I want you to come out to Chelsea with me so I can sell the rest of this dope so that I can get the re-up right."

I said, "Let's go," kind of curious why he didn't call my cousin Tony or Derek but either way I was down. The cab came and we were off. Once we got there he gave me 20 more dollars and pointed to a sub shop where he wanted me to eat and chill and play video games, basically just hold a brick of dope while he sold it by bags and bundles.

Things were flowing smoothly for about the first half hour. He came in twice and I handed him the work like he instructed me. I had my back to the corner playing Pac-Man but I could see the chef pointing to me through the reflection off the game. I looked up and saw two plainclothes officers. One asked me my name then asked the sub shop owner if he minded them taking me in the back to search me. That's when they found three bundles. Before arresting me they said they knew the drugs weren't mine and said if I told them it was Tony's they'd let me go. I said I don't know Tony. They called me stupid and put the cuffs on me. While pulling off in the cruiser, me and Tony made eye contact. I smiled. Seeing that this was my first arrest, he nodded his head and I could read his lips saying "you know I got you." This happened on a Friday. However, even though they said it would probably be no bail required, my mother wasn't able to come get me until Monday so I spent the weekend in DYS.

Upon my release I heard more yelling from my cousin Tony than I did from my mother. In the back of my mind I wanted to tell Tony what I was about to do but I knew he would have said and I felt like I owed Tony McDonald that after all that he'd done for me. So, at that point it was like, fuck it. All I could say to my cousin Tony was, "Yeah, you right, I should have talked to you first." Within two months I ended up getting six months' probation.

Now with being stabbed four times and getting arrested, my street credibility definitely went up. I started having sex with more girls and noticed that more dudes would go out of their way to get to know me. Granted, I didn't make any money selling drugs with Tee McDonald. I still got the feeling I was ready to start pumping on my own. Being that the majority of the new members of Junior Corbett were from Blue Hill Avenue and Deering Road, that became like our second home. Mattapan had caught on to the crack wave and fiends were everywhere. It wasn't long before me and Vidal started hustling for ourselves. If Deering Road was moving slow, me and Vidal would go hustle at the end of Theodore Street where a group of older dudes from my neighborhood had moved down to and started getting money. The main person getting money on Theodore at the time was an older dude we called Beefy. Me and Beefy were cool, he saw me with all the other younger dudes growing up in the neighborhood and seemed to like me, that's until one day we got into some words over me selling my crack on what he considered to be his block. Beefy was a big dude probably weighing about two-seventy to two-eighty at the time, and here I was at five six weighing no more than one-fifty. After a small exchange of words with him being pretty aggressive I walked off upset saying, "Ok, cool, be out here when I get back," insinuating that I was going to get a gun. My friend Bumpy had a twelve gauge shotgun, and granted I really didn't have any intentions of shooting Beefy, I wanted to go get it then come back with it to basically to show him that I wasn't going to tolerate him disrespecting me. While a little more than halfway to Bumpy's house I heard something fall down behind me. I looked back and it was Beefy jumping off of a bike with what appeared to be a twenty-five caliber handgun. I was shocked and nervous at the same time because even though I made that threat I knew that Beefy was a serious dude rumored to have shot people in the past. With anger in his eyes he asked me "WHAT THE FUCK YOU GOING TO GET!" I stood there speechless paying more attention to his pistol as opposed to what he was saying. While ranting he raised the pistol, pointing it in my face. Believing that he came to shoot me, I raised my hands up then asked him not to kill me. After giving me what seemed like a speech on how to be a gangster, he got back on his bike and took off.

My mind was in two places, part of me was relieved that I didn't get shot, while the other half was sucking up what he said about making threats. After that day I vowed to never tell someone what I'm going to do to them; if I'm going to do it, just do it. That definitely was a learning experience that I'd carry with me forever!

Back then a Dominican by the name of Santos was selling three grams of powder for $100, so I had to quickly learn how to cook. Deering Road would make about $1,500 a day but being split up by 10 people I would only bring in about $100 and something a day and wanted more. There were streets close by doing about $7,000 to $10,000 daily, like Wilcock, Theodore and the building on Norfolk Street, and knowing that really started to aggravate me.

I met with Vee one summer night and told him I had planned on robbing and shooting someone from one of those streets in order to lure their customers up to Deering Road. At the time I drove a gold colored Chevy Chevette with stolen plates for which I paid $300. We rode through one of the streets a few hours earlier just to check the scene,

We said what's up to everyone that was out there so that we didn't indicate that we were up to something.

Later that night around eight we parked on the next street over walked around the corner with guns and yelled, "Get down, don't move!" to dudes who took off running in between two houses. But the third kneeled down yelling, "Please, no, Mike McNeill, please!"

Vee pistol whipped him for yelling out my full name, then we took off running to the car. Once we were in the clear, we both busted out laughing at the fact that he still knew it was us while we were wearing masks.

Now over the last couple of years my cousin Tony had taken exception to the fact that I was fully in the streets plus things had started to go downwards for him and his boys. Derek had got murdered while Tony McDonald was on the run for a shooting, and as for my cousin Tony, though he didn't have a drug problem he still had checked into First Academy drug program in order to get less time for his drug conviction. My relationships with the people I met in Four Corners started to get strong, especially with Big Chuck and Ray Dog more so than with anybody else. Once Ray moved from Four Corners to Ashmont, I started going by his house discussing my newfound ambition to be a rapper. He would hear me out but I could tell by his response that he really didn't take me seriously, but it was cool because in the same way Tony McDonald used to give me clothes, Ray Dog would give me a couple things that dudes around the way didn't have. It was mostly jerseys and T-shirts he wasn't wearing anymore.

In ninth grade I was put out of Hyde Park High School for getting caught with the knife the same year Tony Hurston's cousin Rock came to live with his mother and his brother Sean. Rock was a bulky kid with a good heart but had a very serious persona for his age; he was a trustworthy person, and everybody that knew him felt the same. After being kicked out of HP, I ended up in English High School. That's where Rock ended up coming for his freshman year, but we were getting to know each other in the streets. The time we spent in high school was making us friends. It was also where we discussed that we both had dreams of being rappers. Jermaine Spencer also went to English at the time and also had ambitions of being a rap artist; he was a bit more seasoned than me and Rock, seeing that he had done a couple shows and had some recording equipment in his basement. He invited me and Rock to come over to record and it was there we started our rap group, FOA or "Funky on Arrival".

I was maturing and just becoming a whole different person in general. Though I was still close to my own homeboys from JC, I had accumulated a few friends outside of them that I had grown to have love for like Calvin Murphy. Calvin and I met ninth grade in Hyde Park before I was kicked out for the year, and despite my school change, me and him still hung out. Calvin had a big family, three brothers, a little sister and a nice home with his parents still together and I admired that. We were together so much that his brothers started calling all of us brothers and his parents started calling me one of their sons and letting me know that I was welcome in their home. Calvin sold drugs on Norfolk one of the neighborhoods that was doing about $10,000 a day, and within days of us hanging out he made it to where I could pump out there.

At first not everyone agreed on me being out there especially with my rep of being from Junior Corbett, but after being around me for a few days and seeing how much love I had for Calvin they knew I wouldn't violate them on the strength of the respect I had for Calvin and it went the same way with my boys. Granted, Calvin had grown up with Sean Jenkins, one of the main dudes in our crew at the time. My boys liked him and accepted him the same; he was just cool like that. Ray Dog from RSO had a personal relationship with Tony Johnson. A lot of people considered Tony Johnson the leader of Corbett

Street, and at this time I started to see Ray Dog intertwine with the original Corbett Street members a lot more often; the same with Big Chuck, and though Big Chuck did not hang around our neighborhood as much it was well known that him and Tony Johnson were partners and were making a lot of money together.

By this time me, Rock and Jermaine started recording songs together and it was clear that Rock had an aggressive style of rap that stood out. His delivery was comparable to Ice Cube from NWA and while I was still trying to find my style. Jermaine had a way of flowing the beat, kinda like Big Daddy Kane and sounded dope doing it. RSO had seemed to be blowing up at this time; they had a hot album out and had been featured on the cover of a local up-and-coming magazine started b ay Jewish kid attending Harvard in Cambridge named David Mays. Shortly after the article came out I saw Ray Dog on Morton and was excited to tell him about my new group FOA. He smiled shaking my hand and saying, "That's what up, keep doing your thing, mizz," then reached in the glove compartment, pulled out a piece of paper and a pen and wrote down a number, saying, "Yo, call this number and tell him I told you to call and set up an appointment to be interviewed and perform live on the radio."

Happy as hell I said, "Good looking, dog." I couldn't' wait to tell Jermaine and Rock about what we were about to do. The streets had started to become more dangerous; shootings were happening more randomly and granted we did interview at the radio station where I had to meet Dave Mays for the first time, our rap group had taken a backseat to gang banging and drug selling, and although we were still tight and in contact with each other we all sort of took on our own agenda. Jermaine started hanging with his friends he grew up with on Greenwood Street more often while Rock started selling more drugs with his cousin Hurts on Wilson Street. As for me I was tampering with love for the first time. Toy Tavarious, a pretty Cape Verdean girl with long hair, nice titties and thick hips. Although she had a couple boyfriends before me, she told me she was still a virgin and I believed her because of how tight she was when we first had sex. That alone had me open and wanting to keep her around forever.

My friend Calvin just got caught with a AK-47 and a .22 revolver, so with him being gone the mood changed when I came to the hustle around Norfolk, plus with Wilson pumping down the street it had slowed down a lot. So, I just stopped going around there period. There were rumors floating in the neighborhood that Rock had shot a couple of people, and on top of making money he was now wearing some big flashy jewelry; it became noticeable that his street recognition had grown. I started to feel a certain way. It was like I was stagnating. I was still hustling, just not taking it to the next level. Being that neither my father nor my sister's father was around I took it upon myself to look over my sister in a fatherly way even though she was older. Any guy came to the house to see her I would let my presence be known in a way that they knew I that I didn't appreciate them being here. Me and her would often argue about it but that didn't lure me from doing what I felt like I was supposed to do, till I met one that fit my standard of approval. Then came Keith Patterson, a slim, pretty smooth guy who worked at Mass General Hospital with my Aunt Jean. My Aunt Jean often spoke of him as being responsible and respectable, so this was the first guy my sister dated that I didn't feel the need to try to intimidate. As their relationship grew so did me an Keith's; he took me to his neighborhood where I met his cousin Kenny and his two best friends Corey and Darrel. We clicked instantly to where we would call ourselves family. It took me no time to realize Keith was up to more than just working at Mass General, from the fancy Alpha Milano, custom-made jackets and jewelry, I knew he was hustling at a pace that I had never seen anyone do. His job was a front he used to keep the heat off of him and once I realized that I saw that as one of the smartest things I had seen a street nigga do. Throughout all of these new things I was experiencing I was still writing my raps.

I hadn't heard from Jermaine in like a year and Rock started to take his music to another level; Ray Dog was hanging around my neighborhood every day by this time and had got wind of Rock's music and immediately put them in RSO. Though I was happy for Rock on one hand, I was sad for me on the other; I felt left out seeing that I'd known Ray Dog first. He never gave me that opportunity; it was like the first time I really learned that friendship is friendship and business is business. After hearing the first song Rock recorded with RSO, "Shoot a Mother Fucker," in a minute it was evident that Rock had natural talent and deserved to be put in that position Ray Dog put him in. Rock being the true friend he was he said to me, "Don't worry, Mizz, just keep writing and when I blow I'm going to see to it you're next." That made me feel good because the type of person he was I knew he meant it. From that moment there I started to step my rap game up .

Things between me and Toy started to fall apart. She started going to clubs that we both were too young to get into by using someone else's ID. Everything became an argument: out of the blue she started to act as if she didn't love me anymore, then that day came when she called and said we should break up. In the back of my mind I knew she had met someone else, but I still begged her for a chance to fix whatever it was that was wrong, but by her response it was evident that she'd been gone well before she officially cut things off between us.

A couple of months went by since we broke up and I hadn't heard from her at all, but I had started to hear rumors about her being with some dude that drives a 190 Mercedes-Benz. I called and asked her about it all she said was "Why?!" with an angry tone and hung up, which verified to me that it was true.

Nothing seemed to be going right for me at this time and I wasn't making money. Ray Dog seemed to be overlooking the fact that I could rap. On top of that I lost my girl to someone with a Mercedes; that alone had me jealous and I hadn't even seen who he was. Just the fact that he had a Mercedes made me feel like a loser.

Dudley Station was the place to be every Friday and Saturday night; it was where a lot of crews and females went and hung out, after two o'clock the money getters would come through showing off their cars, jewelry and clothes while chicks looking good after the club were seeing who was getting money. One night me, Hearst, Rock and Shep were out chilling parked at Ugies, while leaning up against Shep's car. It was as if I could feel someone looking at me under dark black tinted windows as a pretty royal blue 190e Benz rolled by, and there was Toy riding in the front seat with Corey, who I met a few years ago through Keith Patterson, my sister's ex-boyfriend. Me being immature and still in love with Toy instantly got upset and felt disrespected. I went from bringing my gun out of the house when I thought I might need it to carrying it every day, intending on doing something to Corey over Toy. Although my friends were willing to ride with me on mostly anything, no one was with me shooting someone over a girl, not even Vee and Gerard who usually were down with whatever I wanted to do. It just wasn't cool.

One night after leaving a KRS one performance at Channel night club with Ace, strapped with a Browning nine, I had him unknowingly drive me to where I thought Corey might be by telling him I needed to see someone about something. Upon arrival we were swarmed by police not knowing that about 20 minutes earlier this older dude I knew from my cousin Tony named Ceilly and his crew from Columbia Point had gotten arrested for a retaliation shooting around there. Once we were searched, I told the police that Ace didn't know I had the gun. They were familiar with Ace and still locked him up anyway. Once we were in the paddy wagon I told Ace that he didn't have anything to worry about because I was taking responsibility for the gun. I could see in his face he was relieved as he said, "I feel you, that's some real shit."

After Ace's second court appearance the judge dismissed the case on him seeing that I constantly said that he didn't know I had the gun. As for me, I went on to do time after losing the legal search and seizure motion.

My first full day in prison was like something you see in the movies. The first person I saw that I knew was Little Deek from Forest Street. Once we caught each other's attention we smiled, laughed, slapped five, and gave a brief hug before going into more serious issues. He said, "Yo, you know that Mike Barton is here, right?"

Although that name did ring a bell at that moment, I couldn't remember where I'd heard it so I asked who he was. Deek replied, "He's one of those guys that had something to do with Tony Johnson passing, so watch yourself and be careful."

I said, "All right, cool, you too," as we shook hands one more time before he went his way and I headed back to the J building which was the intake section of the jail.

Once I got back to my cell I barely spoke to my roommate other than saying "what's up" after he stuck his hand out to give me five. My mind was running too many places at once. For one, this was my first time doing time, which was already exhausting and, two, I was thinking about what Deek said and wondered why he felt the need to tell me about this Mike Barton dude. Feeling a little stressed, I dozed off into a nap for a couple of hours until I was awakened by the doors opening and an officer yelling, "Chow time, chow time!"

Like everyone else I got up, put on my state jacket and got in line to walk to chow. Within minutes I was approached by a muscular person that stood about 6'1" or 6'2" weighing about 270 asking me if I knew who he was. I couldn't recall ever seeing him before; I figured this must be the person named Mike Barton that Deek warned me of. At the time I was weighing about 145 and was a bit nervous, but I knew the importance of never showing fear so I just said, "No. Why, should I?"

He stared at me for a second as if he was going to throw a punch, then just turned around and walked to the front of the line mumbling something I couldn't hear but I could tell by his actions that our conversation was far from over.

It's rec time in the prison; the jail had a gym that had two floors, a basketball court on the top floor and a weight room environment on the bottom. Once entering, inmates had 15 minutes to choose where they wanted to be before officers locked the doors separating the two. On this day being my first, I chose to sit up top and chill sort of just feeling things out, plus I had that nigga Mike Barton on my mind because I knew that conversation wasn't over, and then he came standing in the doorway looking around like he was trying to find someone. As soon as we made eye contact he waved his hand to me as to signal me to come downstairs, so I did. Still a little nervous, but I knew I had to go to face him; an whatever it was that he wanted to do downstairs. Once we got to the lower part of the gym I followed him to a table that was on the blind side of the gym. The first question he asked me was, "Are you Mike McNeill from Corbett Street?"

Now me already knowing the situation figured once I said yes we were immediately going to start fighting. Even knowing I didn't have a win, I knew I couldn't take a short, so I braced myself looking him in the eyes and said, "Yeah. Why, what's up?"

Without answering me he asked, "Do you know who I am?"

I said no even though I did, then he said, "I'm Mike Barton. Now you know me?"

I took a deep breath and said yeah, still expecting some type of violent gesture. Instead, he gave me like a little grin, then asked me, "Where did you hear my name from?"

By this time I had sensed that he didn't want to fight me, but was more concerned with what the streets and people on my side were saying about his participation in the situation. So that's when I said. "Yes, I remember your name, you're one of the people that had something to do with Tony Johnson passing."

The look on his face went from a grin to a more shameful look as he began to go more in depth about what really happened. Mike Barton could easily beat me up; there was nothing I could have physically done to him at the time, but instead it seemed like he wanted to be heard and after a good 40 minutes of hearing him out, it seemed like we instantly became cool.

For the next couple of months before he was shipped out he shared various things about doing time and working out I didn't know, plus, we boxed and trained often which helped me become more confident with my hands. I must admit that even under the circumstances we became homies.

Months passed now and I was still working out; my body had made minor changes so my confidence was up. By this time Mike Barton had been classified and shipped out. The prison had begun to change. The faces changed, more younger people started coming in that I was familiar with from the street. Even though they weren't from my neighborhood, the fact that we were all young and upstate for the first time we became tight. It was a good seven of us that stuck together from the mess hall to the rec yard, and I could tell that from sharing this moment in our lives that we would always be friends. The morning came when it was time for me to leave. I was woken up by a CO telling me to "pack it up, because you're leaving after breakfast." Granted, I was comfortable being with my new jailhouse friends. Of course I knew there would be a time we'd split and I would be off to hold my own once again on this five year sentence. On my way out I hugged, and gave five to everyone I had become tight with before walking to the transportation pod.

Once arriving at the new prison, I started having some of the same feelings I had when I first got to the last prison, though my face looked mean I was curious what lay ahead and if I would have another Mike Barton type encounter. The cells seemed a little smaller but the environment was the same, over the last few months I learned all of the prison ethics, basically give respect and you get respect but if someone comes at you sideways you straighten it, period.

While entering my new cell I was relieved to see that my cellmate was someone close to me in size, so that if there was an altercation at least it would be a fair fight. Once we spoke and shook hands the air was cleared, I sort of knew immediately that we would click or at least be able to live cordially while I'm here for the remainder of my time.

Our relationship went from not knowing one another to becoming friends fast. After we started talking, we realized that we had a lot of friends in common on the streets. He knew and had hung out with a few people from around my way, so he had said in several conversations. Although I did feel like he was telling the truth I still called my boy teddy to see what he knew about him seeing that teddy was one of the main people whom he said he knew. Once Teddy confirmed that they were cool, I figured that if there was anyone in there that I would trust it would be him. Over the next few months of being cellmates me and Eddie became really cool, with him being two years younger than me, I sort of started looking out for him like a lil brother. Another thing we had in common was that we both knew that once we got out of prison" we wanted to focus more on getting money as opposed to just indulging in gang violence. Our release dates were close to each other, with me getting out first, five months earlier than him.

CHAPTER TWO

By the time it was time for me to be released, I considered me and Eddie to be real friends, I couldn't wait for him to get out so that I could introduce him to Vidal, Calvin and the rest of my crew that he didn't know. We had plans on hooking up on the streets and I knew that we would because the bond was just that tight, being cellmates with someone watching each other's backs has a way of making you all like brothers. When I was released my mind was focused on the main thing me and Eddie spoke about, which was getting money. I could have easily got an eight ball and hit the block, but after doing time I had a chip on my shoulder and felt like I was bigger than that and should be doing some bigger things.

At the time one of my older dudes from Corbett named Michelet let me know that he was doing really well for himself selling weight. Seeing him ride through and drop off work gave me a sense of how I wanted to do things, and I knew in order to get to the top I had to start from the bottom, so I asked him if I could work with him selling weight so that I could learn the game. At first he just smiled, till I said, "I'm serious, I'm trying to get my clientele up so I can do my own thing." He shook his head walking towards his car telling me to come and jump in so we can talk. We rode for like two hours while he asked me questions like who can I serve and where can I hold some coke; by the time he brought me to my crib I had an ounce in a plastic bag bagged up in all balls and a new beeper. I felt like the man that quick. It took no time for me to get my name up, the coke was good and I knew damn near everyone on the ave that was selling crack. Within days I was selling anywhere from 10 to 16 balls a day, and that was without having my own car. I trusted Michelet and appreciated the position he was putting me in, so we came to an agreement: I would sell the work, only taking out money to get through the day while he saved up, and once we reached a certain point he would give me my own, and I would go out on my own, then buy my own weight from him. We started to spend money together on some things like clothes and restaurants and a couple of cars, which obviously put my plans on going solo back a bit, but I was cool with it for the moment seeing that I was driving now and looking fresh. People started talking about me saying, "Mike's getting money," plus I had my first car, a Volkswagen Fox, with white alloy wheels and tan interior. My head was blown and nobody could nobody tell me shit, it didn't matter to me at the time that he held the money.

A couple of months passed by and I get a call at Mom's house saying, "What's up, bro, it's Eddie. I'm home early from good time." We both could do nothing but laugh being so happy to hear from one another. It felt good to tell him about what I'd been up to while telling him I was about to put him on.

A little later that day I went by his mother's house to see him, feeling welcome as his mother said hi after I spoke, saying, "Eddie has been talking about you and the two of you being friends." It took Eddie no time to start hustling.

Days after the meeting at his mother's house he called me with his plan, he said he was going to start pumping downtown, saying that he just needed a little something to get started. Although I didn't agree with this plan seeing that it was major hot downtown and I didn't want to see him get locked up, I respected his mind and knew he was as focused on getting money as I was so I gave him an eight ball to get started. The next morning he called me saying, "Bring three of them, it's rocking down here." After serving him the three, within four to five days he called back giggling like, "What up, Mizz, come by Mom's with a half."

In my mind I was thinking, *damn, even though I'm selling weight I still ain't getting it like Eddie, especially with the arrangement I have with Michelet.* This was the beginning of me feeling as though I was doing too much, not getting enough money and could do better on my own. Though Eddie and I were still close, we were both chasing money to much to really have time to just hang out, even when I'd go downtown to serve him we would just shake hands, hang for a brief second, say a word or two and keep moving because he usually had someone with him. Seeing Eddie prosper opened my eyes and put a dent in me and Michelet's relationship. I was no longer cool with him holding and building the money. I wanted mine in a stash that only I could touch. Seeing that we just re-upped, I told Michelet that after we finish this package, I was ready for him to give me mine, whatever that may be, so that I could start making my own moves.

Within the next week between Eddie and his boys and my customers on the Avenue, I had to have sold at least 8 to 9 ounces, I had $1,300 and two balls left when Michelette called me sounding hysterical like something was wrong. He spoke with a deep Haitian accent so when he's hyper or yelling I could barely understand him, all I could really understand was come by princess house. Princess was his girlfriend at the time but me and her were pretty cool before they got together seeing that I used to mess with her sister a little while back. Once I got to Princess's house and walked up the stairs I noticed that the door had seemed two have been kicked in. Once I walked in there were clothes and boxes of items scattered everywhere. Michelette looked at me and said, "I can't believe this shit; somebody broke in the crib and took everything."

I stood there quiet for about a minute trying to absorb everything, I could tell by his actions and how he was moving that he was lying, but the look I got from Princess when we caught eye contact was what really told it all. It was as if she felt bad and didn't want anything to do with it.

I was mad as fuck but not able to prove anything at that moment, so I just said a few words then left. Not only did I just lose someone I thought was a friend, I also lost my connection because I knew we were through dealing with one another after that. I called Eddie and told him that I had two balls left, seeing if he wanted them. He said no, he'd just bought an ounce for a cheaper price than I sold him last week. His swagger had changed over the last month, even though he was still cool, I could hear he was starting to build more confidence, especially after I told him what happened between me and Michelet, He said, "Man, Mizz, fuck trying to sell weight anyways, bag them two balls up in dimes and come downtown and sell them for 20s." Although I appreciated the invitation and could definitely see how he was coming up, I still had something in me that wanted me to come up my way, on my own; plus, being on parole I wanted to make paper but take less risk until I was off, and although downtown was pumping it was hot.

A couple months passed and I hadn't heard from Michelet since the staged robbery, I had spent the majority of the money I had left over from hustling with him, though I was selling a few 50s here and a few 50s there, I was basically just staying above water. By this time my boy Calvin had come home on probation. Once we got up it was just like old times, things hadn't changed a bit. Norfolk was making a couple dollars but it was far from the $10,000 days it used to, plus the police had taken notice of the way we used to hustle in the hallway and had gotten a key from management which made it hard to get money. Basically, it wasn't worth it plus Calvin was telling me stories he had heard about all the money that was getting made downtown by the pimps and how dudes were getting triple the amount of money on their packaging down there. Seeing that I hadn't heard from Eddie in a while, once Calvin mentioned downtown I immediately thought of him seeing that that was where he started hustling as soon as he came home so I called him. I could hear it in his voice; he was happy to hear from me saying, "What's up, Mizz, what's good with you?"

We spoke for like two minutes before him asking where I was so that he could come check me. I said, "Mom's."

He said, "Cool, I'll be there in a min." Later, I heard a horn blowing outside and went to the door; it was Eddie, and his friend Keith sitting in a silver and black Audi that looked clean, damn near new. Eddie got out, we shook hands and hugged before he said, "Get in and check it out. I just bought it." In my mind I was thinking, *damn I've been bullshitting*, but at the same time I'm happy as hell for my nigga, especially knowing he just started from the bottom no longer than six to seven months ago. I was proud of him, he had money in his pocket, looking fresh and driving nice and still hadn't forgotten about our bond. He invited me to come get money with him, and seeing how he had come up I had no choice but to say hell yeah. Before he left my Mom's house, he told me that had nine ounces and remembered that I gave him his first package, and that he would give me anything I needed when I'm ready to get started. We laughed, hugged, then shook hands one more time. Before he left, I told him, "I'ma hit you up in a few, good-looking."

The whole time my focus was on trying to make money in the streets, my parole officer was on my back about me getting a job; he had made threats of sending me back before but this time when he came to my house for a visit I could tell he was serious, still I gave them the same story, I'd been trying to get a job but every time they run my CORI they won't hire me! It got to the point where he said he was going to help me get employed. I said, "Cool, thank you," just trying to buy myself some time seeing that I would get off parole in five months.

With Calvin being home and me having no intentions of getting a job, we started riding around making moves. Calvin and a pretty well-known dude named Ron had become friends, which seemed seem to fit seeing that me and Ron were cool form our mothers being friends and working together at Polaroid. Calvin knew some people in Brockton that were getting thousands, and we figured that would be a good spot for us to start getting money. However, still trying to move slow till my parole was over, I didn't go out there immediately. Within weeks, Calvin and Ron were out there getting money. Spring Street became the spot, I would come out there, flip a couple dollars and jet, just enough to keep money in my pocket until parole was done. But Calvin and Ron started making real progress, they even got a crackhead to give them the keys to his apartment so that they could hold their rottweiler and work there, basically having some type of foundation while they're getting it. Even though me and my man Calvin spoke daily, at this point a good month had passed since I saw him, basically he stopped coming to Boston period because the money was coming so fast out there. The same way Eddie had once told me to come downtown to hustle, Calvin was telling me to come back out to Brockton because it was rocking. One night Calvin called me seeming upset, which was rare seeing how smooth he was, so I knew something was wrong. I asked, "Are you straight?"

He said, "Yeah, yeah, yeah," not wanting to talk on the phone. He asked where I was so that he could come holla at me, and I told him at Mom's.

"Ok, I'm about to come through." When he came to me, Calvin was driving a Chevy Chevette with stolen plates. That's how we rode back then, we called it ghost riding. He had a small cut on his eyebrow, telling me some dude in Brockton hit him with a bottle and was acting tough because he was deep with some other dudes. I didn't need to hear why, the only thing I wanted to know was where could we find him; Calvin knew the nigga's address, I didn't want to just fuck the dude up, so I told Calvin to drive to my cousin Tony's house so that I could get Tony's 30/30 rifle, then we went to pick up Ron so he could ride with us. Ron was as mad as I was, that was the moment I knew he loved Calvin as much as I did. Seeing that I had the rifle, I played the back seat. Every corner we pulled up on was empty. It was as if the guy that did that to Calvin knew that Calvin was coming back to straighten what had happened.

Before leaving, Calvin wanted to try one more spot so we rode to the other side of Brockton where it was said that one of them lived. Soon as we pulled up there was a person in the driveway, by this time we were frustrated and ready to shoot anybody and leave. Calvin yelled out, "There's one of them right there!" That's when I stuck the rifle out the window to hear "click!" He looked at us and took off to the back of the house -- me being so anxious plus never shooting a rifle before, I forgot to load the shell in the chamber. I loaded it while getting out to chase him but once I got behind the house he was gone; he must have went inside the house. We all just laughed while heading back to the highway to come back to Boston, but at the same time we all agreed that it wasn't over, saying, "It's cool, we will definitely get with them niggas."

Coincidentally, at this time Calvin was dating Carol Brown, who was the sister of Bobby Brown, one of the singers from the New Edition and had been going out to Canton to see her for some time now and told me about Carol's girlfriend Mary Karr who he believed I might be interested in. I said fuck it, and rode out there with him one night to meet her. Me and Mary instantly hit it off. We laughed, ate Chinese food and drank while the whole time her and Carol constantly said I looked and acted like someone they knew but couldn't put their finger on it. The next day me and Calvin rolled back out there and in conversation I mentioned that my last name was McNeill. Mary and Carol both got very quiet for a moment as if I said something wrong, then Carol yelled out, "Oh shit!" asking me is my father's name Will, but they call him Mac?

At that moment I was shocked, now with a curious look on my face I asked, "How you know that?"

With a surprised look on her face she replied, "Your father's dating my mother and is at her house right now!"

Now me not hearing from or seeing my father in a few years, I wasn't all excited about seeing him but the fact that this type of coincidence could be happening did intrigue me. She grabbed her cell phone, calling her mother saying, "Ma, ask Mac if he has a son named Michael."

Still shocked as if she couldn't believe this was happening, Mrs. Brown already knowing about me just said, "Yes, why?"

Carol told her I was there at her apartment; they spoke for a moment, then Carol hung up saying, "Come on, let's go up the street to my mother's house."

The moment I walked in and saw my pops, the inner kid inside of me came out as I hugged him. Yes, I had questions and was still upset with him, but I loved him so much that at that moment I was just happy to be reacquainted with him. It was a pleasure to meet Mrs. Brown, she was very nice to me and very accepting from the moment we were introduced. I sat over there for about an hour or so catching up with Pops and getting to know her better. Pops was well dressed and kind of chubby like he'd been eating good; it was easy to see that he was being well taken care of and me knowing that he still had warrants out for his arrest for the incident with my mother, I knew he wasn't working.

Me and Pops took a walk and spoke about some things, but really didn't go deep into the past. He just stated that he missed me and my sister but had to get some things straightened out before he could come back around. Meaning with the law. Me being older now and not as emotional as I was when I was young, plus going through things myself, I could feel him and understood better. Once again, we hugged before I left, telling each other that we loved one another and promising to stay in touch. After saying bye to Mrs. Brown on my way out the door, she hugged me telling me that I am always welcome and to not call her Mrs. Brown anymore and to just call her Mom like her other kids, I appreciated that; it comforted me and most of all I appreciated how she was taking care of my father and that he was safe!

My parole officer was on me heavy now, he got tired of me saying I couldn't find a job and there were only three months left before I wrapped up, so he went out of his way to find me one. He called and gave me the name of the manager at Burger King in Mattapan Square, saying he's waiting for me to come fill out application, then I can start. I just said okay. This was on a Friday, so I spent the whole weekend thinking about what I was going to say to my PO on Monday, sort of figuring I was going back to jail because I just wasn't going to be flipping burgers.

After being a little stressed all weekend, Monday came and at about five in the morning my doorbell rang. It was my PO with the State Police officer coming to bring me back. He started to ask me questions on why I didn't go to the job, but at that point I knew I had to wrap up so I didn't answer, staring at him like *fuck you*. After being home on parole nine months, it was finally time to wrap up my bid, which I was cool with seeing that I was tired of having to answer to someone. Seeing that my time was so short and not mandatory, I was sent to a low security camp in Plymouth.

While pulling up in the van I saw a couple of familiar faces that I knew, one being Kevin Lucas from Humboldt and another being Ant Barton who was the nephew of Mike Barton, whom I had been cool with for some years now and actually hung out in the streets years before. Granted, Ant Barton was related to Mike Barton, with whom my older crew had problems. Me and Ant had been friends since kids, and even though he wasn't a part of Junior Corbett, he was one of those cool dudes just into girls and clothes, so it was easy for us to pick up where we left off in the streets. Time was easy there, nobody wanted problems; it was actually a nice place off up in the woods, they had picnic tables that you sit on and chill when your visit came. A beautiful pond to walk around and a cameraman to take pictures of you all at the end of your visit if you wanted that. The coolest thing about the camp was the outside food boxes. Every weekend your family could bring or mail you a box of canned goods and boxed food. My mother would send one up twice a month and on the other two weeks Mrs. Brown would send one. I had only seen Mrs. Brown twice before I got locked up, but she still was there for me when I was down; we would speak on the phone at least twice a month and when we did the conversations were the same as if I was talking to my own mother. It's fair to say that's where our relationship flourished, I knew officially she cared about me and I was going to consider her my stepmother, whether her and my father stayed together or not.

After about seven months into the year I was doing, my then girlfriend Linda sort of faded off and started doing her own thing. Mail and visits came less often, while Ant Barton was getting visits on the regular, he had two girls coming to see him on a frequent basis so I asked him to see if one of them could hook me up with a friend.

Within a couple days he told me his girl Donna was going to bring her friend Tameko up to see me this weekend when she comes up.

I replied, "Cool, cool, good-looking," as we laughed and made jokes about how I was going to be acting when they came.

Tameko was cool, she was single and I could tell by the look in her eyes she fell for me instantly. In my mind I didn't want no girlfriend because I knew once I got out I was going to be running the streets and fucking with all types of chicks, plus trying to get on my feet so having a relationship was the furthest thing from my mind.

But after the visit she immediately started doing things for me like sending money, buying clothes and sneakers, accepting phone calls, in a way it's like she made a decision that she wanted to be with me and was going to do that no matter what it took. For the last few months of my bid she didn't miss a visit and granted, I had my mom's house to go to, she was working on having it where I could come stay with her when I got out. So, subconsciously without it being said she became my girl. I stayed at her mother's house with her for a few days in a row as soon as I got out, but even though her mother was very nice to me I just felt like I needed to be at my mother's house till I got on my feet. On my third or fourth day of being home I called my father and Mrs. Brown to thank them for looking out for me on my bid, sounding excited and happy Mrs. Brown said, "You're welcome, baby, but listen, Bobby and Whitney are getting married and I want you there."

I didn't know what to say. I didn't have any dress shoes or a suit that could fit me seeing that I had gained a good thirty pounds. But before I could find the words to say, Mrs. Brown said, "Don't worry about nothing, we'll get you set up once we get there, just be ready to go once me and your father get there, ok?"

I said okay and packed the few things. Tameko brought me some underwear and I was ready. Once getting into New Jersey I felt kind of out of place but still went with the flow. Mrs. Brown didn't expect for me to be as big as I was and figured I could fit in one of the extra tuxedos and shoes that were at the hotel. The wedding had a color theme so it was important that everyone had on lavender and these were the only option left. I appreciated her too much to make anything seem complicated, so I squeezed into one of the outfits and made it work till the reception. Being at the wedding did something to me, seeing all the stars of that era in one room together gave me the incentive I needed to start taking my music more seriously. From that point there, I was sure what it was that I wanted to do with my life, So I thought. I was home the next day from an experience that I would never forget, but now it was time for reality to set back in. I was fresh out of jail and I had nothing and needed to figure shit out. I was over Tony Hurston's house and we were speaking briefly on the passing of his cousin Rock and how he was in the process of signing a solo deal with Tommy Boy records. Rock was killed in an altercation down at a nightclub while I was locked up. Even though I'd heard about Rock's passing when I was in jail, seeing the look on Tony Hurston's face as he spoke about it brought all the pain and memory of our relationship back. Rock wasn't just one of my boys, he was my friend. Once word got out that I was out and over at Tony Hurston's house, a few of the fellas came through to check on me. While downing a few beers and having some general conversation, Tony Hurston told me about an African dude named Eddie that had been getting paper and had been asking for me. I was kind of tipsy at this point, so I really didn't care nor was I coherent enough for it to dawn on me who he was talking about, so it sort of went in one ear and out the other. My cousin Tony was doing pretty good for himself hustling with his boy Beefy, he had a new young girl named Tammy, and from how I saw it, things were going good. He introduced me to Tammy's mother who was older than me and Tony, but at the time was still looking good. Off the rip she was being flirtatious, which I liked, seeing that the only girl I fucked since I'd been home this time was Tameko, so all them hips and ass was looking good!! And I was being invited over the crib! It was easy to tell she wanted to fuck me and I wanted to fuck her more!

After having some of the best sex in my life at that time, we laid up conversation about something that fully had my attention. Pimping and hoeing. She told me about this pimp nigga named Derick that she was just with and how she used to go out, get money and bring it back to him, and though it sounded easy it just didn't seem like what I wanted to be doing at the moment. I figured that if it's meant for me, then it would come back around once I was at least somewhat situated, so I passed on the opportunity to have been chosen.

CHAPTER THREE

At home close to three weeks now, I was hungry. Poochie and George were two dudes I knew fairly well but didn't consider them friends. They had a crack house in Mattapan that was said to have been making thousands of dollars a day and I decided that I was going to go lay them down. I called Smacks and Og, who had already done time for drugs and a body knowing he was going to be down with it. I'd been in this crib with poochie and George before so I didn't think that they would expect anything of me stopping by, but by the look on George's face once he opened the door I could tell he expected something. Once George closed the door behind himself, I pulled the .357 out and fired a shot in the celling as a warning, yelling, "Go get me everything!" I didn't have any hard feeling towards them at all, I actually liked them, this was just business so I stated that as long as no one tried to bullshit me, no one was getting hurt. After taking whatever drugs and money we could find, me and Smack bounced to my cousin Tony's house to split up what 'lil bit of shit we took. It really wasn't much, but enough to get off empty.

Within a few days of the small money robbery, I was at Mom's house doing some push-ups, maintaining my size when I heard something sounding like loud mufflers outside. I looked out my room window but couldn't see anything; by the time I decided to go look out my living room window my doorbell rang twice.

Curious and sounding angry, I went to the door and yelled, "Hello, who that?"

A soft toned voice doing their best rendition of a polite person replied, "Hi, it's Eddie, is Mike home?"

I opened the door and instantly me and Eddie both just started laughing and slapping five before we hugged. The noise I was hearing was coming from him and his man's BMW's, a green five series that his man Turtle was driving and a brand new black three series that Eddie was driving. It was evident that Eddie had taken things to the next level. I totally forgot that Eddie was African, seeing how light skinned he was, but at that moment it dawned on me that this was who Tony Hurston was talking about when he said someone had been asking about me.

After chopping it up on my porch for like five minutes Eddie told me to come on and, "Let's take a ride, we going to get you some clothes." I locked the crib up and was ready! Turtle left his car at my house and we all left in Eddie's BMW. Shit was tight, brand-new inside. I had noticed Eddie had a little Rolex with diamonds on the bezel signifying that he had come a long way from selling Jums downtown. When he said "shopping" I figured we were going to Marshall's or Filene's to get me an outfit or maybe two, but we ended up downtown at Copley Plaza in stores I had never been in like Neiman Marcus. After looking at the price tag I picked up one shirt, and one pair of jeans, and then Eddie said "yo" with a grin on his face. "Go ahead and get some clothes, man. Fuck the price, get like five pair of jeans and five shirts." Once the cashier rang it up, it was over $1,000. After shopping, the conversation got more serious. We started talking business and formulating a plan so that I could eat with him. He told me that he had been seeing my crew out but was waiting on me to come home to do business with them, so that I could play the middle to certify everything went smooth.

Once we got back to my house Eddie gave me $300 for my pocket and said that he'd be back tomorrow with some work.

Not knowing what he was bringing, I just said, "Cool, good-looking fam. I appreciate you and I got you."

I'ma hold it down," he said. "I got you already, I'll see you tomorrow."

Early the next morning he came through like he said with 4 1/2 ounces of coke; I could tell it was good just by looking at it. The first person I wanted to see was Vidal so I could hit him with something to help him get right. Calvin was back in jail on a probation violation but still the first couple dollars I made I sent him a couple of dollars for his commissary. I wanted to give him a little sign that I was making moves.

Shit started flowing right, immediately I brought Eddie around the way to meet a couple of my friends he didn't know, and he ended up introducing me to his clique he was hustling with and paper was being made. Within the first month and a half I had $10,000 stacked, which was the most money I ever had in my life and was feeling myself.

Tameko ended up being more useful than I thought at the beginning, getting the rentals, plus holding and stashing the bulk of the packages I was getting. She even brought some customers to the table, she introduced me to Ant Barton's ex-girlfriend Donna's people that were hustling out of all three floors of a house on Greenwood Street. The same time my clientele was getting stronger, Ray Dog [Benzino] approached me about being a part of a rap group he was putting together. I still had dreams of being a star and I was still writing music from time to time, so I was like, "Hell yeah, let's do it!" But once he explained the theme of the group, and said it was going to be made up of a variety of rappers from the city, I was skeptical but still in all I respected Ray [Benzino] and knew the influence he had over source and figured if he's going to put his all into this it had potential to work, so I agreed.

After my first song with RSO, called "9:15" which was a tribute to my clique 915, my rap skills started to get noticed. Even with me hustling at a fast pace I still found time to write music and practice my craft, wanting to be a standout on this up and coming project we were working on. Plus, with the majority of my crew was helping build the label so I felt obligated to be one of the best if not the hottest. My cousin Tony and his girlfriend Tammy moved with her mother to an apartment on Franklin Hill Ave. By this time Tony was close to her family, especially Deno, Tammy wild cousin who never left the house without a pistol. Around this time Tony's cousin Sheldon had started coming back in forth into town, and although Sheldon was my second cousin we never viewed it like that; we were blood and that's all that mattered!

Sheldon had started coming back in town more often and was staying with his girlfriend Asia on Hardworthy Street, but the two of them were basically always together over at Tony and Tammy's house. Once I met Sheldon's girlfriend Asia, I started messing with her girlfriend Mia, her roommate at the time. It was beneficial for me, as I happened to meet a Dominican dude named Burto that sold coke and seemed to have it or have access to a lot of it. It wasn't long before I started coming through Tony and Tammy's house cooking up and passing out work. Me and Eddie's relationship was still good with no bumps in the road at this point, but I was getting bigger and felt like it was time to move on and get my own connect because regardless to how cool we were there was no way he was going to sit and let me become bigger than him on his watch. We were friends but competitive like that, and I respected it.

Burto's mother lived right across the street from Asia and Mia's place, so often I waited over there when waiting for him to drop off a package. I'm a generous person, so Asia and Mia knew that whenever I conducted business in their apartment I would leave a few dollars. One time I came over while waiting for Burto to bring me a half of a key, and the only person that was home was Asia. At first I thought nothing of it seeing that she was Sheldon's girl, but once she changed clothes putting on some tight shorts as if she wanted me to pay attention to her hips and ass, I was turned on even though I was feeling like I was in violation. Nothing happened between us that day, but after Burto brought me the half a key we stared in each other's eyes as if to say, "yeah, we fucking the next time the opportunity presents itself."

I was on a half a key now and had at least $1,500 in my stash. My clientele was getting crazy, every day I was moving at least $3,000 in eight balls and I felt like it was time to get a 'lil something to help me stand out! So, I went and financed a bright red Acura coupe that had chrome factory rims on it with a tan leather interior. It was hot for that era. Granted, things weren't right between me and Tameko, I still felt that she was a big part of why I was in the position I was in and felt that she deserved to be riding nice as well for all that she had been doing, so I went and got her an all-red Volkswagen Cabriolet with a black leather interior in it, then had "915" embroidered in red letters in the headrest. By this time me and Tameko moved out of her mother's house and into an apartment close to where I grew up on Morton Street, which I fully furnished with all-black leather furniture. Yet it started to be days on in before I saw her, because of me staying out sleeping with other women.

After buying the Acura, pussy started coming more rapidly. I was fucking Tammy's mother, one of Tammy's girlfriends and Sheldon's girlfriend Asia's roommate Mia along with Tameko whenever I came home, and now I'd met a female named Cynthia whom I was starting to spend most of my time with when I wasn't serving plays. Not only was I getting money but my skills as a rapper were starting to improve, it seemed like the more things I experienced in the game the more I had to write about, Ray Dog [Benzino] was over halfway through the album he was putting together and it seemed like on every track I got on I could do no wrong. My verses started to be so vivid that every time people knew that it was time for me to get on a track they would fill the studio knowing that I was going to up the ante from the last one. My style was being compared to my favorite artist Scarface but with my own twist, and the streets were starting to love it. Ray Dog [Benzino] did it big in the sense of promoting the album, flyers, posters even snippet tapes were being given out to people as a sample of what was coming out. At the time I was a movie on my own; not only was my name ringing from music and money making my violent rage started to take front and center when I started shooting niggas over money issues to the smallest things like verbal disrespect. Owing me money and moving my work slow was acceptable but owing me money and avoiding my calls just wasn't. One afternoon I rolled by Kingsdale Street where this nigga James who owed me a few dollars was hustling. I had called him several times the previous day to see what's up and got no answer. By this time I was heated and I didn't give a fuck about the money, so when I pulled up the only thing on my mind was punishment. With my cousin Sheldon driving, we pulled up on him and seeing that people were out there and it was broad daylight I just said, "Wassup, fam, jump in for second." The look on his face was like a kid knowing they're in trouble but at this time he knew there was nothing he could do but get in and let things play out.

Pulling off, I hadn't even asked about my money yet and he immediately started with a bunch of excuses on why he hadn't called me. Once Sheldon took the first left I pulled the pistol out turning my body halfway in the back seat and slapping him in the mouth with it. My intention was to make him get out, then shoot him wherever we pulled over. But before we could get to that point he jumped out of the back seat while the car was moving going at least 30 miles an hour. Sheldon stopped and closed the door. It was obvious he was hurt by the way he was laid out in the middle of the street, so we just left.

After getting out of Dodge, me and Sheldon looked at each other and started laughing. At that point I knew Sheldon was down for whatever by how composed he was in the middle of the situation. I highly respected my cousin Tony and trusted him so in my eyes he was my main man, the coke was cooked at his crib and id leave him with instructions on what to do with it once I was gone. These were the years before trap music in our city; no one was blatantly speaking on whipping coke and I was doing it, though me and Eddie weren't hustling together he still went out of his way to come show me how to turn a half a key into a whole one. That's just how we were, super competitive but still there for each other.

Once I stacked my first $100,000 I started sharing the secret or how I was stretching the coke with certain members of my crew. My home boys Bum and Wizz had been hustling with Bob Blan, this dude from around the way that had been getting money years before I started getting to it and was said to have plenty change. Bob also knew about stretching coke and had made hundreds of thousands moving coke from here to North Carolina, so Bum and Wizz were up on it but I'm not sure if they actually knew how to do it. I personally became good at even finding a less complicated way to do it than the way Eddie showed me. No matter what my day consisted of, rarely a day that went by that I didn't see the majority of my crew, if not the whole clique, seeing that we all hung at a local bar called Frank's Place on Morton Street. Frank's didn't serve food nor have the best music but even though we didn't own it, it was our spot, a spot where we could relax and have open conversation about money, drama, music, just anything that needed to be discussed. It was no secret that we frequented the place, so all the females that came there knew that they were basically for our picking. Having money has a way of empowering a person and it was known that I was getting mine, and even though years had passed and I was emotionally over my first love toy I became curious on how she looked at me now seeing that I was getting money and she had left me years before when I was broke for someone who was in the position I was in at that moment. I had my boy Sean Jenkins reach out to her through his baby's mother, Tara who is Toy's sister. Within an hour I got a call back and I could instantly hear a tone of respect in her voice that had to come from what she was hearing about me in the streets.

After talking with her for like twenty minutes, I realized that I might have certain feelings for her that just might be there forever whether we're together or not. Sex immediately came to my mind but I wanted more than a night at a hotel. I wanted a situation where I could have fun, be sexual and passionate and make love to her all at the same time, so I asked her to go skiing with me and she said yes she would love to go. We planned it, and we were off to a ski resort the week after we spoke. The trip was good for me; I got to get away from the game and still make money by leaving everything in Tony's hands. I got to see for the first time how he would hold shit down without me right in the mix of everything and it went well.

As for me and Toy, the trip was cool but emotionally I just wasn't there, in the back of my mind I kept saying to myself that if it wasn't for me having this new profound life and money she wouldn't be here, which kinda made me uncomfortable about the whole situation and really ready to leave after the first night. But I smiled and stuck it out seeing that I paid for it, the sex was good but the whole situation just didn't feel genuine. The whole point of me going was that for some strange reason I wanted her to see how I'd changed now that I had some change with hopes that she would regret leaving me when I was broke.

After the trip me and Toy spoke off and on but nothing serious. Although she didn't go out of her way to show it, I could tell she was feeling me again and was willing to be in a full relationship with me again if I was willing. But neither my mind nor my heart were there; the fact that she was expressing interest was satisfying enough for me so I just stopped the little bit of calling I was doing, as she did the same, to the point where our communication just stopped.

The vacation state of mind I was in was short-lived seeing that this nigga named Bing who owed $10,000 was saying he had some complications which I didn't give a fuck about nor wanted to hear. I just wanted my money. I went by Bing's house on Monday, aggressively expressing that he needed to have that for me by the end of the week because I was getting fed up with his excuses. He said okay and that if not all of it, he'd have more than half on Saturday. I said "cool" and left. At that time I was driving a rental minivan, and had Teddy Rux and Hakeem's younger brother Kari with me. No more than ten minutes after leaving his crib we noticed a Mustang with a white guy in it that seemed to be following us. I was driving and at that time didn't have a license. After taking a left turn then a right with them still behind us, it became evident that he was following us for sure. So, I figured okay, let me pull over so we all can get out and once we get back in I can let Kari drive seeing that he has a legitimate license. We pulled up at Harry the Greek's and went in. I purposely spent about 15 minutes buying some boots to try to shake them off but once we came out there he was parked right behind us waiting. I stared at him as I got in the van with Kari driving now.

Within the next five minutes we were being pulled over and swarmed by police, some in uniforms, some in suits and some detectives screaming, "Get out, get out with your hands up!" with their guns all drawn being overly aggressive as they pulled us out. After searching us and the van thoroughly, the head officer asked our names. Once I told him mine he replied, "Wow," with a funny smirk on his face, then continued by saying, "So you're Mike McNeill, huh? You're only about 150 pounds soaking wet and there's all this noise being made about you. I expected you to be much better."

I just sat quietly, unamused by his sarcasm. After staring in my face for another 5 to 10 seconds he said, "Well you all can go now. I just felt it was time for us to meet, and you will be seeing me again," with that same stupid grin.

With Kari driving we pulled off discussing how it had to be Bing snitching because he didn't have my paper. At that point I decided, fuck that money, I'm killing him for that. A decent portion of the money I was making was coming from Greenwood Street. Ant Barton's now ex-girlfriend Donna would collect the money from all three floors after making one big order a day instead of having me run back and forth.

Tameko and Donna were still friends but spoke less since the days of them coming up to Plymouth to visit me and Ant Barton in jail. Donna's Aunt Louise was a hell of a cook, her food was the closest thing I had tasted to my mother's in years, and seeing that she always offered me a plate when I came by, I started to make sure I had time to eat whenever it was time to go through there and serve the play.

After several months of doing business with Donna we built some chemistry; the first few times I would come over she would ask me about Tameko and how she was doing, but once she stopped asking about her I could tell she had become attracted to me. It wasn't long after that that I became cool with her brother Ducky and her cousin Mike, and just started fronting them work myself instead of waiting on them to call.

One day after eating some steak and rice downstairs at Louise's house I said to Donna, "Damn, you always looking good when I come over, wearing those sundresses as if you be wearing them for me."

She smiled while walking out of the kitchen saying, "Maybe I have been." That's when I knew she wanted to mess with me. I didn't say anything else to her besides bye when I was leaving, but I knew I was going to call her later that night to see if she wanted to come out.

My connect really liked my red Acura seeing that it was bright red. Even though he had the money to just go buy one he knew he couldn't just go buy a red one as well, so he offered me a kilo for mine. By this time I had ridden it for a few and put a few highway miles on it from riding up to New York tricking so I said, "Yeah, fuck it, let's do it."

Loyde was another person from my crew who was getting money at the time, he had a silver 325 BMW with white interior and alloy AC snitcher rims on it that I was in love with. I called him and told him, "Give me a price and I'll come buy it cash," seeing that I just got rid of the Acura.

First he said, "I'll think about it then get back to you." Within a couple of days he called me saying, "Give me 25," and I didn't hesitate. Even without touching the kilo I got for my Acura, I met him at his spot and got the car with the title. I had a few cars at that time, but the BMW was my favorite. When I used to ride to the clubs downtown on the weekend my nigga Calvin would call me on Mondays complimenting me on how I looked in the car. He was still locked up in South Bay but his cell faced the highway. I'd say "good looking" along with something else to reassure him that he was going to be straight once he got out, on top of keeping money on his books; he was my nigga like that back then.

After the police followed me from Bing's house I figured I wouldn't call him for that money on that same weekend, wanting to just sit for a sec and see how he played it, and sure enough he didn't call me neither. Now either he was just saying fuck me and the money he owes me, or he did put the police on me and they're waiting on me to call him again. Either way both of those were violations enough for me to kill him.

A week had gone by and it was Saturday, two weeks later from when he was supposed to have made a payment on that tab and I got a call from one of my young boys, Moe Black, telling me that the nigga Bing's in Grove Hall seeming to be just hanging and chilling. I said, "Ok, cool, keep ya eye on him, I'm on my way." It so happened that I was close by with Teddy coming from serving a play on Intervale Street and had my pistol on me. I switched seats with Teddy, letting him drive just in case the situation was right enough for me to shoot the nigga right there and just pull off. Grove Hall was way too packed for me to stank him right there, and besides the people that spoke to me as soon as I pulled up, there was a detail cop overseeing the area that I'm sure had peeped me pulling up. So, I quickly contemplated a new approach. Teddy pulled alongside of him standing on the sidewalk and Bing instantly started saying some stupid shit about losing his phone and not knowing how to get in touch with me. I just played it cool as if I wasn't upset and there wasn't a problem, calmly saying, "Ooo, ok, well jump in so I can give it to you."

Without me even saying it, Teddy knew the play and we started driving off looking for somewhere deserted for whatever it was I was about to do. Once clear from the crowd I could tell he sensed there was about to be a problem, by how he started talking fast and making promises, then bullshit stories, which got me even more upset to where I turned around punching him in the mouth saying, "Shut the fuck up, bitch!"

Teddy sped up but forgot to lock the doors. Bing knew I was taking him somewhere to stank him. Teddy was doing about twenty-five miles an hour heading towards our neighborhood. Once Bing saw me pull the pistol from my waist, without hesitation he opened the door and jumped out rolling into a parked car. There were a couple of cars behind us in traffic but at this point I didn't give a fuck, telling Teddy to stop the car. Killing this nigga was on my mind, but clear thinking kicked in. Instead, I put the pistol on the car floor and grabbed a half full fifth of Hennessey we were drinking, then got out and just busted him over the head with it. I knew the people behind us were watching the whole thing and most likely got my license plate number.

After a few days he was released from the hospital, only to be snatched by the Feds with Poopy and them, and from what I was told he tried to snitch on me after being arrested and the Feds disregarded his statement saying that he should have said that when they came to visit him at the hospital. Anyhow, I then lost a punk ten gees and more importantly, I knew for sure that the Feds were on me.

Regardless of all the 'lil bullshit I was going through, however, all wasn't bad that summer. Me and this female I met named Cynthia had started to get serious and at the time I was beginning to believe that I was falling in love with her. On top of that my boy Calvin had gotten out just in time to enjoy the end of the summer with me.

The day after Calvin came home I took him out to get fresh. It reminded me of what Eddy did for me when I came home. On top of buying him some clothes, I bought him a car so that he could get moving because I knew that I was about to hit him with some work soon as I re-upped.

Within days he had a half a key in his possession and was off and running. After about a week the Pontiac I bought

Calvin ended up becoming a shelter for a blue pit bull puppy he bought seeing that he was instantly getting money and was driving rentals and had no need for a hoopty. Things between me and Tameko were going from bad to worse, and it got to the point where I started coming in and out only to stash and sell drugs. I knew she was in love with me and I did truly appreciate everything she did for me from the time I was locked up and the things she did to help me get to the point that I was at then, but nothing was going to change. I just wasn't in love with her and she was hurting.

Sheldon and his girlfriend Asia broke up, but Asia was still hanging around Franklin Hill Ave with Tony's girlfriend Tammy, and every time we saw each other, her flirting became more obvious. By this time I'd had sex with three more of Tammy's friends and even though Asia and Sheldon broke it off, me and Sheldon were family plus getting money together, and at the time I was under the assumption that he still had feelings for her, plus things got serious with me and Cynthia. We were having unprotected sex and I was really feeling her and started staying over her house every night.

CHAPTER FOUR

The Wise Guys album was finally completed and I must say even though I didn't like any of the artists personally except Main Tee from JP and Cordell from Academy Holmes, all of them had talent and the album was hot. Ray Dog [Benzino] named us the Wise Guys, and the anticipation of the album quickly became the talk of the town seeing that someone from the majority of all the neighborhoods in Boston was on it. Me and Ray Dog [Benzino], although still tight, seemed to have accumulated some competitive ways. I could've been wrong but I felt that he felt a certain way about the fact that me, Little Mike, who used to come to his house and get clothes with dreams of being a rapper but barely could, then came upon a couple hundred thousand, top-notch street respect from numerous violent acts and was being spoken about for my rap skills in a way that he wasn't. Even still, I must say he never let the emotions I felt he was hiding get in the way of how he dealt with me, he always kept things professional and would strive to bring the best out of me as an artist and I appreciated that.

Some months had passed and me and Eddie hadn't spoken, not that anything was wrong, it was just that we were both busy doing our own thing, but he was still my man. Eddy called one day congratulating me on what he had heard about me getting money out here on top of the Wise Guys album. He knew as well as anyone how hard I worked on my rap skills being that I kept him up many nights in jail practicing my skills and letting him hear shit and asking his opinion on it. I was definitely getting money, but when it came to drug dealing Eddie and his crew were the talk of the town. Even though a lot of stuff was left to speculation, it was being said that Eddie was getting like 20 kg a month where I was only moving 3 ½ to 4 a month. Before ending our phone call, Eddie giggled while telling me that he had some bricks of something good for a good price. I told him I'd holla at him knowing I wasn't seeing that me and Haburto were like partners now and things were flowing smoothly.

My friend Jenks and Eddie's friend Turtle were pretty cool. They hung out often, even went out of town together a few times to Turtle's mother's house in New York. Turtle even gave Jenks work for free so he could get on his feet something like a few 4 ½ probably up to a half a key in all, which was cool. He feared Jenks but really liked him as well and wanted to see him doing good. Turtle was cool like that, that's what Eddy liked about him, he was strictly about money. Turtle liked having Jenks around him, seeing that the streets were well aware of how nice Jenks was with his hands. He was tall with long arms, kind of slim but the boy could fight and had a gun game, but most of all he was a big part of 915 and had us to back him on whatever.

Calvin had been home for a good two months now. We were chilling one sunny Saturday, riding a rental Caddy he had when I got a phone call from Vidal sounding upset telling me to come to his crib in the brick. I got there and he was breathing hard, furious, telling me that the Kos niggas just shot Chris. Without asking any more questions I said, "Come on." Vee had his Glock on him while I stopped down the street at my mom's to get my Taurus nine I had over there, then we went hunting. We didn't have to look long because as soon as we went to Mattapan Square, there they were at the tow lot across the street from the Mobil Gas station. I told Calvin to park on the corner next to the school while me and Vidal got out and slid next to a dumpster across the street which was on the path that they had to take in order to get back to their hood.

Two cars deep they pulled out of the garage heading in our direction, unaware that we were there until we jumped out from behind the dumpster, both firing at them. Between me and Vee, we let off at least twenty shots but God had to be with them because later that night we found out that no one got hit, but the message was still sent, which was that no disrespect will be tolerated.

Even though no one got shot I was satisfied with the example that was set, plus I would definitely see them again soon seeing that Cynthia lived in their neighborhood. Along with that, we all hung out at the Rolls Club in Mattapan, so it was only a period of time before we got into it again. Chris was cool; they only shot him in the leg, it was more about the disrespect than anything that had me on my shit.

Me and Tammy's mother Darleen hadn't dealt with one another in a sexual way in over a year now, but I still cared about her and seeing her starting to deal with some old demons and starting to get high again bothered me. Even though I knew she was going to buy drugs with the money, every time she asked me for money I gave it to her. I never forgot about the conversation me and Darleen had about pimping and hoeing, so when my cousin Tony called me one day saying that Darleen's boyfriend Derek beat her up, I already knew what it was about. Still, in all she was a part of my family now and my ego wasn't going to let the incident pass without saying a word to the nigga about it.

After getting Derek's cell number, me, Tony and Sheldon left. Calling him but getting no answer, I left a detailed message on who I was and how upset I was about him putting his hands on Darleen. Within the next ten minutes he called back speaking with a 'lil bass in his voice asking who I was and if I was a pimp.

I replied, "Fuck who I am or what I am over the phone; where are you so we can talk in person?"

He paused for a moment, which told me he was nervous but still said downtown on the track. I said cool and hung up. I didn't know what he looked like; my plan was to just get out once we got there and ask who's Derek.

When we got there I saw a couple of older guys dressed pretty sharp walking opposite side of the street of some white girls looking as if they were keeping their eyes on them, so I figured that one of them must be him. I double parked and jumped out aggressively asking, "Yo, which one of y'all is Derek?"

Nervously looking, they all shook their heads saying not me, then I asked, "Do y'all know who he is?"

One of them said, "Yeah, he just left," but saying it in a way to let me know he didn't appreciate me questioning him. I pulled out the .357 revolver I had on me then said, "Yeah, well listen, y'all tell him Mike McNeill came looking for him and the next time he puts his hands on Darleen I'm gonna kill him and whoever with him."

They were looking scared as shit as they both started shaking their heads with one saying, "I will, I'll definitely get in touch with him and let him know you came looking for him."

I politely said, "Ok, thank you," while putting my pistol back in my pants and left.

Me and Cynthia had been dating serious for six months now. She knew about Tameko but never stepped out of place and questioned me about her because she knew that she was there before her. With all the unprotected sex we were having it wasn't a surprise to me the day she called me saying she just came from the clinic and they confirmed that she was pregnant. My first thought was, *damn, I ain't ready for a child,* but by how happy she sounded when she told me I knew her decision was made and she was going to have it regardless, so I never reacted in any negative way and just jumped on board saying things to comfort her.

Fuck it, I'm about to be a father! I called my clique telling everybody, wanting to go out and celebrate. Within a couple of hours, me and about fifteen of us had went down to Mr. Allen's clothing store buying suits and accessories for the night. That night we went to the Roxy's night club and I jacked close to five gees on champagne and drinks. Overall, it was a good night, one I'll never forget. Any time I would waste money like that or make a big purchase I would put pressure on niggas that owed me money. This heavyset Jamaican dude named Jimmy had been owing me five thousand dollars for a few weeks now, when usually he'd pay me in full on a weekly basis.

After picking up my cousin Tony I went straight to Jimmy's house instead of calling him. Coincidentally, he was pulling in at the same time as me and Tony which was perfect. We were in a rented Expedition, so the truck wasn't familiar to him as I rolled down the window asking him what's good with you, he gave me a stupid grin saying, "I was wondering who y'all was while I was parking."

I replied, "Yeah, yeah, jump in for a minute, let me holla at you." Once he closed the door, Tony pulled off and we started talking. "What's good, do you got that for me?"

Once he said no, I didn't even want to hear the excuses. He started saying people were complaining about the work having too much soda on it. Knowing that I did stretch the shit out on those last two keys, I started to sympathize with him. At first, I just said, "Yeah, well just give me the rest of my shit and I'll move it."

Now he was stuttering saying it's gone but he's waiting on his girl's taxes to come next week to pay me. That's when I got upset asking, "Well, if it was so fucking garbage how the fuck you sell it?"

After a couple more of his stuttering words I pulled my pistol out pointing it in his face yelling, "Lift your shirt, do you have a gun on you?"

He started screaming, "Naw naw, Mizz, please, I promise I'm going to pay you!"

I said, "I knew something was wrong, I called you twice last week and you didn't answer, now you telling me this dumb shit." I told Tee to pull over, then handed him the pistol and got in the back with Jimmy and immediately started fucking him up and going through his pockets for whatever change he had on him. Once I finished, I told him to get the fuck out and that he better have my money next week or else I'ma put more than hands on him next time.

Big Mike from Greenwood Street and Donna's brother Duckie owed me some money and as usual they were on point with it. My stomach still felt empty from throwing up the night before from drinking, so some of their Aunt Wezzy's food was just what I needed and it so happened that she made some of her homemade beef stew that I loved.

While sitting down having a big bowl, Donna finally came downstairs and spoke. "Hey, Mike."

I replied, "Hello, Donna, you look nice."

She smiled while saying thank you. Her ass was looking fat, plus I could tell that she was putting on a 'lil extra bounce to it for me. I asked, "Where your boyfriend at?"

She said, "I'm single. I haven't messed with anyone since Ant." By the way she said it I believed her; the fact that no one hit that pussy in a while turned me on. The freak inside me had me thinking, *damn, that pussy must be tight if no one hit it in all that time.* That's when I threw it out there asking, "What you doing tonight?"

"Nothing."

"Yeah, can I come pick you up tonight so we can hang out for a few?"

"Yeah, I don't see why not."

With a sort of Grinch looking smile on my face I said, "Ok, ok, I'll call you a 'lil later when I'm on my way."

Finishing up my beef stew, I left to go serve a few more plays. After setting things up with Donna for the night, I went over to Hardworth Street to meet Burto. He had been waiting on something to get in town for a few days now and I wanted to find out what was good with it without speaking about it on the phone. Once I got there he told me that, "It will be here tonight," and that it was actually here in a U-Haul as we spoke.

I said, "Cool," then gave him five before getting out of his Land cruiser. While walking back to my car I noticed Asia and Mia walking up the street with 'lil bags in their hands like they just came from the store. Mia yelled out, "Hey stranger!" referencing the fact that I hadn't called her nor answered my phone when she called in close to five months.

I smiled and said hi, feeling like a kid that just got caught doing something wrong, then Asia spoke. "Like, hey, what's up, Mike," having this sneaky type of smirk on her face walking a step behind Mia knowing that she couldn't see it. I had just seen Asia a couple of days ago over at Tammy's house but I could tell by the way she spoke that she wasn't telling Mia about how often she saw me on Franklin Hill Ave. I wasn't in the mood to entertain the situation at the time so I just said, "All right, y'all take care," and jumped in my car moving fast like I was handling something.

Knowing that I had plans to hook up with Donna tonight, I stopped by Tameko's, chilled for like an hour, then went over to Cynthia's and took a nap. That way neither one of them should be calling my phone about anything later. The nap ended up turning into me falling asleep for like five hours. I laid down at five and didn't wake up till ten minutes to ten and had four missed calls from Burto. I finally called, and he sounded upset but still all ready to get this 44 thousand and get two of the keys off from wherever he was holding them. Seeing that I didn't have a license, I didn't like driving that dirty at that time of night and knew that if I had Cynthia or Tameko drive me there were gonna be some questions like when I'm coming back if I left the work at either of their houses at that time of night. So, I figured, fuck it, I'ma have Donna drive me to get it and leave it at my cousin Tony's crib till the morning. That way we could just leave from there and do us.

Once I told Donna my plan, she said no problem in a way that had me thinking, yeah, fucking with her gonna work; plus, she was pumping anyways so I could just hook her up with a 'lil something extra for holding me down when I cook it.

I called Tony after picking it up and he said he wasn't home, but Tammy was and that he would call her now to have her waiting on me in the hallway.

Once I pulled up and walked to the door, Tammy grabbed the bag looking in my car smiling saying, "Damn, another girl," seeing that she knew of at least eight different females I had sex with including her mother and three of her friends. I just smiled saying, "Chill, chill," then started laughing; we were cool like that at that time. She was like a 'lil sister to me. I headed back to my car telling her to tell Tony that I'll be back early. Once the work was situated, I was well rested and ready to chill. Me and Donna went downtown, ate at Legal's and talked for a couple of hours while having drinks. After flirting for months, now I was ready to fuck and I was pretty sure she was too. I asked her if she was staying with me tonight, and with a cute smile on her face she said yes, then we had one more round of drinks and left.

The mood was right; we were at the Marriot hotel in Cambridge both full and tipsy, when we started sexing. I could tell after a good thirty minutes that nobody ever fucked her like I was and she was falling in love with me from every stroke and by the minute.

Next morning after I dropped Donna off, I went straight to Tony's to get the work so I could go to Tameko's and cook it up. It was a 'little bit after noon seeing that we stayed till checkout.

Once I rang the bell, Tammy answered saying, "He not here, you just missed him," while buzzing the door for me to come in, already knowing I was coming to do something concerning the work. After unlocking the door, she must have went in to the bedroom and got the bag because by the time I came up the stairs and in the house she was coming out handing it to me asking do I want this?

I said, "Thanks," noticing that she was wearing a thin silk kinda see-through robe with Chinese imprints on it and appeared to have on no panties or bra underneath it. After grabbing the bag and getting ready to leave, I couldn't resist not looking at her nipples that were poking through the robe, and by eye contact I could tell she noticed me looking.

I said thank you, turned and headed back down the stairs. She said, "Bye, Mike," saying my name in a way she'd never said it before. It was definitely different from how she said it around Tony.

Once I got to me and Tameko's house the energy was the same as it had been lately. She was quiet, getting dressed and ready to leave and seemingly had an attitude. It was around the first of the month this day, so I gave her the thousand dollars for the rent on top of a few extra dollars for herself. Granted, I was no longer into her physically, I never had a problem with giving her money and gifts seeing that she was there for me when I was at the bottom.

I was in the middle of cooking up when Jenks called me wanting to come see me, saying he needed to holla at me for a min. I said, "I'm at Mek's, come through."

About twenty minutes later he got there and said the usual, "What good," at first.

I replied, "What's good."

He asked, "Yo, you still be fucking with your man Eddie?"

I replied, "Not as much as I used to, but we still cool!"

Jenks said, "Fuck them niggas. I been calling Turtle's bitch ass an he ain't been answering."

I said, "Yeah," in a joking way, "he probably tired of givin' you free shit!"

We both started laughing, then he said, "Yo, we should just rob them niggas and take everything, I heard Eddie had a million dollars somewhere."

Immediately, I said, "Naw, cuz, that's my man, he's cool as hell." Even though we didn't speak every day, he was still my man. To me, we were still as tight as we was when we were locked up, plus he looked out for me; he was the reason I was on my feet the way I was at the time."

With a dry tone, Jenks said, "Yeah, I feel you," seeming disappointed from my response. Then he gave me a handshake and left. In my mind I knew that this wasn't the last time that I was going to hear about this.

Granted, I was getting plenty of money at this time, but I still wasn't getting it like this older local dude named Phil. It was said that Phil had millions of dollars and even if his net worth was being exaggerated I knew he had plenty of cash. One night me and Cynthia were out in the same club and from the corner of my eye I could see her and Phil having a conversation. My first instinct was to go over there and make my presence known, but then I thought about it said to myself, "Naw, I'ma just chill and let it play out, then use them talking to my advantage." Part of me was bothered that Cynthia even gave him the time of day while dealing with me. It hurt my ego more than my feelings, but once she told me that he gave her his number I figured I have her set him up for me to rob him in order to prove her loyalty to me. Within days of them meeting, Cynthia and Phil started going out on dates with Cynthia coming back reporting everything to me in detail. Within the first week I knew where he lived, where he hung out, and what other cars he drove other than the bright red five series that he was known for. After a good two weeks had passed I told Cynthia that it was time for her to cut ties with Phil because I had enough information on him to do want I wanted to do. Although she said ok, I could see it in her eyes that she wasn't being fully honest with me. Knowing that I had plans on running up in Phil's house Saturday, Cynthia called me that Friday sounding sad telling me that she doesn't think that kidnaping him was a good idea. It was obvious to me that in that short amount of time she had caught feelings for Phil. Granted, I didn't cut Cynthia off for that, but it did leave the relationship tainted!

Muffin, who was one of the premier hairdressers at the time, was having her first show and by the way it was being spoken about, this was going to be a big event. Though I already had a closet full of high priced suits and clothing at my mother's and Tameko's, I still wanted something that was going to be a definite standout at this event, and at this time there was no classier place to shop then Neiman Marcus. Once I got to Nieman's I came up with an animal theme, I bought a pair of gator skin shoes with the matching belt, then found a rare, thin brown camel fur vest to match, but the piece that put it all together was a raccoon fur coat that I bought for $4,000.

I was killing 'em once I got dressed for the function. Calvin made a joke saying, "Damn, boy, you sharp. I'ma call you Crocodile Dundee tonight." We laughed hard, then headed to the spot. The club was packed with girls looking extremely good wearing close to nothing and it was wintertime. While I was at the bar I had seen my cousin Tony's girlfriend Tammy and a couple of her friends there. I spoke, saying, "Hey."

Tammy smiled saying, "Hey, handsome, looking good," then introduced me to her friends. I saw that there were a couple I didn't know. I bought them all drinks and started to walk off when she gave me an innocent hug with a small kiss on the cheek saying, "Thank you and be careful tonight." Although it seemed innocent, it did dawn on me that this was the first time she had ever touched me.

The night was dope. On the way to get in the car and go to the food spot, I bumped into Princess, Michelet's ex-girlfriend whom I hadn't seen since Michelet passed away, nor since I had been getting money. She was looking good and was tipsy. After we complimented each other, she asked for my cell number saying she had something she wanted to talk to me about at another time. I gave it to her and left, thinking nothing of it.

Me and Calvin were down at the food spot now and it was packed inside and outside. While trying to find a parking space we happened to pull up on my cousin Sheldon out there arguing with Damien, one of Eddie's boys that I had my own relationship with from being upstate with him. Calvin pulled right over knowing I was getting out to assist Sheldon. I was figuring I could easily squash this once I told Damien that Sheldon's my people, but instead he went off, saying, "I don't give a fuck who he is he is with, this bitch nigga that got a problem my uncle!"

I was heated now. Still dressed in my shoes and sharp clothes, I asked Sheldon was he strapped, knowing that he always was. He said, "Yes," and lifted his shirt showing it to me. That's when I took the pistol and shot Damien in front of everybody, then jumped back in Calvin's bright red Caddy and left. Knowing that I couldn't kill him in front of everybody that was looking, I only shot him in the leg and with me knowing that Damien wasn't a hoe ass nigga, I knew this was the beginning of a war. Once we were in the clear, me and Calvin spoke seriously about the issue for like two to three minutes, then started laughing like "fuck him" while on the way to where my car was parked. Sheldon met me within the next 20 minutes to get his gun back, seeing that I had one already in my car.

It was about three o'clock the morning now and my cell phone was blowing up from a number I didn't know and I was thinking it must be about me just shooting Damien, so I answered, "Hello, who is this?"

Sounding all tipsy, the caller replied, "HI, Mike, it's Princess," in a way that I could hear that she was glad that I answered. I could've sworn she about to say she saw what happened, seeing that so many people were out there but she didn't. Instead, she asked me what was I doing, I said, "Nothing. Why, what are you doing?"

She replied, "Just getting home, about to shower. Do you want to come over?"

Although Michelet was dead, the fact that she was his ex-girlfriend came to mind for a brief moment when she asked that but now, horny and tipsy myself I said yes, got the address and slid through.

I got in her apartment, and she's half naked in a nightgown sipping wine. My dick got hard as shit, though I was a little surprised because she seemed to have really loved Michelet when he was alive and I couldn't have expected this moment to happen. After sitting on the couch across from me the first thing she said to me was, "Mike, I'm sorry."

With a confused look on my face and my dick getting soft, I asked, "Sorry for what?"

She replied, "Remember back in the day when Michelet told you my apartment got broken into?"

Remembering the situation well, I said yes, then she said, "Well, it was never broken into, he staged everything so that it looked like it had been when you came over, but I never felt right about him playing you like that when you all was supposed to be friends and I want to get that off my chest."

She shocked me with that, seeing how long ago that was, but the first thing that came to my mind was that look on her face that morning I came over to her and Michelet's place. It was as if she wanted to tell me he was lying back then. I said to her, "It's cool, that's just how some niggas be," but in my mind I was thinking if this nigga was still alive I would have killed him for that now, no matter how long ago it was.

At the same time, I was climbing on top of her kissing her neck and rubbing her titties while unbuckling my pants. After busting a couple of nuts that night, I left early the next morning. Even though I considered her pussy to be good, I didn't intend on going back and making this an ongoing thing. Seeing that I'd had sex with her sister in the past, once seemed to be enough.

After getting dressed at Tameko's house, then stopping by Cynthia's house to see how she was doing, I went to meet Sheldon over at Tony's house to get the full story on what happened before I pulled up to the food spot last night.

Once I got there Sheldon wasn't there yet and wouldn't be till later in the evening. Still, me and Tony chopped it up about the hair show and the shooting. Once Tammy came out of the back room she barely spoke as she usually did around Tony, and at that point I had noticed that there was a pattern formulating in her behavior seeing how she just hugged and kissed me on my cheek last night. This morning was way different, she didn't even mention to Tony that she had sed me there, and even though I didn't pay it complete attention I definitely started to notice things.

Later during the week Ray Dog [Benzino] had called me telling me that we was going to New York this weekend so that me and a couple more members of the Wise Guys could do a track with Mob Deep. Granted, I was never into East Coast music, Mob Deep's shook ones was my shit and I was excited about meeting them. Not wanting to put the highway miles on my car, I went and rented a new Jaguar for the trip not knowing that Ray [Benzino] had rented a minivan and had planned on the artists riding down together, which I wasn't with anyways.

So, when the day came for us to go I pulled up with Vidal in the car ready to follow behind them. Ray [Benzino] had a new silver bug eye Benz back then and didn't have any intention of riding in the van but by the look on his face he seemed to have a problem with me not getting in the van. We had a few words over it with him saying he was trying to have the artists build some type of chemistry. I said I go to New York all the time, and didn't need to be around them to do what I had to do. After it was all said and done, I ended up just following them in the Jaguar.

Ray [Benzino] was the boss of our record company, but I was bossed up in the street and that seemed to have made us clash a lot. Other than Darrell Allen, Belnel Mike, and Duke, the artists in the group wasn't getting no money at that time and depending on Ray [Benzino] to do certain things for them that I didn't needed him to do.

We were at the studio now in New York and Mob Deep finally came in. After Ray [Benzino] introduced us, I shook hands with Prodigy and he held my hand for a second turning my wrist towards him so he could get a closer look at my gold Rolex. I figured to see if it's real. After checking in for a quick sec peeping, it was official. He said, "nice watch," I said thanks and moved on.

After Ray [Benzino] played the track and gave us a brief description on how the hook sounded, he gave us like a half hour to write a verse. Shortly after he said, "McNeill, you ready?" wanting me to go first. Not feeling really confident in what I wrote, plus nervous because Mob Deep was there, I sluggishly said yeah, then went into the booth.

Once I started recording, I began to make mistake after mistake. Ray [Benzino] still holding onto some feelings because I didn't get in the van with the other artists, had started to indicate he was frustrated, which embarrassed me and led me to become frustrated, too. I took the headphones off and came out of the booth without laying a verse, saying, "I see how you're trying to play me, nigga, an you know I ain't the one for this hoe shit."

Being upset as well, he said, "What the fuck are you talking about? If you ain't ready, you ain't ready, if you can't do it you can't do it."

I tore the paper up with the verse that I wrote on it, then said to Vidal, "Come on, dog, we out," leaving and slamming the door behind me.

Once me and Vidal got back on the highway heading home, Vidal expressed to me that he felt I should have finished the song, and deep down I felt the same way, realizing that the only one I was truly upset with was myself because I really wasn't ready for that moment and had realized I wasn't as good as I thought I was. That was truly a learning experience for me, that night, I learned the difference between being a rapper and being a real rap artist.

Arriving back in town I immediately heard that Damion was out of the hospital from me shooting him in the leg and was talking greasy about what he was going to do when he sees me. I never saw him do it or even heard about him doing it, but by his aggression I did assume Damion would shoot but still I didn't give a fuck because I kept a pistol on me at that time and was definitely about that trigger play however or whenever it came.

Days after, when Ray [Benzino] got back in town we got up over tony Hurst's house and spoke about the incident. We laughed about a few things that happened that night, shook hands and hugged. That was the first time we actually got into a heated disagreement, and in a strange way it kind of made us a little tighter; well, at least for the moment.

Sheldon's ex-girlfriend Asia had given up her apartment on Hardworthy Street in order to go to a shelter so she could get a Section 8 certificate. Over the last year her and Tammy became tighter to where they were together all the time during the day when Asia wasn't at the shelter. At this time me and Calvin would go over Tony's every day. Tony and Tammy's crib became like the spot to meet up at during the day and chop it up, and though me an Asia smiled, winked, and flirted for some time now and it was obvious that there was an attraction between us, we hadn't gone to the next level till one day she was running late on making her curfew at the shelter and asked me if I could give her a ride and I did. We spoke briefly on the way there with her telling me that she had a weekend pass that coming weekend and didn't have to be back at the shelter till Sunday night once she left that Friday. I asked her did she have a babysitter and she said yes. Sex instantly came to my mind. I said, "How about I come get you Saturday so we can hang out for a few," and she said yes, smiling while liking how I started to rub her thighs. Pulling up at the door to the shelter she said that she'd call me Saturday from over at Tammy's house and that I could come get her from there if I wanted to.

I said, "Cool, I will," and pulled off looking through the rear view mirror noticing her shaking her ass a lot harder than she usually did to turn me on in case I was looking.

Cynthia was like seven months pregnant now, I still had Tameko in the cut and I was dealing with Donna on the low, starting to have real feelings for her. My emotions were everywhere, but at the end of the day my mind was focused on money!

One day while at the Mobil gas station on Blue Hill Avenue, an old school pimp gone legitimate businessman named Ill Will pulled up. Granted, at this time we didn't know each other personally, but we spoke when noticing each other in passing so it was only right I took the opportunity to go over and finally introduce myself. He was in a black Mercedes-Benz with gold rims, so I started the conversation off by complimenting how clean his car was.

He said thank you, then told me he liked the way my BMW was sitting as well. After shaking hands and exchanging names he handed me a business card telling me about his auto body shop down the street, saying if I ever needed anything done to let him know because he does good work, on top of telling me about a couple of cars he had down there for sale I might want to see.

I said okay knowing I wasn't interested in buying a car nor did I need any work done to my car at that moment, but I still figured that I would stop through if for nothing else than to further our relationship seeing that he seemed like someone that's been around and knew a few things I could learn about, so I said cool. We shook hands, then I left.

A couple of days had passed and for the most part it had been a good week. I collected some long overdue money I had in the streets, plus I sold all the work I had and my connect said that we would be right back on Sunday, so I was feeling good. It was Friday and seeing that I didn't have any priorities, I figured I'd get dressed sharp putting on my Versace pants, shoes and shirt. I was driving a rental Lincoln seeing that my car was at Ike's rim shop getting a rim fixed that I'd bent on a pothole earlier in the week.

Around two o'clock in the morning, I'd just left Frank's place figuring I'd take a 'lil cruise before going over to Cynthia's house for the night. I saw some dudes from Intervale I knew hanging in front of the Jamaican club 3C, so I pulled over to say what's up for a second. Then, out of the four of them that was out there, three of them just said "what's up" back to me after I said "what's up" showing some love. Then there was Black. Seeming to be drunk, he looked me up and down seeing that I was in Versace dress clothes from head to toe. Slurring, he said, "What's up, pretty boy," with this dumb look on his face that immediately upset me. Having my pistol on me, I wasn't worried about anything but seeing that I was cool with and getting money with certain people from the vill, I just told him to watch his mouth and started walking back to the rental. Once I started to pull off, he said something that I could barely hear but me already being upset I wound down my passenger window telling him I'm coming to his house in the morning to whoop his ass.

He said, "Yeah, whatever," but in a weak tone like he didn't expect me to say that. Then I left, so upset that I didn't even feel like joy riding anymore and just went to Cynthia's house to get some sleep.

The next morning at about nine o'clock I called my nigga Beefy to ride with me to his house so I could whoop his ass like I told him I was going to. After I rang his bell, he came to the door with a stupid look on his face saying, "Ooo, you at my crib."

I said, "Yeah, nigga, just like I said I would be; now come out."

He said, "Ok, cool, give me a minute," then closed the door calling a couple of his boys to tell them what was going on.

One of his boys that I was cool with as well named Lil Alan came right over with a video camera laughing and saying, "Let's go around the corner to the park then y'all just shoot the fair one."

I replied, "Fa sho," then me and Beef got back in the car and went to the park. When we got there, Black was bouncing around like he's a boxer. I just charged him and grabbed him and started beating his ass till niggas broke it up saying that's enough.

When I finished, his eye and nose were bleeding. I shook hands with Alan and the couple other vill niggas out there and left. Once me and Beef were in the car we started laughing, with Beef saying, "That what's up, my nigga, you whooped his ass an I gotta call Alan later to get a copy of that tape."

I didn't care to see it; so long as respect was put back in order that was enough for me. By the time afternoon came I had over twenty people calling me saying they'd heard about what happened or had actually seen a copy of the tape. Asia called me later that evening saying, "Hello, Mike Tyson, I was just wondering if you were still coming to get me today."

I said, "Yeah yeah yeah, but why you call me Mike Tyson?"

She said, "I had overheard that you had a fight this morning. Are you ok?"

I said, "Damn, word travels quick, huh? Yeah, I'm alright, and yeah I'm trying to pick you up at like nine o'clock," and then I asked, "Where you gonna be?"

She said, "Where I'm at now, over Tammy's house."

I said, "Cool, I'll see you around nine."

Trying to sound all extra sexy she said, "Byyye," before hanging up.

As I always do before I disappear for the night, I started to ride around seeing my chicks so that they didn't call me for anything later.

First I stopped by Greenwood to see Donna since her brother Duck owed me a couple dollars. I chilled over there with her for like an hour eating food and making sure everybody knew that I wouldn't have any work till tomorrow, so that there wouldn't be any need to call me. Once I left there, I stopped by Cynthia's for a few, then went to Tameko's to get some rest. Then I got dressed for the night. Though getting some rest barely happened because once I got to Tameko's house we conversed for a few minutes, and from how nice she was being after not seeing me in like five days I could tell she was horny. Granted, we didn't have much of a relationship; still, one thing about her was that she was a freak and I hadn't met anyone up to that point who could make me enjoy a dick suck like her. So, once she reached for my zipper I laid back ready for her to suck my dick and make me cum while making herself cum as well at the same time from playing with her clit.

After the dick suck, I got a quick nap, then got up and got dressed and was ready to fuck Asia for the first time seeing that I remembered times that Sheldon would boast saying that her pussy was good when they were together.

Arriving at Tammy's house to pick Asia up, my conscience started bothering me a bit hoping that Sheldon didn't pull up while we were leaving together, even though they hadn't been together in a while now. I must say I was still feeling a 'lil guilty that she was his ex. I ran up the stairs really quick to holla at Tony before we left, and Tammy opened the door for me to come in. I spoke knowing I said it loudly enough that she heard me but she didn't respond. I could see in her face that she had an attitude for what I didn't know, but still I went into the back room and spoke with Tony about some business for a second, then me and Asia left. Once we pulled off, I was sort of curious what or if something had happened, so I asked Asia what was wrong with Tammy. It seemed like she had an attitude when she let me in. Asia said, "I know her and Tony weren't arguing; if you ask me it seemed like she was cool all the way up till the point when I told her that you were on the way to come get me."

I drove and thought about it for like five seconds, then just blurted out, "Oh, she must've wanted you all to hang out tonight." Knowing I'm thinking it's something else, I turned up the radio and started rubbing her hand and thigh as to say "fuck whatever it was." Even though I told Asia that I needed to stop by my spot for a minute, I was pretty sure she knew what it was that I wanted to stop by there for. Once I started touching her she stared into my eyes as to say do whatever you wanna do. I liked that, her submissive attitude was turning me on. I could tell from the moment I picked her up that her main purpose was to satisfy me and she was willing to do that by any means necessary. Before I gave her any type of sign that I was being aroused, I gave her a couple of slight commands like come rub my back, come sit over here, just a few things to show my confidence and take control, seeing that I could see that what she needed was a man who knew he was the man and I definitely knew I was the right person for that!

I put my bare dick in her before ever touching her body with my hands after telling her to come bend over on the corner of my pull out couch. This was the first time a woman gave me all of her and I liked it. I already had her respect and by the things she was saying while I was in her, I knew she was offering me her heart, so after enjoying her entire body I unconditionally felt like I owned her once we were done.

After dropping Asia off back at Tammy's house the next morning I realized I liked her, not really sure to what extent but

I did know I wanted to see her again. It was like I felt a sense of ownership, like in the way people feel about their property in cars. It was weird, but for real to me and a clear sign or how far from reality this lifestyle had taken my mind.

The Wise Guys CD was starting to do well in the streets, it got to a point where It seemed like every car that drove by was playing our music. Ray [Benzino] was happy he was recouping the money he put into the project, plus he was starting to make money from it, but most of all his business relationship with Dave may have gone to another level this year. Me not being very business savvy at the time outside of anything but selling drugs didn't understand it, but I can remember one day me and Ray [Benzino] were talking and he told me something about Dave giving him more points in the company, meaning the source magazine and stated that things were about to start changing. I figured that he was just going to start getting a bigger monthly check, but found out later he was speaking of ownership and had access to millions of its network and more power over decisions being made.

Within a couple of months our company office went from being in the back room at my boy Bum's house to Ray's [Benzino] building, a studio in Canton that had four offices in it, with a trailer in the back from which the promotional team could work. Along with working side-by-side with Ray [Benzino] in overseeing the majority of the Wise Guys endeavors, Bum also had another job at Mass General Hospital. His schedule became too hectic to retain both and raise kids, so it was time to give up one of the jobs. The hospital was the obvious choice. For the people that worked in the position that Bum did, the head of the hospital let them lease an apartment in the privately owned development connected to the hospital for a very good rate. Seeing that Bum was leaving the job and still had his lease, he offered me the apartment at $500 a month and I took it. It was dope, it was on the top floor overseeing the city from Mass Ave. through downtown. I consider my man Calvin to be a pretty stylish person, so I just gave him $10,000 and told him to go get new furniture and style for me. The outcome was nice, everything all black like Scarface's furniture; and it fit my taste.

I was happy to have my own spot that only a couple of people knew about with an underground garage that made it all the better. This happened to be a special time in my life. I easily had $200,000 put up and a couple of kilos, my music career was taking off, and then the most cherishing moment of them all happened.

One day I was on my way to the studio to record and had to make a U-turn after receiving a phone call that evening from Cynthia's girlfriend Nettie yelling, "Hurry up, Mike, hurry up! Cynthia's in an ambulance on her way to the hospital; her water broke, she will be having the baby soon."

I was ecstatic asking what hospital are they going to while doing a hundred on the highway. I made it just in time and this became the most sentimental time in my life at that point. I was holding Cynthia's hand while she was squeezing mine trying to push out my baby, and then it happened – he was finally here, a tiny little baby boy with a forehead and a nose like mine. At that moment I was one of the happiest people in the world and was proud of Cynthia after actually seeing what she just had to go through. I stayed up at the hospital for a few hours, but still had business I needed to attend to. If Cynthia needed anything specific, I would of course get it for her but I had to go. I kissed her and left, assuring her that I'd be back as soon as I was done.

At that point I knew that some things in my life were about change. Here I was stressing on how I was going to tell to Tameko about my child, feeling kind of guilty knowing it was going to crush her feelings, and somehow she had already heard about him. After getting back to the hospital with Cynthia and the baby for like an hour ignoring my cell phone not knowing I had ten missed calls from Tameko, here she was busting in on us at the hospital crying and yelling and asking me, "Why why why couldn't you just tell me; why did I have to hear it in the streets! You're wrong, Mike, you're wrong! After all I did for you, this is how you treat me? Mike, you're wrong!"

She was so hysterical that I had to get up to physically remove her from the room, a little nervous of what she might try to do to the baby. I was hurt seeing that I hurt her and knowing that I should have handled this more like a man, but at this point it just was what it was. Once Security approached us outside of the delivery room, Tameko and her cousin Nicole just left.

Cynthia was obviously upset, but I got a sense that she could feel Tameko's pain seeing that she's a woman as well and was more disappointed at me for letting it get to that point more than anything. After bringing my son Michael McNeill, Junior home I knew it was time to go at least have a conversation with Tameko even though I knew our time together was over. It had been a few days now since she came up to the hospital. I walked into her apartment and she immediately started crying. I tried to answer all her questions as truthfully and fully as possible without hurting her any further, but it was what it was. I had a child now and was ready to attend to this new chapter in my life. There was no need for me to pack my clothes, seeing that she had two trash bags full of my things waiting by the door. After answering the same question over and over a few times I figured it was time to leave. She asked me for her house keys which I left on the counter with $3,000 to help her out while she got used to handling things on her own; it was the least I could do seeing that she was there for me when I was broke and now it was over between us.

As if I didn't already have enough going on with females at the time, one day while leaving Tony's crib another one of Tammy's friends named Schree caught my eye, and it wasn't long before I started making time to spend with her. Dealing with Schree was quite easy at the beginning seeing that she wasn't the type of female to hang out all the time, she was actually in college at the time and seemingly willing to except whatever time I had to offer which worked perfect for me. I found Schree to be beautiful, she had long black hair and a petite figure sort of reminded me of Pocahontas, and it didn't take long for me in my sick mind to start having feelings for her as well. I've had several one night stands over the years but once I liked a female, I was considering her to be mine no matter how many other relationships I was already in!

After having my son, Cynthia could not have sex for a few weeks letting her body heal up. During that time was when my sexual relationship with Donna and Asia started to flourish. I was having sex with them at least four times a week apiece, several times I'd leave one and go to the other. I was not wearing condoms with either of them so often I'd expressed to them both how important it was to me that they didn't sleep with anyone else, not realizing that the cycle was something to which I was becoming addicted. Outside of being signed to Ray's [Benzino] label, me and Ray maintained a personal relationship that our mutual friends called crazy. It was like we couldn't really chill around each other for long periods of time, but when we were not around each other for a while, there was much love once we hooked up. After hearing that my son was born, he insisted that I let him be the godfather and regardless of our ups and downs the fact remained that he was rich and responsible, and as hard to see as it may seem I knew he really cared about me and my well-being, so I agreed.

Within days, my connect Haburto called me sounding hysterical and when he got like that I could barely understand him, but there were a couple of words that he said that I could understand, like "rob me" and "come by my mother's house" that let me know what he was talking about. A couple of months back he had gotten set up by a longtime friend of his to get stuck up for a kilo and must have seen or bumped into the person that did that to him. Me already having my pistol on me stopped what I was doing to race to his mother's to see what was up because even though he could barely speak English, nor did we even hang out, we still had a relationship that was tighter than a buyer-seller relationship. Once I got there he told me that the so-called friend that set him up was recently seen going into his family's house off of Humboldt Ave, and hadn't come out yet and he wanted to go deal with him before he left and disappeared again seeing how long it'd been since he heard word of him since being robbed. I parked my car, grabbed my pistol from underneath the seat and jumped in with him. He had a .357 Magnum revolver on him as well and was seemingly upset, and although I'd never been in a situation like this with him before I could see that he was serious and ready to get at the nigga. Once we got there, just to clear any speculation that I might have had, I blurted out, "Yo! You know we killing this nigga if he still there, right?"

With a serious look on his face he replied, "Yeah yeah yeah."

I just said, "Cool," while cocking a shell into the chamber of my nine.

We got there and he immediately saw a car that he was familiar with while driving slowly up the street from the apartment that he was in. I said, "Cool, let's just park further down the street far enough that we can keep an eye on the door, so that way when we see him come out we can run down on him when he starts walking down to his car."

He replied, "Okay," clearly letting me take control of the situation, then he found a park down the street with no cars in front of us so we could easily pull off after marking him. After sitting for no more than 20 minutes, a tall heavyset Dominican dude came out the door looking both ways before heading towards the car. Haburto pointed him out to me. The plan was to run up on him, get close, then start shooting. But as soon as I got out the car, Haburto jumped out yelling something to him in Spanish then fired two shots in the air.

By the time I started running down towards him the other guy had crouched down in between two cars and started firing shots at Haburto. That stopped me in my tracks to where I ran across the street in between two other cars and started shooting at him. Between the three of us at least a quick 30 shots had gone off. While shooting at us and running at the same time, the Dominican dude took the first left. That's when me and Haburto ran back to the car and pulled off. I was heated but waited until we were off the scene and clear of police before I went off on this nigga. Once we pulled back up to my car I said, "Yo, all that shooting in the air shit I saw you do could have got us killed," I was telling him with my voice raised. I said, "If you're going to be about it, be about; if not, leave it alone."

I could see in his face that he was ashamed that I'd seen him shooting in the air. After chastising and schooling him a little more, I gave him a handshake telling him to be careful out there and to call me if he needed me. By this time I calmed down, jumped in my car and left.

Vidal's birthday was coming up soon, and even though we didn't hang out as much as we used to back in the day, I loved him like a brother and wanted to show him some love, so I planned a little party down at Frank's for him. Our whole team was going to be down there anyway. I brought a cake and invited some people who usually don't come down there to come and told the bartender to serve people drinks and keep tabs on how much he gave out and I would pay him at the end of the night.

I was glad to see that there was a big crowd. While parking I happened to notice Ray [Benzino] leaning against his car talking to my cousin Tony's girl Tammy. For some reason I got instantly upset. It was weird to me, it was as if I was jealous and had no relationship with her outside of being friends. She noticed me walking up and ended the conversation and headed inside the bar. Once I reached Ray [Benzino] I gave him my handshake but kept the convo brief with an angry look on my face as if to alert him that I didn't like what I just saw. Then I walked in the bar myself. Soon as I got in I went and got Tammy and asked her if I could speak with her before even saying hello to anyone, upset and not knowing why. We stepped outside in front and I said, "Listen, all of these dudes in here are my niggas and I would appreciate if you could not let me see shit like I saw when I pulled up. You Tony's girl and I ain't trying to have no problems occur between one of my niggas and my cousin. Feel me?"

Already tipsy, she looked at me, smiled and touched my face seductively saying, "You got that, boo!" Then she turned around to walk back into the bar with an extra shake on her ass and a smile on her face saying, "You better get yourself together before you go back in because your feelings for me are showing tonight!"

I came back in smiling with the persona that I'm ready to drink and be the life of the party, all while I have on my mind how the chemistry just changed between me and Tammy. Although I stayed away from her for the rest of the night and did my best not to look at her, that situation was stuck in my head and wasn't going anywhere anytime soon.

The night was good, no problems, everybody got along good, and the bartender only charging me $1,200 for the bar. Me and the rest of my team hung until about 3:00 to 3:30 like we always did, talking and shooting the shit, then I left.

Pulling off, I came to a stop at the first traffic light on Morton and saw a pretty white girl next to me in an older model canary yellow Cadillac staring at me with a smile on her face. I let my window down to speak and she did the same. After saying hi and us both exchanging names, I told her to pull over for a second so we could speak for a moment. I found it weird that here's this pretty white girl riding around at this time of night by herself and she seemed not to be afraid nor nervous a bit about being in the hood. After pulling over and walking to the window, the first thing she said was, "You're cute."

I said, "Yeah, you too," then pulled out my phone with confidence as to say I'm sure I'm getting the number. I asked for it, and she gave it to me saying she had to go take care of something and would be tied up for the next hour or two, but I could call her afterwards so we could talk if I wanted to.

I said, "Cool," walking back to my car as she sped off like she was late for something. Being that I was half drunk and tired from Vidal's party, I knew I wasn't calling her that night but was so curious on what it was she could have possibly had to take care of at that time of night made it a priority to reach out to her first thing in the morning.

After sleeping late from being hung over, I had to get right to some business that had been calling me earlier. Tony's boy Keith had been waiting for me at Tony's house for a couple of hours to bring him a half a key. Once I got there, the situation between me and Tammy came to the top of my mind. While I was counting Keith's money, Tony was asking me how was the party, saying it in a way that let me know that him and Tammy didn't discuss it and it was possible that she didn't tell him she was there.

I just said it was cool, then asked why didn't you come. He whispered to me that a new little bitch that he'd been trying to fuck for a while had called him to come over and he ended up getting some pussy. I said, "Okay, player, then put the money I got from Keith back in the bag," giving both of them a handshake saying, "I'll be back later, I got a couple things to take care of that I'm late for."

While I was going down the stairs, Tammy was coming up. I could tell she had thrown on anything to run to the store because of her hair wrap and morning slippers. Once we caught eye contact she smiled and said, "Hey, Mike."

I said, "Hey, Tammy," then she asked if I was leaving.

I said, "Yeah, I got some things to handle."

She said, "Okay, have a nice day. I'm about to cook some breakfast and it will be some extra up there if you want to come back."

I said, "Okay, cool. Thank you."

She smiled, letting me know last night was on her mind and said, "You're welcome."

While heading back to the spot, I noticed a dark tinted up Astro van high beaming me as to say pull over. After squinting my eyes and looking intensely, I could see that it was Eddie smiling and pointing for me to pull over. Once I did we jumped out shaking hands and hugging, showing that love that we always did when we hadn't seen each other in a while. After going through the basic "how have you been" and "where have you been at," I asked him who was in the car with him. He replied,

"Come on," while walking back towards the van saying, "It's Day Day and Ron, plus Ron said he knows you an y'all cool."

While I was heading towards the passenger door, Ron got out smiling, saying, "What up, Mikey," and we slapped hands while he was asking me, "How's Theola doing?" That's my mother's name, which he knew because growing up my mother and his mother worked at Polaroid together and were good friends.

I said, "Good, man, thanks for asking," then I asked, "How is Ada?" which is his mother's name.

He said, "She's cool, just working."

I said, "That's what's up, make sure you tell her I said hello."

He replied, "Will do."

We shook hands one more time, then I left, telling Eddie that it was good to see him and that I would call him a little later so we could catch up on some things seeing that we hadn't seen or heard from each other in a while. Granted, Eddie had just spit a nice price to me four a couple of keys, it still wasn't lower than what I was getting them for from Haburto. Even though I had a half a key left, I wanted to re-up now seeing that I was leaving in a couple of weeks to go stay on Martha's Vineyard for a week. I called Haburto twice and got no answer. Being that I hadn't heard from him since we had the shootout with the dude that set him up, I instantly started to think that he was acting like a little bitch because of how I yelled at him for shooting in the air.

Then I got a call back from one of his cell numbers I was familiar with. It was his girlfriend at the time Joanna, telling me that Burto went to Santo Domingo for two weeks but he left his phone and something behind just in case I called. Then she said, "I'm at my house, you want to stop by and see it?"

I said, "Okay, cool," then went through. Joanna was beautiful and on this day she looked sexy coming to the door in some Spandex shorts that showed the imprint of her pussy lips and a T-shirt with apparently no bra on, and with a smile on her face. Once she came to the door, my dick got hard as shit walking into the house. She said, "Hold on," while reaching on top of the cabinet pulling out a key that Burto had left behind. I looked at it making sure it was closed, then sat at the table and started counting the money out in front of her. Then I asked, "When is Burto coming back?"

With an attitude in her voice she said next week. Me, detecting that something was wrong, sarcastically said, "Damn, why you didn't going on vacation with him?"

She said, "Because he thinks I'm stupid, he says he's going to see his kids but I know he's going to fuck and spend time with his baby's mother too, so fuck him."

Shaking my head with a smirk on my face I just said, "Damn!"

After I let her count the money while I was getting ready to leave I asked her, "So, what you get into tonight?"

She said, "Nothing, I'm not going nowhere. I'll be here dressed like this all day. I got a bottle of tequila in the cabinet, so I'll have a few shots after I eat but I'm staying home alone tonight."

I smiled and giggled with an evil grin on my face saying, "You should save me some of that tequila."

She smiled, saying, "It's plenty."

Then I could tell we were on the same page so I said, "I'll be back tonight."

Still smiling waiting to close the door behind me, she said, "We'll see. I'll be here if so!" While pulling off to go put the work up, I started to think, *damn, that was too easy, maybe she's trying to use me to get back at him and this could possibly fuck our business relationship.* Then I figured, *fuck it, I ain't even coming back; plus, I have plans on calling that white girl Gretchen I met last night to see what she's about once I get done taking care of my business for the day.*

When I dropped the key over at Cynthia's house, she got an attitude. She grabbed the bag to put it upstairs and screwed her face up, saying, "Don't you think it's time to cut this shit out?"

Then I said I got to do what I got to, and while walking back out the door, having to get the last word, she said, "Do whatever! It's just time to start leaving me out of it. I have a child now to keep in mind."

I was pulling off upset now myself, but quickly realized that I was only mad because she was saying the truth and I said to myself that I would make that the last time I involved her in my business.

Ever since me and Tameko stopped dealing with each other and I gave her back her keys, it seemed like placing all my shit was starting to be difficult. I already knew the Feds were aware of who I was, so for me to just have money, drugs and all the guns in one spot would be stupid and at the moment I had forty thousand, two handguns and my Teck 9 all in my spot down on Mass Ave that needed to be placed somewhere else ASAP. Back then me and my sister were tight and would look out for each other. I could have easily brought the money to her but she already had two hundred thousand at her house and didn't want me running in and out and possibly attract attention seeing that my stash was there. Knowing that I would need this forty within days to re up, I kept it close. Things between me and Donna were progressing, even though outside of having sex we really didn't spend that much time together, she was the type of girl that never ran the streets or did the clubs, which made it easy for me to trust her and I felt it was time for me to put some trust in her.

After getting dressed I called Donna and told her to meet me on Greenwood cause I needed her to do something for me. She said, "Ok, I'm here," with no questions asked. I separated things into two different bags, putting my Teck and thirty gees into one bag and ten gees and one of my handguns in another, keeping one gun on me.

Right before pulling up on Greenwood, I called Donna and told her to come downstairs and bring her car key; by the time I pulled up she was leaning against her car waiting on me, never saying what it was I got. I said, "Open the trunk," and she did. Then I said, "Bring this out to your mom's house for a few days for me."

After me giving her a kiss, with no questions asked she pulled off seconds behind me after saying, "I'll call you when I'm on my way back."

The other bag with $10,000 and the Glock in it I brought to my man YG's crib and told him to hold it and to take whatever he needed to pay for the rental house I was about to stay at on Martha's Vineyard, seeing that we had to pay for it in advance.

Within the next few hours, Donna called saying that she's back from doing that for me, which was putting up the Teck and money. As for Cynthia, I just told her that after thinking about what she'd said, I realized that she was right about me keeping drugs and money in her house and after I moved what was there I wouldn't bring anything else around her and my son.

Within this same week Ray Dog [Benzino] calls me from New York telling me that it's important that I be down there for a studio session that night by eight, and with it only being around one o'clock in the evening I had plenty of time to make it. Sort of needing some alone time, I just went home and got a couple thousand for my pocket and headed to New York by myself. Getting there a little bit early I went shopping, then I got me some weed before finally going to meet Ray [Benzino] at the studio. Walking in the studio the first person I saw was my boy Vidal's sister Ebony braiding Ray's hair. After giving her a hug, Ray [Benzino] stood up giving me a handshake and a hug like never before, smiling and asking me am I ready! Me thinking that it was just another studio session, I nonchalantly said, "Yeah, let's get to." Within about five minutes of me listening to the beat playing, Mr. Scarface of the Ghetto Boys walks in behind me asking Ray, is this him? I was so shocked I couldn't say shit for a second. Here I am in the studio with my favorite artist apparently about to do a track. Having none of my boys with me, Vidal's sister Ebony was just as good in encouraging to do my best seeing that she knew how much I listened to Scarface's music and how special that moment was for me. After messing up several times from trying to over exceed, I finally got through my verse to a song we called the forty-four caliber killers.

Around this time, Asia called telling me that she was about to receive her Section Eight certificate and planned on giving me a key to her apartment when she gets her place. All three of these women started to play a certain role in my life and I didn't see me not wanting to deal with any of them any time soon.

I pulled up at Frank's later that night to meet up with Ray [Benzino] so that I could hear the final mix on a song that we had done the week before called "Co-defendants." It was dope, it featured me, Terror, and Tang the Juice spitting street lyrics over the instrumental to Genuine Wind's hit single "My Pony." Ray [Benzino] loved this song so much we must have sat in his car listening to it and smoking blunts for at least an hour replaying it over and over with him saying to me, "McNeill, you killed this verse real shit," and I can't lie, to hear him say that made me proud. I felt like I was on top of my game and getting noticed for getting better. Before getting out of Ray's [Benzino] car, he used the moment to speak on something I could tell had been on his mind for a minute saying, "McNeill, how long do you plan on selling drugs?"

The question shocked me, and I had no real answer for it, saying, "I never thought about it, but why?"

He said, "Because, my nigga, you gotta feel yourself getting hot and with me having more ownership in the source, the Feds could try to take the company away from me and Dave if they could prove that I knew you was selling drugs and I employed you." He was explaining to me how conspiracy works, then he said, "Plus, I care about you, my nigga, and I'd hate to see you get locked up for years over that little bit of money when we got an opportunity to make millions together."

I couldn't say anything besides I'd think about that and start figuring shit out. I gave him dap, then we both got out and went into Frank's to holla at niggas. After a couple of drinks it dawned on me that I still hadn't called Gretchen, the white girl I'd met after Vidal's party, so I hit her up. She answered sounding polite, talking sort of like a telemarketer saying her name was Tiffany which was different from what she'd told me last night. Not knowing this was her, I asked if I could speak with Gretchen? She asked, who's this, sounding surprised that I said her name. Once I said, "Mike from last night," she said, "Oh," with a sense of happiness in her voice saying, "I'm sorry, it's me; how are you?"

I said, "I'm good, just chilling, what's up with you?"

She said, "I'm okay." Now sounding like something was wrong that she didn't know me well enough to talk about; she asked, "Where are you?"

I said, "Frank's place close to where I met you last night, that little bar right across the street from the police station."

Then she said, "Okay. Well, I'm on my way to take care of something for like an hour or less, how about we get together for a minute once I'm done."

I said, "Cool, stop by here when you're finished and call me when you're outside and I'll come out."

Just to boast to her a little, I mentioned that I was in a different car seeing that I was in a rental the night we met and now in my BMW, I gave her a description of it then said, "That's just in case you pull up looking for the rental."

Just like she said, within an hour or a quarter till she was outside calling me to come out. She was also in a different car, a new model Dodge, smiling from ear to ear once I sat in the passenger seat. After saying hello being extra smooth, I complimented her and the car asking her if it was hers. She said, "No, my girlfriend Jen's."

First thing that came to my mind was dope, she's got someone for me to hook my man Calvin up with. Every word I said she stared into my eyes paying close attention to everything I said and commenting on how I said it.

While I was talking, her phone rang and she said, "Excuse me for a second" and asked me to be quiet for a moment while she answered. "Hello, this is Tiffany, how may I help you?" Then she spoke for a minute like she was taking an order. She asked me to reach in the glove compartment and hand her a pen and pad, then she wrote down an address saying she would be there within an hour. That's when it became obvious to me that she was working for an escort service.

Once she hung up she said, "Okay, I'm about to go take care of something, I'm about to go see this trick in Lynn," while grabbing and rubbing my hand saying, "I want to see you after."

I said, "Cool," trying to act like I'd been in this situation before by saying, "I'll be out here, just call me when you get back around."

She said, "Okay," while still smiling as she pulled off. Within five minutes of her pulling off she texted me: "I want you!"

Me not knowing what was really taking place at the moment sort of ignored it, especially when I noticed I had two missed texts from Haburto's girl Joanne asking me if I was really coming back over? Even though earlier I'd decided that it wasn't a good idea to go back over there and fuck with her, she was texting me now and I was tipsy from the couple of drinks I'd had and ready to fuck. Now I was back thinking about how good her ass and pussy lips were looking in the spandex, so I called saying I'm on my way.

Sounding extra sexy she said, "Okay; I'm waiting."

When she let me in, she was naked, wrapped in a towel, her body still damp from just getting out of the shower smelling clean like Irish Spring soap. Once she locked the door, we wasted no time and started kissing as she let the towel fall to the floor then sat back on the couch unbuckling my pants, biting her bottom lip staring up words into my eyes while I was now anticipating her sucking my dick. Then she did, I was whispering, "Damn, this feeling good as a mother fucker," and even though this is Haburto's girl and I'll probably have no respect for her once we're done, still at this time I came to realize that this was the most attractive woman I'd ever slept with. Her face resembled Jennifer Lopez's as well as her body, and I became fully committed to the moment. Once I was borderline about to cum, I softly pushed her away from my dick, then bent down in front of her in between her legs. At first, I hesitated for a second just rubbing her thighs being that I'd never ate pussy before, but

I was so horny and eager to please her that I was ready for this to be my first time. First, I licked and started sucking on the outside of her pussy lips, then I pulled back the skin so that I could lick the clit like I saw in several pornos. By her reaction, I could tell I was doing it right. She was rubbing my head, moving her waist slowly, speaking Spanish and English saying, "Yes, Poppie!" I had two condoms in my pocket but we were being so passionate that night to do anything other than lay on top of her and put my bare dick inside her wouldn't have felt right after just making her cum from the oral sex. We fucked hard and soft but once we were finished it felt like we made love by the way we fell asleep holding each other like we were in a deep long-term relationship.

Next morning, I woke up to 10 missed calls, one from Donna, Cynthia, and Asia but seven from the white girl Gretchen. After calling Cynthia back to check on my son, I called Donna and Asia back, all three of them seeming to have an attitude, all apparently because I didn't answer the calls last night but I really didn't give a fuck; my selfish behavior only had me focus on my own well-being. Before leaving, I had Joanne bend over and fucked her from the back one last time not sure of what was going to happen between us once I left, seeing that she was still my connect's girl.

Later that day after taking care of the few business moves I had, I figured I'd stop by the pimp nigga I met at Ill Will's auto body shop and chop it up with him for a few to try and pick his brain. Soon as I walked in, he smiled as if he was glad to see me asking what's going on? I nonchalantly said, "Ain't shit, I just wanted take a look at them couple cars for sale you had spoken on."

He showed me a couple of older model Mercedes-Benz's, saying, "This is where the money's at. You can buy this off me for a couple thousand and make almost 20 once you finish doing everything I tell you to." Being that it was only a couple grand I bought it, for one to learn some new things and for two to build a business relationship with him. Seeing that it was said that he used to be a pimp, I figured I'd talk to him about Gretchen not really trying to get advice, but to seem like we had a few things in common seeing that we were now about to bust a move together.

After telling him about Gretchen setting up calls in front of me, and then all the missed calls I woke up to he said, "Man, the bitch was trying to choose you and you didn't even realize it," me being dumbfounded at the time.

I asked him what he meant by "choose me?"

He said, "Give you some money to be with you," then asked her name. After I told him Gretchen, with his hand over his mouth with an exciting expression he said, "Oh shit, Gretchen," and then described her to the tee.

I said, "Yeah, that's her."

While giggling, he added, "That's Derek's bottom bitch, and I heard she was running around here loose, that's a good bitch; she be getting paper."

I said, "Yeah, well I have to hit her up in a minute and see what's up with some of that."

"Yeah, you better because trust me, no money like hoe money," he said and we both laughed.

Then he said, "Listen, if she saying she want to be with, you make sure she give you some money so that you know that she's not just playing games with you, because them hoes do that when they suspect that you ain't a pimp; they be trying to get some free dick. Tell her you want some money and Derek's number so you can call him and tell him that the bitch with you now so that there's no problems and it's all pimping."

I said, "Ok," and gave him two grand for the car telling him that I'd be back for it tomorrow.

While getting back in the car I was anxious now to call Gretchen and see what was going on. She said, "Glad you're all right, I was a little worried when you didn't answer last night," and then she asked what I was doing.

I said, "Nothing, wanting to see you, where you at?"

She said, "I'm in Quincy at my girlfriend Jen's house, this is where I'm staying for a few till I get myself re-situated, seeing that I just moved out from my man's place a couple weeks ago."

I said, "Okay, where's that?"

She gave me the address then I headed that way acting like I didn't have any idea of anything. Once I got there and in the apartment her girlfriend Jen came out of the bathroom looking down walking into the bedroom and closed the door; not fully aware of how this pimping thing works, I didn't know she was avoiding eye contact with me because she had a pimp and wasn't allowed to look any black man in the face unless she was choosing.

Me and Gretchen talked for like 20 minutes with her doing most of the talking, asking me questions about girlfriends, who I live with, and how I get money.

I said, "No, I don't have a girlfriend, and I live by myself, but as for how I get money that's not something I just discuss with everybody, maybe one day we'll get close and I'll tell you about it."

She said, "I can respect that," while touching and checking out my Rolex. Granted, I didn't immediately ask for some money like III Will told me to. I could tell she was on me and that I'd get to that real soon by how tight she hugged me after asking for one on my way out the door. Once again when I left she texted me like 10 minutes later, but this time saying: "I want to be with you." At that point, I knew I had her and instantly started feeling a little different, sort of like I'd just won something.

Several hours had passed, and now I was over at YG's house checking out a brochure of the house that we were renting down the Cape in the upcoming week when Gretchen called me sounding scared, upset, and hysterical all at the same time. I told her to calm down because I couldn't fully understand her speaking so loudly. She calmed down a bit and asked, "Where are you?"

I said, "Close, why, what's up?"

She said, "Derek just came to Jen's, banging on the door threatening to fuck me up if I don't hurry up and come back to his house, and I don't want to be with him anymore."

I said, "Yeah, so what is it that you wanna do?"

She said, "Be with you."

I was happy but not trying to sound like it, saying, "That sounds good, but I'm not accepting any game playing, nor any lies or disloyalty."

She said, "I've been nothing but honest to you since I met you and don't plan on changing."

I said, "Cool, well grab your clothes and all the money you have and have Jen drop you off to me at Frank's."

She said, "Okay, give me like 40 minutes to an hour because I have $500 on me but stashed $2,000 at my mother's. I want to go get it."

Trying to sound all smooth, I said, "Cool, I'll be there," then hung up the phone and started laughing all excited with YG, saying to him, "Ya boy's a pimp, it's time to start getting some hoe money."

Excited for me he said, "Okay, pimping!" then I left to go sit at Frank's and wait.

In the middle of my second shot of Remy she called me almost an hour later on the dot saying, "You can come outside. I'm here."

Once I got outside, I purposely tried looking at her girlfriend Jen in the eyes to see what she'd do; it was just like at her house, she looked away.

I took Gretchen's two duffel bags and put them in my trunk as she hopped in my car, telling Jen that she will call her once she's dressed and ready for work. So, as I got in the car, before I could even put it in drive she handed me a knot of money, saying it was $2,500.

I just nodded my head, then took off to bring her to my apartment down on Mass Ave. Now that she gave me some money, I felt it was time to do something physical to take charge of her body, so I stuck my hand in her bra and rubbed her nipple with my index finger, then seeing that she had on a skirt I put my hand in her panties and started fingering her. She started breathing hard and moving her body in a sexual motion while rubbing my dick, so I didn't stop until I pulled up at my building. First thing she said once getting in my apartment was, "This is nice, I figured you had a decent place but I didn't expect it to be this nice."

I moved all my clothes to one side of the closet making room for hers. That's when it really hit me, thinking, *damn, this better be worth it. I'm really moving a bitch into my secret spot.* Not trusting her yet, I took all my jewelry and money out of the apartment and brought it to my mom's leaving nothing worth value there once I left her alone. I sat there with her for a couple of hours picking her mind and helping her feel welcome before giving her the extra set of keys, then leaving to take care of some business. She called me within the next hour saying she was about to leave with Jen to go to work and that she would keep me posted on what's going on. I said, "Cool, be careful."

She said, "Okay," then reminded me that I hadn't called Derek yet to serve, plus, she said that he'd been calling but she didn't answer. After getting that money, I totally forgot about everything else. I said, "Text me his number so I can hit him right now and get his mind right. I'll call you after I speak with him and if he calls you after that let me know."

She said, "Okay, baby," then hung up sounding relieved and confident that I could take care of her. I called him not knowing if I should be rude or polite, seeing that this was my first time serving a nigga so I stayed in the middle saying, "Hello, is this Derek?"

When answering the phone he said, "Yeah, who's this?" with a sort of angry tone to his voice.

I said, "Mike," while putting more bass in my voice than I initially intended.

He said, "Yeah, what's up?"

"I'm calling concerning Gretchen."

He asked, "What about?"

I said, "She paid me and I put her up. I'm just letting you know so we don't have any problems, feel me?"

Instead of answering me he asked me if I was a pimp. Not knowing how to answer that upset me to the point where I just said, "Naw, I'ma killa. Fuck all this talking, do we need to meet somewhere and talk in person?" at the same time realizing that his voice sounded familiar.

Then he said, "Naw, talking like that you ain't no pimp," then he hung up.

I tried calling back and got no answer. Then, about 10 minutes after that, Gretchen called me saying, "He just called me again and I answered because the number was blocked, saying, 'oh, you messing with gang members now. Well, I ain't accepting no serving for you period!'"

I said, "Cool. Don't worry about it, just take care what you need to do and I'll call him from your phone once we get together."

She said, "Okay, Daddy, I'll come meet you once I come from this call I'm on my way to now."

I said, "Cool. I'll be waiting!"

I called Calvin to tell him about my pimping endeavors and her girl Jen, plus to have him drive me just in case I needed to go find this nigga Derek and run down on him. Seeing that I just got a taste of that pimping money and she was out getting me some more, I wasn't about to let anybody or anything coming between this for a while. By the time she came to meet me I had already jumped in with Calvin, strapped up and waiting on her. She got out of Jen's car and jumped in Calvin's backseat handing me $400 that she just made off her first call. Immediately after I said, "Call Derek from your phone and hand it to me." She did and he answered sounding shocked once he heard my voice instead of hers. With an angry tone I said, "I tried calling you back from my phone but you're not answering. I felt disrespected by how that last conversation went and now I want to meet somewhere so that we can get some understanding, because I'm not going back and forth with you over the phone like bitches."

He said, "Naw, we don't need to meet, you can have the bitch. She don't mean shit to me anyways. I'm a pimp, they come and go, so fuck her."

I calmed down saying, "Cool, man, I appreciate it, and would appreciate you not calling her no more," then hung up. Before she got out of the car to go back to work with Jen, I introduced Calvin to her saying, "He's like my brother," and that she should tell her girl Jen to leave whoever the nigga she with and get with Calvin so that the four of us can be around each other all the time making moves.

She said, "Okay, I'll talk to her about it," then got out. With the $2,500 I got earlier, then her just jumping in and giving me $400, Calvin was stoked and wanted in bad. We laughed and talked about it all the way back to where I parked my car. Before getting out, I reassured him that I was going to try to see to it that he at least get a chance to spit his game at Gretchen's friend Jen. He said, "Word," knowing I would because he was my nigga like that back then. Granted, I had well over $100,000 stacked at the time, this money I got from Gretchen felt like an accomplishment.

I stopped by Tony's house to tell him about the pimping. He wasn't home, but his girlfriend Tammy and her mother Darleen were. Seeing that Darleen had been in the game before, I figured I'd ask her a couple of questions and try to pick up a few pointers on how to be a good pimp. The smile Tammy had on her face when I first came in disappeared once she heard me telling Darleen about my new hoe and the money she gave me and how I moved her into my apartment. Darleen was excited for me, explaining things to me excitedly with a smile on her face telling me things, like "The moment she gets out of line, get on her ass, make sure you let her know that just because she's your first hoe, you ain't dumbfounded by nothing and let it be known right off the rip that you're not accepting her stashing any money and that you want it all!"

We laughed about it a little bit while I explained to her how she looks, then she asked me did I serve her last pimp. I said yes, telling her how that went, then she asked me his name. Once I said Derek, the look on her face was priceless. She immediately asked what the hoe's name was, and after I said Gretchen she said, "Oh shit," repeating it three times in a row as if she was shocked about something before saying, "That's Derek I used to be with, I know Gretchen very well. I was with him when he first got her."

Then it dawned on me that I did think his voice was familiar, especially now knowing that I spoke to him before when I called him about putting his hands on Darleen. The whole time Tammy was acting like she was not paying us any attention, but then she said, "Damn, you got mad girls," with a look of disgust on her face on the way out the door, not saying good-bye to me or her mother.

I stayed for about 10 more minutes talking to Darleen, then I left. Shortly after that, Gretchen called saying she'd just left one call and was on her way to another call and would call me when she's done. I said, "Cool, I'll be down at the spot when you finished for the night."

I went home kind of early that night and started sipping on lil' Remy and watching a porno waiting on her to come in knowing that she had at least another $400 for me which would make $800 for the night. I took a shower, then just chilled out naked in my house slippers and robe. She came in somewhere around 3:15 putting her keys and $500 dollars on the table in front of me, saying, "Hey, handsome."

I said, "Hey, pretty," opening my robe and rubbing my dick in an up and down motion telling her to, "come here."

Knowing that I wanted my dick sucked, she said, "Give me a second, let me brush my teeth and rinse my mouth," which instantly made me look at her differently than I initially did and gained some respect for her. She walked back into the living room and I pointed down indicating to her that I wanted her to get on her knees while I was sitting on the couch. She got down moving her hair to one side, then started sucking my dick. My first thought was, *yeah, her mouth's wet, plus I'm horny from the money she gave me and the fact that I haven't fucked a white girl in years,* but after the first minute I had to pull it out of her mouth and tell her to slow down because I couldn't enjoy it with how fast she was sucking it. She said, "I'm sorry, baby, I'm just so used to sucking fast to make a trick cum so I can get my money and leave."

Then I said, "Well recognize the difference and slow down and suck it the right way."

She said okay while looking me in my eyes, now slowly sucking it moaning as if me talking to her like that made her horny. Once I came she got up to go clean her mouth again then jumped in the shower. That's when I counted the money up, then took two condoms out of my wallet, and put them in my housecoat pocket ready to fuck. She came out and we got right to it. In my mind I'm saying I'm sure she's come across all different size dicks, and seeing that mine is just average size it was important to me that night that I was above average in bed. Just to show some complete dominance, I went for the ass first while pulling her hair and rubbing her clit. Once she came, I switched condoms in seconds, then got on top of her staring down in her face saying, "Yeah, this mine now!" After about forty minutes, I came again, feeling confident about the way I just laid it down because it was obvious that she was satisfied by how she started coming for the second time while I was coming.

The next morning, I let her ride with me to pick up money and hand out some work. Even though I felt it was too early to let her see all my business, she was officially living in my apartment, which was eventually going to require all my trust. We picked up twenty thousand and fronted out a half a key; she stayed quiet, only speaking to give me the amount of money I handed her to count.

After running around, I dropped her off at the building with the bag of money saying, "Bring this upstairs with you. I got some other shit to take care of. I'll see you later. Call me when you leave out."

She said ok, then got out. Though she didn't say anything at the moment I could tell she was impressed, which was one of the reasons I let her hold the money. For one, I wanted to show some trust and for two, I wanted her to see that I get my own so that if she thought that she could play with me in any way because she gave me some money then this would signify to her that I didn't need her and I was going to do good with or without her!

As the day progressed, I got a call from Ray Dog [Benzino] sounding excited about a track him, Jeff and JB had made the night before saying, "You gotta hear this, McNeill, it's hard an aggressive. I can't hear no one on this but you, an I want you to come lay a solo to it tonight."

I said, "Cool, I'll be out there tonight."

He said, "Cool, around ten's good."

I said, "Cool," then hung up. At the time, I had about ten to twelve verses written that no one had heard and seeing that we were a group, that was enough music for the next album, but Ray [Benzino] had just raised the bar by wanting me to do a song alone. I knew the expectation from my friends would be high on the song, seeing that I'd been being compared to some of the greats by my friends and that's only from verses I'd done, so to me it was important that I do something special. It had to have all the elements in it that made me stand out as an artist. In order to do this, I needed to mentally be in a special place, and there was no place that could put me there like my old bedroom at my mother's house, so I went there, turned my phone off and started writing. The streets are the streets, and granted I took chances and hustled hard to be in this position, I was in to my music now, my true passion. Ray [Benzino] calling me to do this solo song was big to me! I looked at it as a testament to my progression, and I was going to use this as an opportunity to show how far ahead of the group I really was.

Hours passed and I was ready. I called Calvin to come park at my mom's house and jump in with me so that he could hear me get it in. On the way to the studio, Gretchen called telling me she was getting ready to leave with Jennifer to a call and asking where should she put the bag with the money that I totally forgot about while focusing on the song. I said, "The closet," then told her, "I'm on my way to the studio," and that she could come out there to bring me the money she makes when she finishes. She just said ok, trying not to seem too excited, but I could easily tell that she was.

It was cool though. This way, I could impress her more, plus seeing that she was with Jennifer, Calvin could get the opportunity to say what he wanted to say to her. While in the middle of recording the last verse, I could see Calvin answering my phone and heading out of the studio room. Within two to three minutes, he walked back in with Gretchen staring and smiling at me while I put the finishing touches on a track I called "Treason."

The song was now done and it was hot. Once I came back in the engineering room, me, Ray [Benzino] and Calvin all celebrated like a World Series win while playing it back to hear it from the beginning. I asked Gretchen, "You like it?"

She said, "Yeah, you sound really good," while reaching in her bra to pull out the three hundred she made before coming to see me. I took her by the hand and started walking her back to the car while telling Ray I'd be right back and Calvin to come on. I started hugging her and whispering in her ear, walking through the hallway to the exit saying, "Have Jen get with my man."

She whispered back, "I can't make her, but she did look at him and said that he was cute!"

I turned around to Calvin jokingly saying, "Yo, cuz, it's time to make your move. Jennifer said you're cute."

We got outside, and I kissed Gretchen before she got back in the car. I said, "Straighten that," meaning egg Jen on to speak with Calvin even though she was with some pimp named Blinky at the time.

She said, "Give me a second."

Then she got in and spoke with Jennifer for a moment alone, then the driver's window came down with Gretchen saying, "Calvin, this is Jennifer, and Jennifer, this is Mike's boy Calvin."

Calvin and Jen talked for their first time, within minutes I could see Calvin installing her number in his phone. After a brief convo about my music, I told Gretchen to call me once she came off her next call, then her and Jen pulled off.

Calvin was happy and I was happy for him, because it was going to be no time before he started to get some of that pimping money too.

Within the next hour of listening to Ray [Benzino] mix down the song, we were visited by Willie McGinest and Lawyer Milloy of the New England Patriots. At the time one of my boys named Beef was Willie's bodyguard and spent a lot of time with him in the off season, so once Ray [Benzino] told him about the new track I'd just laid, Beef didn't hesitate to bring him through to hear the joint and just check the studio in general. Willie was cool as shit. Even though he was an NFL superstar, I could still feel the street nigga in him. Lawyer, on the other hand, was a lot different. Although he did speak, I could tell by his facial expressions and posture that he wasn't really feeling being here and couldn't care less about meeting anyone other than Ray [Benzino], so I treated him the same way by blatantly ignoring him, not even introducing myself nor extending my hand out for a shake.

Willie listened to my new track not knowing that it was me. He said, "Yo, he's hot, who is this?"

Ray [Benzino] said, "McNeill! Right there."

I said thanks, feeling validated and shook his hand again. Then he said, "You don't sound like you from Boston."

I said, "Yeah, I heard that before."

Then he told me about his artists and an independent label he was starting called 55 Entertainment. I could tell from that first meet and greet that we had real nigga chemistry and would probably become cooler down the line.

Gretchen called me telling me that she had some money for me and to see, if I was coming to pick it up, instead of waiting on her to bring it home, because if so she would be at Jennifer's.

Then I heard Jennifer in the background yelling out, "Bring Calvin with you when you come!"

I said, "Cool, we on our way."

After telling Calvin what's up, we said peace to everybody and left with me still not acknowledging Lawyer Milloy or shaking his hand on the way out.

Once we got to Jennifer's apartment, she was speaking and looking me in my face which was different from the first couple of times we met. While her and Calvin went into the kitchen and started talking, I took Gretchen into Jen's bedroom and closed the door to see how much money she had for me and to take advantage of the moment and get me a dick suck real quick before she got another call. Without saying anything, I pulled my limp dick out and she sat at the edge of the bed and started sucking it till I came. Soon as I bust a nut, and before fully pulling my pants up I said, "Let me see that paper!"

She went to the bathroom real quick to clean her mouth up, then came back in the room reaching into her bra and handed me three hundred and some change. I rubbed through her hair being sort of rough pulling her neck back slightly as to say "good job" then gave her a kiss on her cheek, saying, "I'll see you at the house later."

She said ok, then then added, "Tell your friend if he wants Jennifer, he should claim her tonight because she just left Blinky and she has some money on her."

I said, "Ok, I will."

Then she said, "Make sure you tell him that he has to call Blinky and serve him."

I told her I would, while walking out of the room and asking Calvin if he was ready. He said yeah, while telling Jennifer that he'd be back later as if he had set it up to come back for the night. Once we were in the car pulling off, the first thing I asked him was, "Did you get some money?"

He said, "Naw, but I can tell I will tonight."

Feeling happy for him I said, "Cool, and when you do, make sure you call the nigga she was just with and tell him what's up, because Gretchen be talking like serven the nigga is important."

We went over a few things while laughing and joking before he dropped me back to my whip. Before pulling off in my car, I wound my window down smiling and said, "Welcome to the pimp game. Congratulations, player," then pulled off.

Although Cynthia wasn't a big complainer, I did know that she had a lil' attitude about me not waking up with her and my son the last few days and figured it was time to go let her know about Gretchen and me pimping. First thing I did once I got in her house was pick up my son and kiss him, then I told Cynthia that I had something I needed to speak to her about. Looking at me with an angry and curious look on her face, she asked me what!

I said, "Listen, I met this white girl a few days ago that runs an escort service and she gave me a few thousand so far to be with me, so as of now I'm her pimp!"

Cynthia replied, "So I guess that's why you ain't stayed here in a few days?"

I said, "Yeah, I've been just trying to get her situated to where I don't have to spend much time with her and still get that paper!"

She asked, "Did you have sex with her?"

Not really wanting to lie, and surprised that she asked me that, I hesitated for a sec and then said, "Naw!"

She said, "Give me my baby, Mike. I can tell when you lying, don't come out the street kissing on hoes then walk in here kissing an touching on him without washing your face an hands."

I said, "Chill out, you got it all wrong; this ain't like some dirty feen bitch. She clean an takes good care of herself."

She said, "Yeah, I can tell by how you speaking up for her that you already fucked her. Me an you ain't having sex no more. I ain't trying to catch AIDS so you can go on with your hoe an them other bitches you was already fucking an leave me alone, cause I'm done!"

With me and her both knowing that I would never let anything like my feelings for her stop me from getting some money, I yelled out, "Whatever! I'm trying to keep it real with you an let you know what's up, an this how you act. Fuck it, I'm out!" while heading towards the door. I then added, "I'll be back later," before slamming the door behind me.

She shouted after me, "No need to!"

I was a lil' agitated but really didn't give a fuck because I knew she wasn't going anywhere. I slid down to Frank's to have a couple of drinks while waiting on word from Gretchen. I pulled up and there were police everywhere. I went inside and all my niggas were in there with looks on their faces like something had happened. I gave everybody dap then asked, "What's going on?"

Bum told me that Belnel Mike and his boys had a shootout across the street and one of them got hit in the neck. Belnel Mike and his boy Duke were in the Wise Guys, but besides that me and Mike were in middle school together and sort of stayed close and kept in contact with one another over the years. So, I called him to check on him to see if he was straight or if he needed me for anything. He didn't answer, so I took it as either they were in the hospital or out riding trying to kill someone for what happened, seeing that over the last couple of years Belnel dogs became a violent street gang looked at by the police for a few homicides and multiple shootings. A couple of drinks and a couple of hours later I went to the spot to wait on Gretchen to come home with some more paper, but I fell asleep before she came in.

The next morning, I woke up with Gretchen lying next to me still sleeping. I tried sliding out of the bed without waking her up, but then she said in a sleepy voice, "There's five hundred in my purse."

I said, "Ok," then kissed her on her head and told her to get some rest while I got up to take a shower. As soon as I got out while drying off, I started thinking about Calvin and his pimping, and Belnel Mike and his man that got shot. I hit Calvin up first asking, "What's good. You get some money?"

He replied, "Yeah, she gave me six hundred."

I said, "Ok. Did you call an serve the nigga Blinky?"

Sounding confident he said, "Yeah, fa sho'." We laughed seeing that we found that serven shit funny. I hung up with Calvin and hit Belnel Mike up.

He answered sounding tired, saying, "What's good, miz? I seen your calls last night but I wasn't in no position to answer."

I said, "Yeah, I figured that. Give me a call when you get to your mom's crib."

He said, "Ok," then hung up.

Dressed and now on my way out the door, I realized I got a missed call and text from Asia saying: "Hi, Mike. I am heading over to Tammy's house and I got the key to my new place in East Boston and would like to take you by to see it. Call me or come by Tammy's house if you have time!"

I hadn't seen her in a while, so I made a mental note to stop by there after I finished taking care of my business, but my priority for the day was to get with Cynthia and get the Benz I bought from Ill Will registered, so I could start making those insurance moves. Cynthia was fully aware of what I needed her to do for me and granted she was still upset about me now having Gretchen living with me, she was still going to handle the business at hand. She answered the phone with an attitude.

Smoothly, I said, "Hey, baby."

She replied, "I'm not your baby, your baby's upstairs asleep." To avoid confrontation, I just overlooked her attitude and sat quietly while she got my son and herself together so we could go get the car situated.

By the time me and Cynthia got the car situated, Belnel Mike called me back now at his mother's house telling me to come by. Pulling up I could instantly see the anger and pain in Belnel Mike's face! I asked, "What happened, bra?"

He said some bullshit popped off and niggas ended up getting into a shootout and Eight ended up getting hit in the throat.

"Yeah? Damn! Is he ok?" I asked.

He replied, "He's cool; yeah, that nigga be home tomorrow."

I said, "Ok, let me know if you need anything; just holla at me an I got you."

He replied, "I know, Mizz, but we cool; we was on them niggas' backs over it last night. We gonna straighten it."

I said, "Alright, my nigga, I'll holla at you later," leaving while a couple of his niggas I didn't know were pulling up looking upset. I could tell they were about to talk about who and how they were going to further their retaliation. Being that this is the weekend of the Fourth of July coming up, and I had a house rented for the weekend down the Cape, I needed to run around and tie up any loose ends. Granted, Gretchen had earned a little bit of my trust, but there still was no way I was going to leave over $20,000 including the money she had with her while I leave for a week.

Getting to my apartment I ran in and out not saying much other than, "I'll be back, I gotta handle something," then left. I grabbed the bag of money from my spot and brought it to my mother's house; then I called everyone that owed me money seeing who had what before I left that Thursday.

Donna still had money and my Tec at her mom's house for me. I stopped by Greenwood to tell her that I was leaving in a couple days for a few days and I could see in her face that she felt some way about what I said. So, I asked her, "Are you alright?"

Looking bothered she said, "Yeah, I'm cool. I just noticed that you been really busy lately an doing you, and I've been wondering where do I fit in, cause lately it seems like I only see you when you stop by here to see Lil Mike or if you need me to do something for you."

I was brushing what she was saying off by rubbing her face and pulling her waist close to mine telling her that everything was good and that once I get back in town, we were gonna spend some time together.

With a frown on her face she said, "Ok, we'll see."

I said, "Fa real, I'll see you when I get back," then went upstairs to holla at her cousin Mike to see if he wanted to see me one more time before I left town.

He said, "Naw, I'm good till you get back."

I said, "Alright, I'm out."

This wasn't the first time me and Cynthia went through this barely speaking shit, so I'd come to know that when she gets like that it means she wants me to come over, kiss her ass and stay the night, basically make her feel important by begging for some sex while she says no knowing she really wants to fuck. Usually after I throw the dick down real good, talk about us being a family for a few, then leave a few dollars for her to pretty herself up she'd be good.

So, knowing that I was going to Cynthia's house that night I figured I'd stop by Tammy's crib to holla at my cousin Tony and pick up Asia for a few, take her to let me see her new apartment seeing that she texted me earlier sounding proud to have her own again. Once I got in Tammy's apartment everybody was seemingly in a good mood. Tony was counting up some money from a couple plays he made, Asia was smiling just happy that I came to see her, and Tammy was cheerful, speaking about the rest of the things she was going to the mall to get for her trip this weekend.

I said hello to everybody; me and Tony shook hands while Asia and Tammy simultaneously replied, "Hey, Mike."

Then I said, "What's up, Tam, you going on a trip this weekend?"

She replied, "Yeah, nowhere far, I'm just going to the Cape for the weekend."

I said, "Ooh, I should have figured that, cause mad people going down this year. Me too. I'm leaving tomorrow, me, an my nigga YG rented a house for five days." Then I looked at Tony and said, "What's good, cuz, you still don't wanna go?"

He said, "Naw, I'm chilling."

I sat next to Asia on the couch and asked her, "How you doing?"

She said, "I'm good, glad to be finished with that shelter and to have my Section Eight certificate."

In the middle of us talking Tammy's mother Darleen came in with a big smile on her face. She looked at me and loudly said, "Hey, Pimping, how's things going with Gretchen?"

Even though it'd been at least a year since me and Darleen had sex, I could tell that she still harbored some feelings for me but had too much pride to act on them knowing that I'd moved on to another chapter in my life. But she was definitely saying it in a sarcastic way having heard that I'd been messing with Asia. I said, "Good good, she getting my paper to me like she supposed to, plus we hooked Calvin an her girl Jen up so he getting some of that hoe money too."

With a serious look on her face she said, "That was dumb!"

I asked, "Why you say that?"

She then told me, "If Gretchen had a friend that was ready to choose, you should have gotten her; you could have had both them hoes."

I said I honestly wasn't thinking about that, plus I wanted Calvin to have her so that we can pimp together.

She giggled while walking in to the back room saying, "Ain't no friends in this game, baby, you'll learn later, one day, that if you gonna pimp you gotta pimp alone!"

Now Tammy's ride was outside blowing the horn for her to come out. She kissed Tony, then grabbed her purse asking Asia what she was doing.

Asia replied, "I don't know," looking at me for a response.

I said, "Come on, I'ma ride out to check your new apartment."

Tammy said, "Ok, girl, I'll call you when I get back."

Asia said bye, then me and her walked out behind Tammy after I told Tony that I'd be back in a couple of hours. Asia hadn't put any furniture in her apartment yet so I knew that asking me to see it was just a way to spend some time with a nigga, plus I figured there's a nice Italian restaurant I liked in East Boston that I hadn't had in a while that we could eat at after checking out her place.

It was a decent spot, nothing impressive but what I did like was that it wasn't right in Boston and I knew I'd feel comfortable stashing money and drugs there. I looked around a couple times and said, "Yeah, this is nice," before grabbing her by the hand and directing her to the bathroom, bending her over the sink and pulling her pants and panties down to her knees. My dick wasn't fully erect so while leaning against her. I said, "Put my dick in," knowing that her putting her hands on it would make it hard. I was squeezing her ass harder than I regularly do and spreading her ass cheeks apart further than usual, fucking her from the back aggressively talking to her saying, "This my pussy," asking her, "whose pussy is this?"

With both hands in front of her on the wall pushing back down on my dick she was saying, "Yours yours!" Within ten minutes I started cumming, with her saying, "Don't pull it out, I'm about to cum!" This was supposed to be a quickie; still, after I nutted I left my limp dick in her for a couple more minutes so that she could cum. There wasn't anything in the apartment yet, so with cum on my dick and in her pussy we both just pulled up our pants and left.

After we ate at the restaurant I liked out there, I dropped her off to her sister's so that she could clean herself up, telling her to call me when she was ready and I'd come drop her back off at Tammy's. I called Ray Dog [Benzino] to see when he was he leaving for the Cape and where the house and boat that he'd rented for the weekend located.

After telling me the location he said, "I'm leaving tonight so that I can meet someone down there I don't want no one to see me with."

We laughed, then I said, "Damn, nigga, you been fucking a lot of these nigga's bitches out here lately."

We laughed even harder, even though me and him were joking, what I had said was true, seeing that over the last year as his position in the source magazine became more identifiable, more females made themselves available to him. Not that Ray didn't have girls before that, but being called an owner and CEO of our record company definitely boosted his stock.

My bags were packed in the trunk. I had the Bema detailed emailer in the week; the main nigggas that I dealt with had been served and fronted extra work, so I was basically ready to go. Gretchen hadn't even been with me a month at this time and I didn't give a fuck. Granted, I liked her and how well she fit in with what I was doing out here. However, I wouldn't let me trying to keep her alter anything I wanted to do or how I was living one bit. I definitely had the my way or the highway mentality. But she was such a good hoe at the time and appreciative, that to an extent I trusted her and kind of just knew she was happy being with me and would be on point while I was gone. Besides, I didn't leave anything in the house worth taking just in case!

I was getting out of the shower down at my spot finally washing the cum of my dick from fucking Asia earlier, talking to Gretchen about my trip and what I expected from her when I get back. For some reason I was under the impression that when I gave her orders and demands I was being a good pimp, so I said, "While I'm gone, I'm still expecting you to call me on the way to and from calls. You hear me?"

She replied, "Yes, I'm a big girl, I'll be alright while you're gone for a few days. Enjoy yourself and don't worry about me because I'm wit you cause I wanna be, not because I have to be." Then she smiled and hugged me while I was naked looking through my closet to put something on. With my bath towel wrapped around my waist, she pulled the towel off and started rubbing my balls, and even though I had a quickie with Asia earlier, and I knew I had to fuck Cynthia the right way later that night before I leave, Gretchen declaring her loyalty to me on top of stroking my dick made me horny again, plus I was thinking, ain't no way I can tell my bitch that be paying for the dick, not while she's horny, so fuck it, let me go ahead and fuck her too. I gave her a small kiss on the lips, then said, "Go get me a condom, then go in the living room and play with that pussy and have it wet for me by time I get in there."

She was a freak, she loved when I ordered and talked to her like that. After like three to five minutes of picking out an outfit and stalling so that she could get wetter I went in there. She was finger fucking and by the expression on her face and how shiny her fingers were, I could tell she already came once. I put my dick in her mouth for a few minutes, just enough to fully get it hard, then I told her to bend over and to keep rubbing that pussy. I put the condom on and started fucking her the same way I fucked Asia earlier, squeezing her cheeks as hard and pulling them open as wide. The only difference was I was pulling Gretchen by the hair and she loved it. It took me a lil while longer to cum seeing that I had a condom on plus this was my second nut but I didn't mind the effort. I figured, shit, this 'bout my money; as long as I keep her satisfied, she gonna keep me satisfied. I nutted, got back in the shower and dressed saying, "No slacking, baby, cause I'm gone. I'm expecting a few Gs to be in the house when I get back."

She said, "Ok, I'll do my best, have fun and I'll call you to keep you posted."

I agreed, then gave her another kiss and said be good before leaving out. I had two Gs in my pocket, all my drug business taken care of, I just dicked my hoe down and she seemed secure, my trunk was full of fly shit, car clean; I was ready to leave in the morning. I called Asia to see if she wanted a ride back over to Tammy's before I left to get up with Cynthia and my son for the rest of the day.

She said yeah, she was ready. I picked Asia up and now we were parked in front of Tammy's house waiting for her to pull up, and after hanging up with Tammy on her cell phone, Asia came out of the blue and said, "Sometimes I get the impression that Tammy likes you!"

I looked at her with my face screwed up and said, "Why would you say some stupid shit like that!"

She replied, "It ain't stupid shit. I've been noticing lil shit lately but I'll keep it to myself just in case I'm wrong but I have been noticing lil shit."

I said, "Yeah, well keep it to yourself because you're wrong and I don't get that impression." Automatically, I started thinking about the conversation me and Tammy had at Frank's, then I started thinking about what Ray Dog [Benzino] said about leaving tonight to spend time with someone he didn't wanna be seen with considering that I did see them talking one on one outside when I pulled up at Frank's that night. Within minutes, Tammy arrived, got out and started getting her bags out her girlfriend's trunk. While getting out my car Asia asked, "When you coming back?"

I said, "I'm not sure, but I'll call you when I do."

She said, "Ok, have fun," seeming a lil sad that she was just getting herself together and really couldn't afford to go.

While I was pulling off, Tammy waved and I waved back letting down my window saying, "What's up, when y'alll leaven?"

She said, "My girlfriend's picking me up tomorrow at seven in the morning. When you leaven?"

I said, "In the morning as well. I'll probly bump into y'all down there."

"It's only so big," she said.

"I know," then I said, "alright, I'm out. Tell Tony I said I'll hit him when I get back."

Ok."

For reasons I didn't know at that moment I felt like I was relieved of something, knowing that it wasn't her that Ray dog was tricking with. I blew the horn and pulled off to go spend time with Cynthia and my son before I leave in the morning.

CHAPTER FIVE

Calling Cynthia was just like I expected, attitude and acting like she barely wanted to speak which I expected, so instead of catching an attitude I played along with it. She said, "I'm not home. I'm over Netty's," sarcastically adding, "If you ain't pimping tonight and have time to see your son, we'll be home."

Within an hour, while waiting on her to get home, I stopped by Frank's to have a couple shots plus holla at niggas to see when they're leaving for the Cape. I walked in and noticed niggas were hyped up and laughing about something. I said, "What's good?"

"Bum," said my nigga, "you just missed it."

"Missed what?"

He said, "Cuz, there was a couple of niggas in here drinking, everything's cool, then Wiz noticed that one of the dudes kept staring at niggas, so I asked him what's up. Is everything alright? Dude started talking shit then shit got crazy, we started beating the nigga's ass, then one of them pulled out a gun, then I bussed him in the head with a bottle an took his burner."

I said, "Oh shit," then we started laughing. I said, "Where's it at?""

He said, "Right here," and showed me a scratched up Glock nine fully loaded.

Then we joked with me saying, "Damn, they need to come back with a couple more of them for us to take," while ordering me a double shot of Remy.

Bum described the dude as having undone braids with a beard and thick sideburns. We joked throwing out various names we could call him since we didn't know his real name. Then Bum said, "That nigga's head was big as shit, I'ma call hem lion head." We fell out laughing but paying close attention to the door and who came in, just in case they tried to come back.

It was over an hour, but Cynthia did call back saying she was home but Michael's asleep, basically saying he should be the only reason I wanna come over. I said, "It's cool, I'm still on my way."

She said, "I don't know what for, he's asleep an ain't nothing else over here for you," then hung right up.

When I got there, she was wearing a sweat suit as opposed to the nightgown she usually put on when she knows I'm coming over, as if to say you ain't getting none! I softly grabbed her arm and tried to pull her close to me. She pulled away and said, "Your son in his crib an don't wake him up when you get in there."

I said, "I'll wait till he wake up," then added, "come here, give me a hug."

She replied, "Naw, I'm straight, you can go hug your hoe!"

I said, "Damn, baby, I know you ain't sweating that hoe? That's just about money." Then I pulled out a knot from my pocket and said, "She gave me this."

She said, "I don't give a fuck about that money, Mike, that money ain't shit. You had money before you met her and I'm not mad at you, you just ain't gonna be sleeping with a hoe then sleeping with me period! I'm not mad."

I said, "I ain't sleeping with her," then touched her ass, but she pushed my hand away.

"Yeah, Mike, tell that to someone else cause I ain't trying to hear it."

I went upstairs and admired my son for a few, then accidentally woke him up by kissing him on his head. Once she heard him crying, she said, "Damn! Didn't I tell you not to wake him up?"

I said, "Chill out, I didn't mean to, but I got him."

She came upstairs to assist me, making sure I was holding his head the right way, then put a blanket over us. Within minutes he went back to sleep. I laid him down next to me on her bed, then took off all my clothes except my boxers and tee and laid across the bed myself. While dozing off, I heard a camera take a picture. I looked up and she was standing in the doorway taking a picture of us, obviously not as upset as she appeared about an hour ago. She put her finger to her mouth and said, "shhhh!" signaling me not to wake him up as she put the camera on her dresser then picked him up to put him back in his crib. With a smile on her face, she came back into the room and said, "You guys looked cute laying there, I had to get a picture of that."

Faking like I was extra tired, I got under the covers and balled up on one side of the bed. She turned the light off making a sighing noise acting like she really didn't want me there, but was just gonna let me stay anyways while taking off her sweat suit and balling up on the opposite side of the bed. I reached over and tried to touch her and she ignorantly said, "No, ain't you tired? Go to sleep."

I said, "Naw, I ain't never too tired for you," while moving closer to her putting my dick up against her ass.

She said, "Well if that's what you really came here for, you might as well go to sleep or leave because it ain't happening."

I asked, "Why, you on your period?"

She said, "No, I just ain't feeling you right now, it's bad enough you fucking other bitches and now a hoe. I just ain't feeling it."

I scooted down underneath the sheets almost to the bottom of the bed and started kissing and sucking on her body from her ankles all the way up her leg to the side of her ass, moving my tongue in the motion you would move it if you were licking a clit; with my head still down near her waist I softly turned her on her back while still kissing and licking on her pelvis and the top of her G string. After eating Haburto's girl Joanna's pussy, I had eaten Cynthia a couple of times and realized that she loved it, so even if she intended on standing her ground and not having sex with me tonight, the fact remained that she loved me and I knew how to make myself irresistible. I was pulling her panties off while still licking on as much of her pussy lips as I could get to till I took her panties fully off when she lifted up so I could fully get them off in the back, then she bent her knees pulling them all the way off herself. While I was sucking her clit and fingering her with three fingers, she started rubbing my head and moaning. After a few minutes I took my fingers out and used her pre cum on them to rub my dick so I could get fully erect. While now sticking my tongue all the way inside her while she spread her legs open as far as they'll go! Within ten minutes I could tell she started to cum, for one by the change in the taste and for two how she started rubbing her clit side to side on the top of my gums. I climbed to the top of the bed to get in her already wet pussy from the side, squeezing her titties, stroking slow and close, I came quick, probably within five minutes but not much cum came out. So I faked it making it seem like I was putting more inside her than I actually was. I had a way of making Cynthia feel like her pussy was the best I'd ever had and that feeling became important to her, it helped her feel secure in our relationship to think that no matter whoever else it was I might have been sleeping with out there, she was still number one.

I woke up the next morning about 4:45 close to five, ready to hit the highway. I slid out of the bed quietly and slipped on my clothes trying not to wake her or my son up. While I was leaving her a few hundred dollars on her nightstand next to the bed, she opened her eyes and asked if I'm leaving. I said, "Yeah, I'm meeting YG at Symco at 5:30."

She said, "Ok, be careful down there."

I said, "I will, plus I'ma keep in touch with you while I'm there to check on y'all."

She said, "Ok, give me a kiss," and after a small kiss we said "I love you" to one another, then I left.

Pulling up at Symco's, I could see YG sitting in his new Lexus coupe looking clean with his hazard slights flashing. I pulled up on him saying, "You good?"

He said, "Yeah, I was just about to call you."

I said, "Ok, let's ride," then sped off with him following me. Once we finally got there, I was pulling up in the driveway saying to myself: damn, this is nice. It was a three bedroom, two bathrooms cottage style house with the landscape very well taken care of. Coming inside I was saying the same: this is nice! Fully furnished with a decent size kitchen. I chose my room, hanging my clothes up in the closet and putting my cosmetics in the bathroom to give the place a home type of feel. I said to YG jokingly, "All this money we paid for this spot you better get some ass cause I know I'm fucking at least three to four new bitches."

He replied, "Well you better catch up cause I got some new pussy coming over tonight. I already set up a few new pieces."

We laughed, then I said, "Yeah, let me get some rest, cuz, so that I can get out here in a few an get started."

A few hours passed and I was up getting showered and dressed to get some breakfast over at the mansion that Ray dog rented. I had my outfits all planned out; first day I came out in a thirty-three hundred dollar gold, red and black silk Versace shirt with some brand new tan Tims. Back then, boots and shorts were in style, and with a gold Rolex on my wrist I was killing em! The mansion where niggas was at was off the hook; it was three times the size of me and YG's crib next to a boat dock with a big ass boat tied down that Ray also rented. I came in asking where's the breakfast, niggas started laughing saying, "You late, fool, but it's a lil something in there left for you." The counters were full of all types of different liquor. While making a sandwich with the rest of the eggs and a few pieces of bacon and pouring me a shot of Remy, I noticed Ray dog wasn't in the TV room with everybody else so I asked, "Where's Ray?"

Hurst said, "Out back on the deck with some skins."

I said, "Damn, he been with her for a couple days now, huh?"

Jenkins replied, "Fuck naw, this one just came this morning, you know that nigga, he den had a couple bitches through here already." We laughed. Noticing that Calvin wasn't there neither, I called him to see when and if he was coming down.

He said, "Yeah, I'll be down shortly. I just have to situate one or two things then meet with Jennifer, then I'll be on my way," which to me meant he had to collect money on some work we had, then go fuck and break Jennifer before he leaves.

I said, "Tight, I'm waiting on you, it's nice out here; hit me when you get around so we can link."

He said, "Ok cool," then hung up.

We were sitting around laughing at old stories, talking shit to one another, getting nice letting time pass so that the town would be packed when we came out deep and do our first walk through, letting people know we were here. YG finally came in, and I was like, "Damn, nigga, what took you so long?"

He said, "One of my lil bitches called me, asked was in I town yet, then came through an brought me some breakfast and an early dick suck when you left."

I said, "Ok, player, she was something new?"

He smiled and said, "Naw, I fucked her before, but she really didn't suck the dick right then, so she came through to get it right, then I told her not to call me no more on this trip."

We laughed, and slapped five, while he poured himself a drink. I could see Ray [Benzino] walking his company to her car through the blinds of the glass door on the side of the house. I happened to get a glimpse of her face and she struck me as being familiar but at the moment I couldn't quite put my finger on from where. She pulled off and Ray [Benzino] came into the house yelling, "Where's McNeill at?"

I yelled, "Out in here, cuz!"

He said, "I didn't know you was here till I saw your car."

I said, "I was here for a minute, plus I was in the kitchen an saw you walking with a thick lil bad bitch, Who's she?"

With his facial expression changing he said, "You seen her?"

I said, "Yeah, I seen her before but I can't figure out from where at."

He said, "Sshhhh chill," then giggled and said, "don't tell nobody, my nigga, that's the cop Derek that be in the bar's girl."

I said, "Yeah yeah that's right. I remember seeing them together."

He said, "Yeah, she's a freak. I just finished beating the pussy up out back, but what's good with you? I'm about to jump in the shower an get dressed so that we can hit the streets an get some more bitches."

"I alright, let's do it, we waiting on you," I said, then he ran upstairs to get himself together.

It was about two o'clock in the evening and I was high from the weed and tipsy from the few shots but still vibrant and ready. Ray came downstairs and we left to hit the town. Females were everywhere looking good. Between my car, YG and the Suburban that niggas were in and Ray's car, we had pulled over at least seven times to holla at chicks in traffic or walking on the side of the road. While parking our cars so we could start walking and mixing up with the festivities, I started noticing mad people from Boston I knew out and about with drinks in their hands laughing and having fun. Within no more than ten minutes of us standing in front of a bodega styled pizza shop, I saw Eddy and his boy Dea Dea and a few other dudes that I didn't know at the time walking up the street. Once me and Eddy caught eye contact we both just started smiling before getting close enough to shake hands. With a slight hug he said, "You looking good," while tugging on my Versace shirt and checking out my Rolex.

I said, "Just chilling," smiling and touching on his iced out bracelet and chain. I said, "I already know how you doing?" asking him in a joking way but serious, "What you put on that, my nigga, bout thirty?"

He giggled and said, "Naw, but close to it."

We were definitely glad to see each other doing well, living up to the things we spoke about in jail. After saying what's up and giving dap to all my crew he told me where he was staying on the beach and said, "Hit me up, my nigga, when you get a chance come through so we can kick it for a few."

I said, "Fa sure, I'ma hit you," while giving his boys dap before they turned around and walked up the block.

Several different groups of females were walking up to us asking aren't we from the magazine, and ain't we the Wise Guys. Ray [Benzino] being the most noticeable was getting the pick of the litter but I wasn't doing bad out there at all when it came to getting phone numbers and setting things up for the night. After directing Calvin to exactly where we were standing, he got there and said, "I just saw Tammy and her girls around the corner."

Really paying it no mind, I said, "Yeah, she told me they were coming."

Then he told me that she'd asked for me. I again thought nothing of it and started asking him about Gretchen and Jennifer.

He said, "They cool shit, last I heard they was getting ready to go out an get us some paper."

I giggled and said, "Yeah, I can get used to this shit!"

Every bad bitch that walked past where we were standing was getting booked. I had happened to be getting a phone number from a very pretty tall girl when I caught eye contact with Tammy standing across the street with her girlfriends. I waved to say hi. She looked at me with an eye squinting facial expression as if to say, "I know that's not all you're going to say to me!"

While logging the female's number in my phone, Tammy and her friends started walking in the direction where Calvin and the rest of my boys were standing. I told Tina (the girl I'd just met) that I'll call her later, then headed back up the street myself. Tammy and her girls were now standing next to my niggas smiling and conversing, basically just saying hi from as far as I could see from where I was standing. I walked up and gave Tammy and all her girlfriends a small hug asking them if they were enjoying themselves. Everyone answered, "Yeah, it's cool, we chilling," then Tammy sarcastically said to me, "I see you are, ain't she too tall for you?" meaning the female that she just saw me talking to! I just giggled not committing to the question.

Ray [Benzino] was inside the pizza shop when they walked up but was still there when they came out; he said, "Hey, ladies, what's up?"

They all spoke back with Tammy putting on an extra big smile looking at me from the side of her eyes. It was as if she was trying to make me jealous and for some reason, I did start feeling some type of way. While saying bye and starting to walk off, Tammy turned around and asked me, "Mike, where y'all going tonight?"

With a look on my face showing that I was obviously upset for some reason I said, "I don't know yet, we just out here really just trying to let them go on their way."

She said, "Oh, ok, well I heard some basketball player named Alonzo Morning was having a party on the beach."

Noticing that I had a problem with something she was still being kind of sassy and sarcastic, I said, "I don't know what I'm doing tonight," being sarcastic now myself insinuating that I might be with a female tonight.

She made a facial expression and shook her head as to say, oh, is that right, then said, "Ok, however, enjoy yourself," then walked off seemingly having a problem with something now herself.

Calvin walked up on my left side making sure that no one could hear him and asked me, "Did you peep that?"

I said, "What?"

He said, "Tammy was just looking and talking to you like she got feelings for you or something!"

Me already thinking about Asia saying that same thing a few days ago, I said to him, "Naw, I didn't get that vibe really," just trying to downplay it, lying to my nigga and I knew that he knew it. Ray's [Benzino] a funny dude, he must have peeped what Calvin saw but instead of speaking to me about something so personal knowing that Tammy was my cousin Tony's girl, he said, "Damn! Tammy got a fat ass," while grabbing his dick, then asked me, "Yo, McNeill, she still with Tony?"

I already knew that him speaking on her ass was just to try to get an expression out of me, so I just said, "Yeah," real quick trying to cut the conversation, but with Ray dog being Ray dog that wasn't good enough. He felt like he knew something and was trying to feel me out to see if what he thought was true. So, then he said, "Oh, ok, cause I remember that day me and her was talking outside Frank's the day of Vee's party, you pulled up and she just stopped talking and said she going inside as if her man had just pulled up. Then when me and you spoke you seemed like you were upset about something."

Squinting my face trying to be convincing I said, "Naw, you tripping; I was cool, as for her She might of thought I was gonna go back and tell Tony that y'all was outside talking but shit, you know me, I got too many bitches an a hoe to be looking out after. I ain't got time to be out here babysitting somebody else's pussy!"

We slapped five and laughed a lil bit with him giggling saying yeah in a way to let me know that he really didn't believe me. Me and Ray [Benzino] are both Cancers, so in a strange way it was easy for us to read one another, so no matter how I stood there and tried to downplay it, I knew he was convinced that there was something between me and Tammy as I started to notice and realize it myself.

A few hours had passed of basically just hanging out smoking weed and pulling hoes when YG decided that we should go change clothes, cause it was getting a lil chilly, plus by conversation it seemed like we were going to end up at Alonzo Morning's beach party and it's always cold late night near the water.

Soon as we got back to the house, I ordered pizza and a sub before getting in the shower. While drying off, I heard the doorbell ring. Thinking it was the food order I rushed to throw something on and get some money to pay for it. By the time I came out, YG was already at the door but it was not the food, it was a female for him. I could barely see her with him standing in the doorway, but once she came in and they were heading to his bedroom she said, "Hi, Mike."

I turned around to say hi and got a good look and realized that it was Michelle, someone that I used to deal with a few years back. YG brought her to his room, then came back out whispering to me asking, "Did you fuck her?"

I said, "Yeah, she's cool, that's a good time."

Then he asked, "Did you get the blowey?"

I said, "Yeah, it's right, too."

Quietly laughing he gave me a handshake and said, "Alright, cool, I'll catch up with you on the beach."

Getting dressed I threw on basically the same thing, changing the jaboes shorts for jeans and instead of the red and gold Versace shirt I put on a royal blue one still wearing the tan Tims; I was fresh, and I grabbed one of the three pints of Remy I had, then yelled out to YG on the way out the door saying, "Gezzy, I'm out." I waited two or three seconds for him to respond but he didn't, but when I listened real closely I could hear him fucking so I just left. I called Calvin to find out exactly where they were, and he said, "We on the beach, fool, an it's off the chain hoes everywhere: this nigga Alonzo got it rocking out this bitch!"

I said, "Cool, I'm about to park in like five minutes, how I'ma find y'all?"

He said, "Once you get here come to the DJ booth, Dave and Ray [Benzino] over here chopping it up with Alonzo plus I'm waiting on you."

I said, "Ok, cool, give me a sec."

I pulled up and like Calvin said, "It's off the hook."

I immediately saw Alonzo Morning and heard him on the mic saying, "We can hang out all night, y'all, and have fun but please put all your trash in the bins an let's not have any problem."

It seemed like everyone was drunk. Ray dog don't even drink and had a cup of something in his hand. I get with niggas and we were chilling. I'm drinking straight out the Remy bottle and smoking mad weed back to back passing blunts. By the time YG came a couple hours later I was feeling nice damn near drunk myself, granted I was coherent, I was definitely in another zone enjoying the moment. In a joking manner but being serious the first thing YG said to me was, "You owe me twenty- five dollars, cuz!"

I said, "Why?"

He said, "When you left a food delivery came."

I said, "O shit," I had started sipping that Remy while I was getting dressed and totally forgot about the food. Not having any change and not really giving a fuck, I handed him two twenties then passed him what's left in the Remy bottle and grabbed a Heineken out of the cooler to change the taste in my mouth.

We had been in the same spot for close to three hours, I was so nice that there were people walking past me I knew that I didn't notice until they spoke to me. Calvin tapped me on my shoulder and said, "Look to ya left." I saw Tammy and her girls in their own lil group seductively dancing with drinks in their hands all looking tipsy.

I went over to speak, saying, "Hi," while asking, "are you all, all right?"

Her girls said yes while Tammy just put on a big smile as if she was happy to see me then started dancing in my direction. She spun around and rubbed her ass on my dick a couple times to the rhythm of whatever song was playing. Before I started walking back towards Calvin I said, "Y'all be careful driving tonight." Tammy stopped dancing with a smirk on her face as to say, "oh, you're leaving," and she yelled out bye loudly and sarcastically, once I started walking away.

Within the next thirty minutes the beach had started to clear out a little bit and from where I was standing, I could see the parking lot. I happened to look over and saw Tammy getting into the passenger seat of a white convertible Jeep Wrangler with the top off without any of her girlfriends around and Big Dave driving. For some reason I got sort of upset and walked fast to the top of the parking lot where they exiting, in order to meet them. Big Dave was a local club bouncer that knew everybody in the hood, and we were cool but at this time I didn't give a fuck about him and wanted to know what's popping! I started yelling, "Yo yo yo!" while flagging and waving my arms for him to slow the motion. Dave pulled over then I walked up to the truck with an obvious attitude mostly fueled by the liquor saying, "What's going on? What's up with you, Tammy?"

Looking surprised seeing that her eyes were closed and her head laid back on the seat, she said, "Nothing, Dave was about to drop me off cause I was ready to leave an my friends wanted to stay."

I said, "Oh, ok, well that's cool, good looking Dave, but I got her. I'm leaving now too. I can drop her off," and although he said, "ok, cool," I could tell by his facial expression he was pissed and was planning on trying to get him some pussy that night. Tammy got out of his truck not even saying bye or thank you to him, and followed me to my car. We pulled off and I asked what direction?

She said, "I'm not sure."

I said, "Well, how was Dave was going to drop you off if you don't even know where you were going?"

She said, "While showing me the key to the house, my girl gave him the address and he said he knew how to get there an would drop me off."

I handed her my cell phone and said, "Call somebody so I can get the address."

She said, "No," while starting to rub my neck and back of my head saying, "I'm staying with you since you're so concerned about who I'm with and where I'm going!"

My dick got harder than a motherfucker; part of me was like, damn, this is my cousin Tony's girl, while the other half was like, damn, she looking good and ready to fuck tonight.

Heading towards where me and YG were staying, I stuck my hand in her shirt under the bra and started playing with one of her nipples with two of my fingers. She zipped my pants down and pulled my dick through the hole in the boxers and jeans and started stroking it softly. I was so horny that I had to make her stop before I busted a nut in the car, and from how she was moving and rubbing her legs together in that skirt she might have even been cumming! By the time we got to my place, without saying it, the decision had been made that we were fucking tonight and we would deal with whatever comes with it after. She came right in and went to the bathroom while I went to my room to take a big swig of a new bottle of Remy and get naked and lay in the bed. She left the door open, and I could hear her pissing then running the sink water too long to have been just rinsing her hands. So I knew she was in there washing the pussy up cleaning off any sweat that might have accumulated from all the dancing she'd been doing for the last few hours.

She came into the room with her panties in her hand taking of the rest of her clothes, then climbing on top of me putting my dick in herself, then started riding me slowly so that she could really feel it. I put a pillow up against the headboard to put my back up against so I could sit up just enough to suck her titties, while still rubbing and squeezing her ass. Within twenty minutes I started to cum, sort of leaning my body to the left so that she could get off of me seeing that I didn't have on a condom, but instead she laid flat across my body wanting to kiss, slamming her pussy up and down my dick real fast, really giving me no chance to pull out.

After I came in her she could feel my dick going limp then started sucking my neck and licking in my ear saying, "Get it back hard." After a couple minutes of soft dick fucking her I got back right, telling her to come bend over the edge of the bed then got back in from the back. I asked one of my favorite sex questions [whose is it?] with her saying, "Yours, baby!" while I'm kissing her on her back reaching under her to squeeze her titties while slapping her on her ass telling her how good and wet it was to me. Once she started grabbing the sheets, moaning, telling me to fuck her harder indicating that she was about to cum, I got excited and was ready to cum again. Since I had already came in her once, pulling out wasn't even an option.

After waiting till I knew for sure that she was cumming I laid across her back pulling her downwards by her shoulder, going real hard until I nutted again. We got back in the bed hugging and wrapped our legs around each other and went to sleep. Things happened so fast that night that I forgot to close and lock the door, waking up to it cracked. The next morning, I went to use the bathroom, closing it behind me when YG came out of his room with a big smile on his face shaking his head giggling and whispering, "You a fool with it, cuz!"

I whispered, "Why you say that?"

He said, "Your door was open when I came in this morning."

I said, "Yeah, you know ya boy was gonna get some skins," really trying to play it off to see exactly what he saw.

Faking, like he was unsure, he said, "When I looked in there to check on you I saw her face; she looked like Tammy."

I shook my head rubbing my hand over my face saying, "Damn, yeah, that's her, that shit crazy. Right?" We started quietly laughing.

Then he said, "At first I saw that fat ass hanging outside the sheets and was like ok my nigga, then fuck something thick. Then I saw her face and was like, aww naww, nezzy tripping," and he started laughing.

I said, "Shhh, be quiet, fool, what time you leaving so that I can let her get dressed and drop her off without you being here?"

He said, "Give me a minute. I'ma bout to go out to breakfast with this lil bitch then come back and get a shower and get dressed in like an hour."

I said, "Cool, I'll be gone and back by then. I'll holla at you in a few!"

I got back in the room and Tammy was awake, wrapped up in the sheets staring at me hugging a pillow. I said, "Good morning."

She said, "Good morning" and smiled at me with a look of satisfaction on her face.

I said, "We off the hook, that Remy motherfucker."

She said, "Ooo, so that's what happened, you blaming everything that happened on the liquor?"

I said, "Naw, I can't say that, but it was nice."

She said, "Well other than you being nice what was it?"

A sense of seriousness came across me and I said, "Damn, Tammy, no matter how I feel we both gotta think about Tony!"

She said, "Yeah, I know that but me and Tony's been going through it lately; even though we still live together and sleep in the same bed we haven't had sex in months."

I said, "Yeah right!" really not believing her.

She said, "No, honestly, I know he's probably sleeping with other women but I don't question him because I don't care. I don't, cause I don't let him touch me."

I said, "Even if I do have feelings for you, what you expect, us to be holding hands out in the streets once we get back in town?"

She said, "Don't get smart, no, I don't expect that, but I don't expect to be treated like a chicken head either!"

Strongly thinking about my cousin Tony I said, "This shit crazy."

She said, "Why, because you have feelings for me?"

I asked, "What make you sure about that?"

She said, "I know you do, you have for a long time now but couldn't say it because of Tony." While she's sitting up to lean over my back on my shoulders, I turned and looked at her for a second then started kissing her leaning her back while climbing on top of her to have sex one more time before I dropped her off.

Getting back to the spot, YG was there with that same stupid smirk on his face as if he's ready for me to explain everything to him in detail.

He said, "You get a car wash?"

I said, "Naw, I didn't even try."

He said, "Was it right?"

I said, "Yeah it was right," speaking in a way like I didn't wanna take pride in it or speak on it at all.

He said, "Damn, you gonna tell Tony?"

I said, "I'm thinking about it but I know that will crush him right now, he loves that bitch. I think it best to keep it quiet and leave her and what happened alone."

Still joking, he said, "Yeah right, my nigga! I saw that fat ass naked; you might not tell Tony but you gonna want some more of that." Laughing, he added, "Trust me!"

I started laughing with him saying, "Shit, I got too many bitches as it is," realizing I hadn't called Gretchen, Cynthia, Donna, or Asia since I'd been down here, figuring I'd call them all back to back before I got in the shower and got dressed for the day.

Once I get over to the mansion that Ray [Benzino] rented with niggas, everybody was chilling getting tipsy and high ready to repeat the night, but once I saw Calvin he had a smirk on his face as if he knew something and was waiting till we got alone to tell me. We went out back to smoke one when he asked, "Where didn't you end up going last night?"

Knowing he assumed something I just bust out laughing then he busts out laughing while I was asking, "Why what's up, cuz," but knowing from how he asked the question that he knew.

He said, "Ain't shit," still laughing, then said, "I saw ya car pulling off from the beach with someone in the passenger seat and was thinking, damn, this nigga just gonna bounce without saying yo I'm out or something."

Still laughing, I said, "Yeah, I was tired, ready to be out."

He sarcastically said, "Yeah I bet!" Then he said, "Then I'm in the parking lot getting in my car and I see Tammy's girls getting in they car without Tammy. I say to myself, this nigga's a fool with it."

We started laughing even harder now with me confessing that that was her in the car with me going back to the crib.

He asked, "You hit it?"

I said, "Damn, yeah," while still laughing.

He said, "You ain't right, cuz."

I said, "I know, that shit was crazy."

He said, "Naw, nigga, you crazy. I don't want shit to do with that when it blows up in your face cause me and Tony cool. That's my nigga."

I said, "Naw, it ain't going down like that cause I ain't fucking with her no more; that was a one-time thang."

He said, "We'll see bout that, just remember what I told you. I don't want nothing to do with it when it blows up," while shaking his head with a look on his face like he didn't believe it was going to be a one-time thing.

As the day progressed everybody seemed to be doing their own thing mostly hooking up with some chick they met over the last couple days. It was around seven-thirty, close to eight and I decided to call Tina, the tall pretty girl I was talking to when I saw Tammy and her girlfriends here for the first time.

She said, "Hello, with all these pretty girls running around here I wasn't sure that I was going to hear from you."

I said, "Shit, you gorgeous. I was going to call you yesterday but me and my niggas sort of just chilled out shooting the shit at Alonzo's morning beach party."

She said, "I was there, too."

I said, "Yeah, it was so many people an it was nice, we could have just walked right past one another."

She said, "Maybe, plus after about an hour of passing out business cards I needed to go take care of a couple things."

I said, "Oh, ok, that's what's up." At the moment it didn't dawn on me to ask what type of business cards she was passing out. I just asked, "What you up to now?" and if she wanted to hook up.

She said, "Yeah, why not," then gave me the address saying, "give me at least a half hour to get ready."

I went back to me and YG's spot to change the sheets and straighten up a lil bit before going to pick her up.

She got in the car looking sexy as a motherfucker wearing almost nothing and some high heels looking even taller than when we first met but looking good! I asked, "Is there anything specific that you would like to do?"

She said, "I'm with you for a couple hours, it's up to you."

Then I asked, "Are you hungry?"

She said, "Not really, but I could eat something."

I said, "Well shit, we could go get a pizza then go back to my spot."

She said, "Cool, sounds good to me."

After eating a couple slices, we were having a couple shots of Remy, smoking one, getting to know one another a lil better; my cell phone went off a few times without me even checking who it is. Then I started thinking, let me check it out to make sure it's not Cynthia calling with an emergency with my son. It was not, it was one of my customers, Gretchen, and Tammy. I said, "Excuse me for a second," while I called Gretchen back in front of her to make sure that she was alright. Before hanging up with her I asked, "How much money you made?" making sure, I said it loud enough so that Tina heard me, sort of stunting a lil bit.

Gretchen said, "A lil over two thousand."

I said, "Cool, I'll see you within a couple days," then hung up, then go right back to talking with Tina but now also thinking about Tammy's missed call, saying to myself damn, she's calling. I should have known she wasn't going to leave shit alone! I reached over and started rubbing on Tina's thighs noticing that her mood and facial expressions changed a bit. I asked her, "Are you alright?" saying it with a strong tone. She said, "Yeah, I'm fine."

I was thinking maybe I fucked up the pussy trying to show off but I was still about to go for it, moving closer to her starting to rub on her titties and kiss her neck. She said, "Hold up a minute, we need to talk about what's going on!"

I said, "Well damn, baby, it kinda obvious what's going on."

She said, "Yeah, I know that but that's not what I'm talking about," while reaching for her purse to get something. My first thought was that it was some condoms, then she pulled out a card with her face on it that read: "professional escort."

I said, "Ooo, that what you meant when you said you was handing out business cards."

She said, "Yeah, I thought you knew me an all my girls are down here on some money shit!"

I said, "Oo, I feel you, I definitely feel you being about your paper, but I don't get down like that. I ain't never paid for no pussy."

She said, "I sort of expected you was going to say something like that once I heard you on the phone asking what sounded like your hoe how much money she made."

I said, "Yeah, I'm bout money but ain't no love lost; now that we got that out in the open, let's discuss how you been doing and how you could be doing if you choose me."

She said, "I'm cool on that. I don't want a pimp. I like keeping my money to myself," while putting her cards back in her purse and standing up as to say she was ready to go.

Without saying anything else I grabbed my car keys off the dresser and headed for the door with her following then leaving out to drop her off. It was complete silence the whole ride there but once I pulled up to her spot I said, "Hey, I hope ain't no hard feelings about the misunderstanding cause I still think you're good people and I respect that you're doing your thing."

She said, "Naw, same here and thank you. I appreciate that and I think you're a cute fly nigga, but I came out to get money to feed my daughter and gotta stick to that."

I said, "I feel you, and be careful."

She said while smiling, "You too, and you got my number, keep in touch, you never know what might happen in the future."

Pulling off, I was thinking, fuck this, I need some ass now and ain't got time for no more of that picking someone up unsure of if she gonna fuck or not, so I decided to call Tammy, saying to myself, shit, we already fucked once. One more time ain't gonna make no difference. I called her and she answered saying, "Damn, I called you hours ago," giggling but sounding like she was trying to check me.

I waved it off and asked, "Where you at?"

"On the beach. Why, you coming to get me?"

I said, "Yeah, meet me in the parking lot in ten minutes."

"Ok, boo," then I hung up.

I was on the way to get her horny off the Remy and by the way she asked me if I was coming to get her I was saying to myself, damn, this shit getting crazy already!

She stayed over again seeming to have less of a guilty conscience than she did the previous night. Before we had sex this time, I suggested we use a condom, she smirked and asked, "Don't you think it's too late for that?"

I said, "We gottta be careful of you getting pregnant," but still I decided to go back up in her bare back. The sex was even better than it was the first time, with her being more vibrant than before. This time when she started cumming she looked me in my eyes and said, "I love you, I love you so much," holding my neck while I started to cum. The first time we had sex I knew I had just fucked her but this time we had been more passionate, and I really didn't know what to call it. Before falling to sleep I had to commit on her saying that she loves me, she said, "I do love you, I've loved you for some time now!"

I said, "Yeah."

Then she said, "Yeah," while kissing me on my chest then saying, "Even if you try to deny it, I know you care about me an been wanting me for a while."

I asked, "What have I done to make you believe that?"

She said, "I see it in your face; any time one of your boys try to talk to me you get upset like you're protecting or saving me from something."

Not knowing what to say to that I just rolled over and went to sleep with her laying on my chest. Dropping her off the next morning it really started to set in, and I came to the realization that I did feel some kinda way about her, granted it wasn't anything stronger than how I felt about Asia, Donna, Cynthia and Gretchen, but it was something! Half of me was feeling bad, like, "Damn, I violated Tony," then in a selfish way the other half of me was feeling bad for myself for being caught up in a life that was impossible to live forever, though I loved myself I started to dislike the person I let this money turn me into.

With my customers calling and me having had enough fun I was ready to leave and get to that key I bought before I left. So, I decided to leave a day earlier to go take care of some business. About twenty minutes before entering Boston I called Cynthia to have her meet me at her house so that I could get the work. While leaving there I called Gretchen to see if she was at the apartment and if not, where did she put the money she made while I was gone. She described one of my leather jackets and said it was in the inside pocket, and said she was at her mother's house but could come down right now if I needed her to.

I said, "Naw, don't come yet. I need to take care of something, but I'll call you when I want you to be on your way."

While unwrapping the key I immediately saw something I didn't like about it; one half was white fish scale and the other half was a tan chalky color. I could tell the key had been opened and recompressed. Knowing that Haburto was in Santo Domingo till the end of the week, I called Joanna to explain the problem to her.

She said, "No problem. I still have your money here; if you want to you can come cook it up in front of me so that if there's any problems with it, when Burto comes back I can say that I saw you do it."

I said, "Cool, I'm on my way." Hanging up with her I called Gretchen and told her to come to the apartment and hurry up, it was important, and to just call me when she's downstairs. Gretchen was driving a rental Pontiac that was in her name so I figured it would be best to let her drive me seeing that I had my Pyrex scale, and work all together. It was the safest thing to do. I called Joanna when I pulled up so that she could come to the door by the time I got out of the car. Coming to the door, at first Joanna had a big smile on her face, that quickly turned into a frown when I saw Gretchen closing the gate walking behind me. Noticing that she now had somewhat of an attitude, it dawned on me that me and her had recently had sex, but I was saying to myself, I know she ain't getting jealous. I spoke with a smile on my face saying, "Hey, Joanna."

She barely replied, saying, "Hey, where's the stuff?" with an obvious attitude.

Then Gretchen spoke, saying, "HI," and got no response, but getting told to have a seat in the living room while me and Joanna headed into the kitchen.

My mind was focused on my money at this point so nothing else mattered at that moment, but looking down I noticed that she had on another pair of those spandex shorts she wore the night we fucked, and I realized that her attitude was most likely because she wanted to fuck again after I cooked the coke.

I broke the key in half showing her the difference and taking the part I liked. While I was cooking it up, she whispered, "Damn, I know I'm not your girl or nothing like that but don't you think it was disrespectful to bring a bitch to my house with you after what we did no more than a week ago?"

I said, "You know that, shit happened so fast that I didn't even have time to think about that. My mind was on my money; I apologize, no disrespect was in intended."

She said, "Yeah, whatever."

After the coke was cooked up and I saw it was good, I told her I'd take it. She went upstairs and came down with half of the money I gave her, passed it to me and said, "Count it." Once I counted it, I leaned up against her flirting while she leaned up against the counter with her ass towards me. She turned around softly pushing me away saying, "You blew that."

I said, "Cut it out, don't act like that. I told you I'm sorry," while still trying to pull her close to me.

She said, "Naw, that's over, plus you haven't even called me once after to even say hi, then you come over with your white bitch; naw! It's over."

I could see it's better this way now instead of later! I said, "Chill out. I'ma call you once I get myself situated, I just came back in town."

She said, "No need to, there's no more work here; besides that half you don't want so I'll have Haburto call you once he gets back."

I kissed her on her lips and said, "Stop acting like that. I'ma call you in a couple hours."

She said, "Whatever!"

While I was walking out, I told Gretchen to come on. Heading right to drop off the work and pick up some money, while driving Gretchen said, "You must of fucked her." I looked at her with my face turned up trying to convince her that she wrong.

I said, "Naww, that's my connect's girl; what would make you say something like that?"

She said, "It's a girl thing, a bitch can tell when another bitch either wants to fuck or likes her man."

I said, "Well you're wrong on this one, that bitch be about money."

She said, "So do I, but that bitch is a bitch an also likes dick."

I just laughed it off and changed the subject as we pulled up to one of my worker's houses so I could drop half this shit off; the other half I brought to my cousin Tony's house to wait for Keith to come get it. I walked into the house with Gretchen. Tony said, "What up, Mizz, how was the trip?"

I said, "It was cool, but I had to get back in town to get back to this paper that was calling."

He giggled, then asked, "Did you happen to see Tammy and her girlfriends down there?"

Instantly feeling like a piece of shit I said, "Yeah, I seen them once out on the beach, they said what's up then kept it moving."

He said, "Yeah, they probably was trying to get away from where you was at so that you didn't see them tricking."

I said, "I'm not sure, we was out there tipsy an high at the time, I really didn't pay them no attention."

He said, "I feel you. I really don't care. I been doing me the whole time she's been gone anyways."

I said, "I hear that but call Keith, ask him how long it's going to take him to get here cause, I got other shit to do."

He called then hung up saying, "He said like twenty minutes, but if you in a rush you can just leave it here. You know your money will be straight here with me till you get back."

I said, "Yeah, good looking. cuz, I'll hit you up when I'm back on this side to see where you at." Then me and Gretchen left, leaving the work.

Gretchen dropped me back at our apartment saying, "I'll call you in a lil bit, I'm going back over my mother's house for a little while."

After getting dressed I called Donna to have her meet me on Greenwood Street so that I could take her out like I promised after I see what's up with her cousin Mike. I pulled up with the windows down and before I could even park, I saw Mike smiling saying, "Yeah, I'm glad you're back in town, I need to see you." I was thinking that he'd finished what I left him and was ready to get some more, which I didn't have at the time. So, I got out of the car shaking my head in a no motion saying, "I ain't even right an won't be till at least tomorrow."

He said, "Yeah, that's cool but I need to holla at you about something else anyway."

I said, "What's good?"

He said, "I got that change I owe up upstairs, but when you're up, I wanna buy a whole key from you."

"Powder," I said, "Damn, player, you been stacking, huh?"

Really curious about how he stacked that type of money so fast, plus feeling some kinda of way about him asking for powder instead of cooked seeing that I made my money off whipping it and getting extra grams.

He said, "Yeah, I been saving but that's not where I got the money from. I refinanced the house last week for over a hundred thousand and the bank's gonna have the check for me Tuesday." His whole demeanor was different. He was trying to talk with me like he wanted me to respect that he was about to be on another level.

I said, "Ok ok, I'm getting a few keys tomorrow," really lying and exaggerating, refusing to entertain his "I'ma baller now" impression.

He asked, "What's the price?"

"Twenty three."

He said, "Cool, now that I'ma be buying powder off you, do you think that you can show me how to do that whip thing?"

In my mind I'm like, damn, this nigga wanna totally do shit like me, but I still said, "Yeah, I got you. I'll holla at you once I get the work."

He said, "Cool. I'll be right back, let me go upstairs and grab that change for you."

Me and Donna started talking. She asked, "Aren't you back early?"

I said, "Yeah, it wasn't all that. I figured I'd come back to get me some paper plus see you."

Smiling, she said, "Yeah, you probly did come back to get money but you didn't come back to see me."

I started rubbing on her thighs, pulling her closer to me saying, "Chill out, you know you my baby."

While turning her lips up she said, "Yeah, me an only God knows how many other girls."

I started giggling, rubbing her hair not saying anything so that I could change the subject. Mike came back downstairs calling me to the hallway so I could count the three g's he owed me. Before I left out, he asked, "So we'll definitely be straight Tuesday?"

I said, "Yeah, I'll hit you soon as," then walked over to Donna and gave her two hundred telling her to get us a hotel room somewhere for the night.

She said, "Ok," and that she'll call me when she does, before I jumped in the car and pulled off. This had been a bad month when it came to the work, not only was I about to lose big Mike, but also everyone that lives in the entire three-family business, which was a big part of how I was making my money. On top of that, basically everyone else I was serving and fronting coke had started complaining about it saying that their customers were saying that it was burning funny and had too much baking soda in it. When I first started buying coke off Haburto it was bomb, every key was fish scale. I could easily tell that he didn't open or tamper with the package, which made it easier for me to get extras with no complaints. But lately the quality hadn't been good; whether it's him or his connect, someone's been cutting the coke, fucking up my clientele. Big Mike was about to get that money from his house and not need me no anymore. That really had me feeling a certain way, and had me look at everything and how my business was falling apart, plus Burto wouldn't be back for another week for me to re-up and give him a piece of my mind about that trash he left with Joanna and how the work hadn't been that good lately, period!

CHAPTER SIX

———×◆×———

Lately, Gretchen had been acting distant, not bringing in much money, which led me to believe that she was stashing some, not really wanting to talk when I asked her to keep me posted on what she was doing, just intentionally becoming difficult to deal with, period. I had too much on my plate between drug dealing, rapping and all of my other relationships to really just focus on her, so I ended up taking on the attitude like fuck it, when she leaves, she leaves.

Over the next couple of weeks Vidal had called me twice telling me that him and the nigga Damien had bumped heads in traffic a couple times and had stare downs and it was starting to aggravate him. Ever since I got caught without my strap at the pay phone, I hadn't taken mine out of the car hoping to bump into him but just hadn't.

That weekend Vidal and Dre had gone out clubbing and ended up hanging out at the after spot till after three in the morning when they bumped into Damien on the way home, standing on the corner in Mission Park, Vee was strapped so he figured fuck it, this is the perfect time to merk this nigga and be done with this situation once and for all. Dre parked on the corner while Vidal got out and ran up on him and shot him once, but before he could get off a couple more shots, Damien's man who was sitting just out of sight with a burner and let off three shots hitting Vidal in the back once. With Vidal now shot, he had to take his focus off Damien and fired back in the direction of where he thought the shots were coming from while running back to Dre's car.

After getting Vidal to the hospital, Dre called me with in the next half hour telling me what happened and where they were. I shot up there like four in the morning and the doctors wouldn't let me in nor give me any information about him being able to walk, which was my main concern seeing that he got shot in the back. While standing in the lobby a couple of detectives and uniform cops came into the hospital speaking to the doctors, so I figured I'd leave till the morning seeing that off impulse I came into the hospital with my pistol on me.

Next morning after barely getting any sleep from feeling like this was all my fault, I went back up to the hospital to check on Vidal. Soon as I walked into his room and we caught eye contact we both started laughing, his girl was there sitting in the chair so we didn't discuss much at all at that moment, but me knowing Vidal, his smile said it all. We slapped five and I softly hugged him and said, "You know I'ma straighten this."

He said, "I already know, enough said."

I said, "I love you, bro."

He said, "I love you, too."

I said bye to his girl, then left to set up the night because even though Damien was in the hospital too, somebody was getting punished immediately over what happened to my nigga!

I got back to my apartment and Gretchen was there seemingly upset about me not answering my phone last night, not knowing what I'd been going through with Vidal. I already had an attitude about the whole situation and really was not in the mood for anybody's bullshit! After being in the house for no more than five to ten minutes barely speaking, I asked, "Where's the money from last night?"

She said, "Ain't none!"

"What the fuck you mean ain't none."

She said, "If you would of answered your phone last night when I called you, you would of known that I didn't feel good an didn't work last night."

I said, "Well you don't seem sick now!"

She said, "Because I'm not," saying it with an attitude.

Me, knowing she was just being spiteful, got me even more upset, then I said, "Bitch, where the money at, stop playing all these games with me."

She started raising her voice saying, "Why didn't you get no money from the square bitch you stayed with last night?"

Now I have never been into hitting women, and even with me pimping for the last year I never put my hands on her, but she really got to me this day trying to try me! I ran up on her and slapped her in the mouth and said, "Bitch, stop raising your voice in here. You must of forgot whose mother fucken place you in, and stop playing with me. Where is some mother fucking money at?"

Now crying she said, "In my purse."

I said, "What the fuck you lying for?"

She said, "I wasn't lying, that money was from the night before. You just never came an got it."

I went in the purse and there was seven hundred. I said, "I'm getting tired of your lil bullshit."

She said, "Do you want me to leave?"

I said, "I don't give a fuck, just let me know whenever you want to, but I do know I'm tired of your fucking attitude."

For the next hour I was there getting dressed neither one of spoke to one another. On my way out after getting dressed, still upset, I said, "At any point you decide you wanna leave, just give my key to Jennifer to give to Calvin an I'll get it from him!"

Outside of Cynthia, Donna and a couple of my customers, I didn't answer my phone much waiting for nightfall to ride through Mission Park and merk any nigga that looked of age seeing that Damien was one of the main dudes from that hood at the time.

Around nine o'clock I switched cars, getting out of my BMW and getting into a rental. I had my .44 bulldog revolver and Glock nine on me, then I called Woodie from Grove Hall to meet me up Franklin Hill Ave. so that he could ride with me.

I pulled up, Woodie jumped in and I handed him the Glock, then he asked, "Who we going to get?"

I said, "Whoever out there since the nigga I want is in the hospital."

He said, "Cool, let's go just point someone out and he dead!"

We got down to Mission Park, and the front of the entrance to the complex was yellow taped off, with a detail cop sitting in his car. The incident with Vidal was a lil bit further up the street so it was obvious that this was a fresh new shooting that happened not too long ago. We sat up straight and kept driving, getting out of the area after seeing detectives ride down the opposite side of the street. I dropped Woodie back off telling him to hold the Glock for a few because once the coast is clear we were sliding back through there!

A couple of days had passed and Vidal was well enough to come home, so I went by his crib to check on him. He had lost a couple pounds but for the most part he was straight and had his cheerful spirit back.

While talking about everything that happened, I told him, "Don't worry about it, cuz."

I went down there the next day looking for anyone of them niggas to hit up but the police were out there like somebody else had been shooting, so me and Woodie slid off but I was definitely on it!

Vidal said, "Yeah, you must of went through there after Fat Allen went through there bussen at a crowd of them niggas that was standing out there earlier."

I said, "Oh shit, Fat Al."

Vidal said, "Yeah, he called me right after saying that he just cleaned the block."

I said, "Yeah, that's cool but it ain't over yet." We both started laughing then hugged.

The Vidal said, "I know!"

Within this week Ray Dog [Benzino] called me to remind me that were leaving for Houston next week, so, on top of wanting to get some revenge I needed to get things situated to where I could leave for a couple weeks and still make money while I'm gone. My clientele wasn't as heavy as it was a year ago, but I was still making a few thousand a week and needed to stay on top of that. Ever since I introduced Calvin to Jennifer it seemed like that's where his focus was. He had stopped serving the few customers he had and basically just left the drug game alone and was fully pursuing pimping. Even still, he was my nigga and had no problem taking care of something if I needed him to, so I knew I could leave him my phone and he'd hold shit down for me till I got back. Even though things weren't like they used to be between me and Gretchen she was still living with me and paying me. We considered ourselves to be working on our relationship although I didn't change anything I was doing. I was still moving the way I wanted to, and it was either she dealt with it or not. And as far as I could see she was dealing with it.

Seeing that I was leaving next week I had made plans on spending some type of time with all the women I considered myself to be seriously fucking. Before I left, Tammy had been calling me complaining about her having to hear about me from both Asia and Sharee, asking when was I going to stop fucking with them. She was so into me at the time that I knew it really didn't matter to her what I did as long as I made time for us to be alone and promised her that soon it would be just me and her.

Things between me and Donna had gotten more serious than everybody knew. The fact that she wasn't up in the clubs every week and wasn't out there making a name for herself said a lot to me. I gained a respect for her that I didn't have for anyone else that I was dealing with including Cynthia, my son's mother whom I was supposed to be in love with at the time. Even with that being said she took a back seat to the fast-paced lifestyle that I was living that demanded that I have whoever and whatever I wanted when I wanted it. Going down in a row, I had sex with every one of them for at least an hour before I left starting with Cynthia, then Donna, Tammy, then, Asia, and even though things were coming to an end between us, Sharee and then finally Gretchen.

The night before I left, I stayed at my spot to cook a key to leave behind for Calvin to move while I was gone. That was the longest, most tiring flight I'd ever taken, but finally landing in Houston knowing that I was going to the Rapp a Lot compound, it was definitely all worth it!

Me, Jenks, Tang and my man Terror flew down together. Ray Dog [Benzino] came down the day before us, rumor was that he had some chick with him from Boston that he wanted to hang out with before the festivities started. Once we got our bags there was a man holding a sign that read Wise Guys who was our driver to the limo Ray [Benzino] rented us for the weekend. The hotel we were staying in was nice, surprisingly better than the ones he usually put us in while he's in some lavish suite on the other side of the town. This time we actually stayed in the same spot as him, just on the lower floor. The spot had a cold fridge, stove, fully furnished with a big TV; in the back was a private beach that you could get to from the back door that was only accessible to the guests.

We were there for like twenty minutes before Ray [Benzino] came downstairs to say what's up and check on niggas. He came in wearing swimming trunks, flip flops with a towel on his shoulder, giving us a half ounce of weed and three hundred apiece to spend while we're down there. I came down with all new clothes and a grand in my pocket, plus I left instructions for Gretchen to Western Union the money she made every night, every day so I was straight, but still took the per diem and weed that Ray [Benzino] gave me before he went back out to the beach with the female with whom he flew in from Boston. Ray [Benzino] called Lonnie Mack and let him know that we were in town. Lonnie Mack is a well-known DJ in Houston and a good friend of Scarface who is a member of the platinum recording group the Ghetto Boys, and the owner of Rapp a Lot record label, J Prince, whom asked Lonnie Mack to show us around and basically looked out for us while we were in town. Although we hadn't met Lonnie Mack till this point, we were all familiar with his name from the few songs that Scarface mentioned him in, and personally I felt it was pretty cool to get to meet him as well as being here in general.

Once Ray [Benzino] left out the back door leading to the beach, curiosity led me to peek out the window to see if I was familiar with or knew the female he was spending time with and surely I did! It was Keisha, my man Chico's new wife. Chico was a dude I fucked with in the street that would get a half a key from me here and there whenever him and his man Cal's connect wasn't on. Chico and Cal were together all the time back then. No more than a month before this trip they went half on a key from me. That's when Chico told me that he was about to get married; even though I congratulated him, I remember saying in my head, *this a stupid ass sucker for love ass nigga* and now look, not even two months later she's out here with Ray [Benzino] sucking and fucking chasing that money.

Within the next hour Lonnie Mack came to the room smiling and being cheerful showing us love off the rip. He stayed for close to an hour talking and getting to know us, plus telling us stories of some of the things he'd seen being on tour with Scarface and the Ghetto Boys and being a part of Rapp a Lot, period.

This was the night of the grand opening to Lonnie's new club on the South Side and he figured since we were in town, he'd ask us if we would like to perform and everybody said yeah. He said, "Ok, cool, that gives me the rest of the day to promote and I'll have y'all a VIP section ready when y'all get there."

Jenks said, "Ok, cool," as if he was speaking for all of us in a managerial type of way. After asking us if we needed anything, Lonnie left saying, "I'll see you tonight," and giving us the address.

Soon as Lonnie closed the door behind himself, Jenks made a statement saying, "That nigga ain't nothing like I thought he'd be like after hearing Scarface talking about him in his music." I knew Jenks was passing judgement on him because of how cool and comical he was being and didn't look at it as hospitality. I didn't take his kindness for weakness and didn't see anything about how he came across as being soft, but that was just Jenks back then. He was quick to look at things for what they appear to be as opposed to looking at the bigger picture overall. There was a pizza shop, Western Union, and a liquor store across the street from the hotel, so everything we needed was accessible and in walking distance. After getting some food, and some Remy, we ate and just stayed getting high and tipsy, wasting time till it was time to go to Lonnie Mack's club, still having intentions on performing.

That night, Ray [Benzino] ended coming back down to our room for a second, a few hours later to see what's up. Once we told him what our plans were, he strongly said that he thought that that was a bad idea and that he forgot to tell us that he didn't want us going into the hoods. By this time, we had already made an obligation to Lonnie and we weren't going to just disrespect him by not showing up, plus we were some real niggas and real recognized real, so I was figuring no matter where I'm at I'ma be straight; as long as I come with respect, I'm gonna get respect!

Nine o'clock and we all got in the limo and left after Jenks gave the driver the address. Upon pulling up in the parking lot to the club, I immediately noticed that us pulling up in a limo had raised a few people's eyebrows being the club was in the center of the hood where limos weren't coming through on the regular. Getting out going inside I could sense that this wasn't going to be a good night by the facial expressions on most of the people waiting in line watching us just get out of a limo then be escorted in like we were some well-known celebrities. After Lonnie got us situated in the VIP and had the waitress send us some shots of Remy, and a bottle of Champagne, he got on the mic and introduced us as his guest performers for the night. Immediately we could hear niggas saying, "Boo, fuck them niggas, go back to New York. Who the fuck are they? Nobody wants to hear that shit." The majority of the crowd had made their decision on how they felt about us soon as they saw us get out of a limo. So, we already knew what it was gonna be once we got on the stage, still we sat there having drinks trying to get comfortable for like a half hour, but the whole time there, different dudes started walking by us muttering disrespectful shit. If we were home somebody would have been fucked up and probably shot, but we were in one of the most dangerous parts of Houston six deep without a strap, getting no love. Jenks said, "The way these niggas in here acting I don't think y'all should perform." Me and the rest of the artists agreed with him, seeing that the tension had gotten so thick we figured it was time for us to leave. But we wanted to bring it to Lonnie Mack's attention before we just walked out. Once Jenks told Lonnie that we weren't performing and were leaving, Lonnie got upset, asking why?

Jenks said, "These niggas in here already booed them and are constantly walking by saying lil slick shit. We just leaving."

Lonnie walked off, grabbed the mic, then got on stage and started to disrespect us in his rendition of a free style saying that our music sucks anyway. He said we were scared, and he don't know why Lil J wanted to fuck with some New York type rappers anyway. He definitely wasn't the same funny joking dude we'd met at the hotel earlier. With the crowd laughing, we started leaving and I could see Jenks and Lonnie catch eye contact with Jenks saying, "You got that for now, but trust me we gonna see each other again!"

We went outside getting into the limo when Lonnie came out looking furious with six dudes by his side asking Jenks what was that he said. I was already in the limo with the rest of the group but got out when Lonnie, the six dudes and what seemed like the whole club, started to surround Jenks and the limo. Being outnumbered there was nothing Jenks could say or do besides accept what it was that Lonnie was saying. There was a short heavyset nigga with him flashing a .38 revolver saying, "Let me do it, Lonnie, let me do it, we'll explain this shit to Lil Jay later."

Lonnie said, "Naw." While looking Jenks in the eyes he said, "You must of gotten me fucked up. I'll leave you niggas out here, I'm definitely not the one," while his man was standing there with his hand on the .38. Then Lonnie said, "You niggas get the fuck outta here before y'all get hurt tonight."

Jenks got in looking mad as shit and partially embarrassed that Lonnie spoke to him like that. Then I got in behind him hearing Lonnie telling people standing in front of the limo to move so that we can leave. The ride back to the hotel was quiet as hell, the only person that spoke was the limo driver saying that he was about to run people over to get out of there. Everybody else, including myself, was too embarrassed to speak, feeling like we just took a shot.

The next morning Ray came downstairs and I started to tell him about what happened. Before I could even finish the whole story, he started laughing hard as shit saying, "That's why I told y'all not to go into the hood. People out here not going to accept you all's music until the world accepts it. All they wanna hear out here is their own or a hit they can sing along with. Other than that, you ain't shit."

I was laughing now too, saying, "Yeah, you right, you right."

He said, "Well, listen, Friday night me an you going to Mike Dean's studio so that you can record a solo track with him."

"Who's Mike Dean?"

He said, "He's the producer that produces ninety percent of Scarface and the Ghetto Boys' music."

"Word. I'm ready for this."

He said, "Make sure," while lighting up a blunt for us to smoke; once the blunt was gone he went back upstairs after saying, "Be ready in a couple hours, I'm coming to get y'all to go up to the Rapp a Lot compound."

After getting dressed I called Gretchen to see how much money was made and to have her send it to me Western Union. She said six hundred and that she'd call me within the next thirty minutes with the Western Union information. I felt smooth hearing her not being complicated at all, it made me feel like the pimp I was supposed to be. Hearing her be on point added an extra something special to an already special trip.

The Rapp a Lot 20th anniversary was basically a big cookout held on Jay Prince's ranch. Soon as we pulled up, I saw Scarface and several different artists that I grew up listening to standing around laughing, drinking and shooting the shit. Once I got out the back of the tinted up Suburban and finally caught eye contact with Scarface, he smiled and yelled out, "Yo, M3 !" then started telling the people standing next to him that me and him just recorded a banger. It felt good to see my favorite artist acknowledge me as an artist, and to see that Face still had the same personality and persona as he did the day we met. It had me saying to myself, *yeah, he a real nigga.*

After a couple beers and burgers, I started to inquire on how big was the ranch. Face started explaining, then said, "Hold on," and started walking towards what seemed like the back of the mansion. Next thing I know he comes bolting out the other side on a big four wheeler saying, "M3, jump on, I'ma show you around." Being that this was the first time I'd ever been on a four wheeler I wasn't hip to keeping my feet on the stand, so within five minutes of riding we had to turn around and go back because I had burned the bottom half of my calf on the muffler going over bumps. Ray [Benzino] looked at it and said, "Damn, McNeill, we should go to the hospital an get that checked."

I was so psyched about how the day was going and being around this environment that I would have rather bled out than left. Scarface asked Lil Jay for a First Aid kit, then Jay told me to come in the house so that he could have someone clean it and properly wrap it up. An older woman whom I never got her name cleaned it with peroxide, then wrapped it with clean gauze and I was cool. I said, "Thank you," then went back outside, got a cold beer and got back to enjoying myself. The burn on my leg would just make the trip more memorable.

While everyone was chilling and having a good time, I noticed a brand new Rolls Royce pull up to the entrance with two guys in it. Not wanting to stare them down, I looked for a moment then turned away, but I did glimpse long enough to notice that they both wore wearing gold Rolexes. Entering the gate, I heard Lil Jay calmly embrace him with a smile on his face and a head nod saying, "Draper." Right then I knew this had to be the Tony Draper that I'd heard about in several different songs from various Southern artists. Tony Draper was another record exec from Houston who was doing real good for himself. At the time, he was the CEO of Suave House records that consisted of Eight Ball and MJG, Mister Mike, Tella, and a roster of other hot artists. This happened to be the year that Draper got a ten million dollar deal for the company, so a lot of people including radio stations were commending him and the label on their accomplishments. While walking past me he said, "Nice shirt." At the time I was wearing my yellow, gold and blue silk Versace shirt with my gold submarine Rolex and iced out gold Wise Guys piece, so I was looking real player. Back in my cool mode, I just nodded my head and said thanks, then his man asked if I minded him taking a closer look at my Wise Guys piece. I said, "Naw," then he lifted it off my chest to check the weight and really analyze the diamonds; then he said, "This shit heavy and icy, this nice."

I said, "Thanks," then stuck my hand out for a shake saying, "My name is Mike."

He said, "What's up, Mike. I'm Fly Guy, that's Tony Draper."

Then me and Tony Draper shook hands before he walked over to speak with Jay Prince and everybody else on the ranch that seemed to be celebrating and congratulating each other. As the night progressed, me and Fly Guy ended up talking some more finding out that we had a couple things in common being pimping and hustling. Also, I told him about the song I was about to do with Mike Dean.

He said, "Yeah, I wanna hear some of your music, matter fact, I'ma get up with you before you leave town so I can hear how the song come out you do with Mike Dean."

I said, "Ok, cool, let's make it happen."

Later that night me and Fly Guy exchanged numbers and made plans on getting up after I finished recording with Mike Dean that Friday, so that we could listen to a few songs and just kick it and compare notes on the "husslen" and pimping. To me,

I felt like he really wanted to get with me to pick my brain and see how real I was about what I told him that I had going on in Boston. Shortly after I embraced Scarface one more time and we left the cookout.

For the next few days me, Ray and the group did a lil shopping and a lil sightseeing for the most part enjoying the weather, weed, and the beach connected to the hotel. Speaking with Calvin he told me that everything's going as expected back at home. So, it felt good to know everything was on point back in town and up to this point Gretchen had been sending me my money every day without any problems, seemingly glad that I was enjoying myself and taking care of my business.

Thursday, I decided to buckle down and get into my craft by writing a couple of songs in preparation to record with Mike Dean the next day while the rest of the artists went out with some girls they met at the mall.

Getting to the studio the next day I was kinda nervous and Ray [Benzino] must have seen it in my persona, while getting out to go in the studio he said, "Loosen up, McNeill, you got this. I wouldn't have brought you here if I didn't believe in you." His words of encouragement definitely helped me take a deep breath and prepare to rise to the occasion. Ray [Benzino] rang the bell and within minutes a short white dude with glasses came to the door saying, "What's up, welcome to the Dean's office!" At first, I thought this must be an assistant or engineer but getting into the studio I realized that this was Mike Dean! He shook my hand telling me to have a seat and make myself comfortable. There were several different plaques on the wall but the ones that stuck out to me were the ones from the Ghetto Boys and the couple from Scarface's solo albums. Ray [Benzino] knew this was a big moment for me, not just the fact that I'm making a song with a platinum producer, but knowing my love for this type of production, and at this point there was no one better to me than the man who produced for one of my favorite artists, Scarface.

Ray [Benzino] lit up a blunt and passed it to me saying, "You got this" while Mike Dean started playing some beats telling me to let him know when I hear one that catches my attention. Within the first three he played I knew I found the one for me. None of the lyrics I pre wrote seemed to be good enough for me at the moment, all that basic killer shit I kicked just wasn't going to cut it for this big of production nor for this moment! After picking the track, Ray [Benzino] and Mike Dean walked out telling me that they'd be back in an hour which to me was well enough time to create a new song from scratch. Being in Houston gave me a vibe that I'd never had when writing music before. Mentally I felt more musically mature, my mindset was that on this one I'm going from being in the mind state of a gangbanger to becoming a gangster!

While writing the song I knew this was something different from all the other music I'd ever done and every time I'd get stuck on a line I'd look up at Scarface's plaques on the wall and say to myself go harder. My confidence was out the roof. If there ever was a chance for me to prove myself, the time was now!

Hour later, Mike Dean and Ray [Benzino] came back in asking if I was I ready. At this point, I was done, basically going over my lines several times in my head trying to minimize it before I got in the booth. This was the first time I felt like a professional. Not only was I proud of the song I wrote, I was also proud of the small timeframe that I wrote it in and was ready!

While recording the song I could see a smile on both Ray [Benzino] and Mike Dean's face which made me more comfortable by the minute. Once I came out of the booth with the song done, they both embraced me with handshakes and hugs with Mike Dean asking me that question that seemed to always get asked when someone heard me rhyme for the first time. "Where you from?"

I said, "Boston."

He replied, "You don't sound like it; you sound like you're from somewhere in the South. Good job, this song a banger."

Before leaving the studio, Mike Dean put a pre-mix on the song, then asked me what's the name of it for his logs. At that point I hadn't even thought about that. I wrote the song and the hook but was viben so hard I hadn't even thought about a name. With smoke in his face from a blunt he was smoking and his head bobbing while listening to the song one more time before we left, Ray said, "Manhood, yeah, let's call this one Manhood," and I instantly fell in love with the title.

The next morning, I woke up with the song and the experience still on my mind telling the group about it and waiting for Ray [Benzino] to wake up so that he could come down with the copy so that he could play it for them. Everyone seemed happy for me, that was sort of a bonding moment for me.

Even though we were a group, I still mentally and emotionally kept my distance from some of them due to the gang conflicts me and my crew were having with their crews. Later that evening Ray [Benzino] finally came down to our hotel suite with the rough cut of the song and I could tell by the vibe and the other artists' faces that they were feeling it along with being happy for me for actually living out one of my dreams. Ray [Benzino] had told us that there really wasn't much planned for the day so we could just move how we wanted, but to be careful and sarcastically saying, "Stay out the hood," referencing the incident that happened a few nights ago at Lonnie Mack's club. The first thing that came to all of our minds was calling some girls over and getting some pussy. But unfortunately, the female that I had sex with while down there had to work that day, so I had planned on just getting high and laying out at the beach when I got a call from Fly Guy, the nigga I met at the Rapper Lot tenth anniversary, coincidentally asking me what's good and if I was free for the day. I said, "Yeah, matter of fact, Ray [Benzino] just told us that there wasn't anything planned for the day so I'm just chilling."

He said, "Good, I'ma be back on that side at like six o'clock, I'ma come get you so we can slide for a few and chop it up."

I said, "Cool, I'll be ready, just call me when you downstairs an I'll come down."

He said, "Cool, see you then," and hung up.

A few hours later maybe a quarter past six, Fly Guy called me saying that he was downstairs. I said, "Ok, I'll be down in a sec," then left out without telling anyone where I was going.

Getting off the escalator I was greeted by a handshake and a smile as if he was glad to see me again and I knew that this was about to be more than just a quick ride and conversation. I usually don't open up to people I don't know about the drugs I was selling, just in case they were police, but I could sense he was a real nigga right off the rip. So, throughout our conversation we almost instantly started comparing prices on kilos, and although he never said that he had it, he spoke in a way that let me know that he had access to it and left the door open for me to initiate a business proposition. While driving we got on the highway and although it didn't matter to me where we were going, I asked, "Where we going?"

He said, "To the Suave House studio." Instantly my mind switched from being a serious drug dealer to quietly becoming a fan now knowing that I was going to the studio where some of my favorite artists like Mr. Mike and Eight Ball recorded their music. This was crazy for me; just last night I did a song with Mike Dean, and now I was going to Suave House. I felt like shit was happening for me and was excited although pride wouldn't allow me to show any expression.

Pulling up to the studio, I remember saying this is nice but it really wasn't anything exclusive considering that we had a nice spacious studio fully equipped with office space, a practice room and an SSL board back at home. But I guess all that matters is the quality of music that was coming out of there, and their shit was dope! Walking in, the first thing that caught my attention was all the posters and plaques of artists on the walls. Looking down the hall, I could see someone playing pool and after staring for a minute I realized that it was one of the Suave House artists Tella, which gave the moment more of a "so fa real" feeling!

After showing me around the front we walked towards the back when Fly Guy introduced me to Tella saying, "What's up?"

"Tella, say 'What's up?' to my man money getting ass Mike from Boston." We shook hands and giggled over the introduction as I told him I'm a fan and that I listen to his music.

He sounded surprised, then said, "Damn, y'all bumping Suave way up there in Boston?"

I said, "Yeah, I mean it ain't something that everyone listens to, but I fucks with it heavy."

Instead of leaving the conversation alone, he questioned me on what's my favorite song on his last album, as if to see if I was just saying that for conversation or was I really listening to his music. I could have easily said, "Girls in the Club Show Love," seeing that was the lead track on the album, but I figured I'd go deeper and pick a song on the album you wouldn't know unless you really listened to the album and said "Twisted," telling him that I love how they used the sample from Run DMC. He smiled, feeling that what I was saying was real shit, giving me another handshake saying, "Ok, that what's up."

While sitting in an office in the back that seemed to be Fly Guy's office, I called Gretchen to check on her and share some of the moments I was experiencing with her, and unexpectedly she had an attitude and was talking slow and quiet like she really didn't want to talk to me. Figuring that she was upset because I didn't call to check up on her the day before, at first, I tried to smooth things out by apologizing and being funny so that I could make her laugh to change her mood, which usually worked. But this time it wasn't, she was stuck on this dry non-conversation attitude and I knew something had changed. Not only in our situation, but with her emotionally. Really not having the patience for her attitude at the moment I aggressively said, "What's up, what's going on" You taking care of shit or what?"

She replied, "Yeah, taking care of shit for myself. I don't have you here to do shit for me, so I have to take care of shit for me!"

Right there I knew there was nothing I could say or do to change how she was feeling, especially from a distance. Still, keeping in mind that this was a pimp and hoe situation, I aggressively said, "Fuck all that dumb shit, how much money you made last night?"

She hesitated like she didn't wanna answer me, then the phone hung up. I said, "Hello hello," reassuring that she'd really hung up on me.

Fly Guy, overhearing us having problems said, "Sounds like ya bitch playing games with you pimping."

I said, "Yeah, the hoe get like that sometimes," then I called her back twice only to get the voice mail, so I called Calvin to see if he'd heard anything from Jennifer about what's going on.

He said, "Naw, but I'll pick my bitch's brain then call you back asap."

I said, "Cool," then hung up and start kicking it with Fly Guy when Tony Draper walked in with a smile on his face.

Draper said, "What's going on, fellas."

Fly Guy said, "Ain't shit, just cooling, Boston was just on the phone having some turbulence in his pimping, his hoe acting up while giving me a handshake."

Draper asked, "What's wrong, Boston?"

I said, "Ain't shit, the hoe always acting stupid off and on, but as long as she get me some paper at the end of the day it's all game!"

He said, "I hear that," then asked how that track came out, saying, "Fly Guy told me you was doing one with Mike Dean last night."

I said, "Tight."

He said, "Spit a verse from it for me."

I spit the first verse to "Manhood," then four more verses I'd wrote that I didn't record yet. By the look on his face I could tell he was feeling my flow. When I finished spitting, he said, "Yeah, you tight, plus you don't even sound like you from up East where you was born."

I said, "Boston."

He said, "Yeah, you different, if I was ya CEO I'd change your name to the Chameleon cause of how you be switchen up flows."

We laughed a lil bit then he asked me if I was I signed to Ray [Benzino]?

I replied, "Yeah."

He said, "Damn, I wouldn't have minded having a tight East Coast artist on the label and you cool as shit."

I said, "Good look," really feeling accomplished to have just been basically offered a deal from someone that just got a major distribution deal.

Then he said, "But it ain't over, I'ma holla at Ray [Benzino] soon to see what's good. You never know, we still might can make something happen."

Within the next twenty to thirty minutes Calvin called me back saying Jennifer told him that Gretchen had been complaining to her about me going in and out of town all the time not really being there to have her back if something was to happen to her while she was working. "Plus," he said, "when you are home you be messing with too many square bitches on top of hustling all the time, It seems like you don't have any time for her."

I said, "Yeah."

He said, "Dog and Jennifer said the bitch said that she ready to go choose up."

In the back of my head I knew it was gonna happen but I didn't expect it to happen while I was on this trip, seeing that she knew that I was coming to handle my music business. I told Calvin, "Yo, get my apartment keys from that hoe for me and make sure if she leaves before I get back that she don't take nothing out the spot that doesn't belong to her."

He said, "Cool."

We hung up and both Tony Draper and Fly Guy almost simultaneously asked, "What's up with ya bitch?"

I said, "My nigga that's pimping too, told me that his bitch told him that my bitch bout to leave me and go choose up tonight."

Draper started laughing, and saying, "Yeah, pimp, that's how it be, they here today gone tomorrow."

I said, "Yeah, I ain't gonna lie, I'ma miss the bitch's money but don't get me twisted, I still got a couple hundred thou from breaking down bricks, so I ain't never really depend on the hoe."

Fly Guy said, "I hear that!"

We sat around for the next few hours drinking and listening to some up and coming music from his artists, viben like we'd been around each other for years. It wasn't no CEO / artist type shit. Draper was cool like that; the fact that he had just deposited a ten million dollar check didn't seem to have him acting funny style at all. With all of us now feeling tipsy, Draper said, "Come on, y'all, let's go to the strip club," then told Fly Guy to lock the truck.

Then the three of us got into the Rolls Royce. On the way there I asked Draper to turn the music down for a sec so that I could answer this call from my man about the bitch. It was Calvin. I answered asking, "What's good. Did she leave?"

He said, "Yeah, I got your keys and she didn't take nothing outta there besides her clothes."

I said, "Cool, fuck that hoe, she was starting to become too stressful anyway."

Calvin said, "Alright, my nigga, enjoy you trip. I'll holla when you get back," then we hung up.

A moment before pulling up to the strip club Calvin called me back. "Say, bro, Jennifer just told me that the bitch just told her that she has a thousand dollars on her wanting to choose me!"

I got quiet not knowing what to think or feel, then Calvin said, "If you don't want me to fuck with the bitch I won't, but if I do at least you can get that thousand, cause she said if it ain't me she just pulling up on some pimp that's been getting at her downtown."

Really not wanting him to, but having too much pride to act like I cared, I said, "Cool, just hold that gee for me. I'll get it with the rest of that other money when I get back."

Calvin said, "Cool, I'll have it."

Immediately after hanging up, Fly Guy asked, "How did that situation turn out?"

I said, "Now the hoe talking about she got a gee on her and wanna choose my nigga."

Tony Draper and Fly Guy both started trying to convince me that Calvin did me dirty on that, and when I said, "Naw, that's my nigga, we like brothers," they both said in different ways that there ain't no brothers in pimpin, steady trying to convince me that Calvin put that whole shit together. It crossed my mind for a second that he could have, because of the way everything went down, but my heart and trust for him, wouldn't let me believe that so I just said, "Naw," making a face that let them know that I was getting a bit sensitive about the situation and didn't want to discuss it anymore.

Fly Guy peeping it just turned the music back up after saying, "Well shit, you bout to get a new bitch tonight!"

It was well known that Tony Draper just got a ten million dollar distribution deal and walking into the strip club all the females acted as if they were waiting on him. Soon as we sat down ten to twelve girls came to our table throwing themselves at him speaking to him as if he had a personal relationship with all of them. After having a couple drinks, and tipping the waitress well, and throwing a few dollars around while whispering in a few of the stripper's ears he was ready to go. While getting back into the Rolls Royce he looked at me and said, "I got four of them bitches bout to meet us at the suite to fuck!"

I didn't even know he had a suite, but I was high and definitely ready to fuck, seeing that my lil bitch had to work earlier. Getting in the hotel I noticed that the beds were side by side with just a lil wall separating the two. Once the girls got there, Draper whispered to me, "You can have any one of these hoes you want, I'm paying." We were about to share these hoes. A good fifteen minutes went by and Draper and Fly Guy both were talking to the females like they had to pull the bitches when I was under the understanding that they were getting paid to fuck! I grabbed the short, light skinned one that was basically trying to handcuff herself to Draper and said, "Come over to this side."

I started opening the packet to a condom while telling her to bend over the edge of the bed, then started fucking her wet but musty pussy from dancing from the back. I came in less than ten minutes becoming the butt of another one of the female's jokes saying, "Damn, you came already?"

I laughed like everyone else in the room but now stroking my dick to get it back hard so that I could fuck at least one more before I left. Tony Draper finally was getting his dick sucked when one of the other girls saw me rubbing my dick and sort of choosing who I wanna fuck next, came over and laid me down on the couch next to Draper and started sucking my dick while Fly Guy was over in the next room fucking. After a couple minutes, Draper took his female by the hand and walked her onto the open bed. While getting up from getting my dick sucked and now putting on a condom, I lay back down for the stripper to ride me, and the night was off the hook!

After about forty minutes everyone ended up back in the living room fully dressed when Draper pulled out what looked like at least two thousand and handed it to one of the ladies and said, "Y'all split this up." Me and the second girl I fucked really enjoyed the sex, although she was getting paid for it I could tell that she found me attractive by how passionate and comfortable she became once we were alone. We fucked hard and fast for a bit, then went real slow as if she wanted to feel the dick hit a certain spot, while grabbing my ass with one hand pulling me deeper into her. She pulled my neck downwards toward her for a kiss which ended up being the moment that she started cumming and whispering, "I like you" in my ear which in fact made me start to cum as well.

Before the night ended, I ended up getting her phone number saying, "I'ma call you when I get back home so that I can fly you up so that we can spend some time together and really get to know one another." While still rubbing my hand and looking me in my eyes like she had caught feelings for me, she said, "I'd love that" but in reality, I knew that this would most likely be the last time we ever spoke or saw each other.

On the way to drop me off, me, Draper and Fly Guy made jokes about each other the entire ride; if there was someone else in the car that didn't know us they would have thought we were longtime friends from the same hood out having fun. Getting out at the hotel, Draper gave me his cell number telling me that he was going to California for a week in a couple of days but for me to stay in touch so that we can see what. if anything, we could make happen.

I said, "Ok, thanks, I appreciate everything," while slapping five, then I got out.

The next afternoon when Ray came down to my room, I told him about my night and that Tony Draper said he'd like to have a conversation with him concerning possibly signing me to Suave House. He looked at me with this disappointed look and said, "I don't need to speak with Draper, I got bigger shit planned than Suave House, just chill, my nigga an let me drive." Granted I felt like a big opportunity was passing me by, I had to respect how far Ray had brought me to this point and the things he made happen for me, so out of respect and loyalty I just shook his hand and said, "You got that, I'm with you!" and left the conversation alone.

A couple days passed and we were leaving, on the flight back was when it really hit me that all the extra money I was getting from Gretchen was gone, along with thinking of how I truly felt about Calvin having Gretchen now, when I'm the one who introduced him to Jennifer and helped him start pimping in the first place, half of me was like, "this my nigga" but the other half was looking at it like he overlooked all that I'd done for him for a bitch ... matter of fact, my bitch!

After getting home and getting myself together I called Calvin to get the money from the work and that last gee from Gretchen. While speaking with him in person I got that feeling you get when you feel like someone's not telling you the truth, but regardless the fact remained that she wanted to be with him. I had too much money and pride to let either one of them assume that they fazed me but I definitely saw a gap in me and Calvin's solid relationship that I never knew existed till that moment. I took that money, then ran around collecting all the money from work fronted out prior to my trip. In all I had close to fifty thousand and figured I'd wait till the next morning to re-up considering what time of day it was. Plus, I was tired from the flight and wanted to just go to my spot and lay down, get some rest and start over fresh in the morning. Surprisingly, I was going through way more changes over losing Gretchen than I expected, half of me was feeling embarrassed knowing that the streets were about to know Calvin got my bitch. Secondly, I was realizing that I cared about her more than I knew now that she was gone.

Jenkins and everyone else had returned home from Houston a day before me and Ray [Benzino] seeing that Ray [Benzino] wanted to get the full mix of my new song from Mike Dean before we left, so I figured I'd go over my man Sea Wood's crib that night to say what up to the fellas before I went home. Soon as I pulled up, Jenks came off the porch telling me to take a walk with him so that he can hip me to something. Immediately, I got an eerie feeling from his demeanor and felt that this wasn't going to be something good. He said, "Earlier, me, Greed and Monsta rob your man, Eddy's boy Jimmy for a whole one and like twenty gee's!

Before saying anything I just stood there shaking my head trying to take it all in, feeling disrespected because he knew that me and Eddy were cool. I said, "Damn, dog, I told you that Eddy was off limits because he's my man!"

Acting as if he didn't know that the shit they took from Jimmy was Eddy's, he said, "We didn't take shit from Eddy, we got Jimmy, plus I told that nigga that if he said anything about what happened we'd come back an kill em. Trust me, he's not even going to say anything to Eddy about what happened."

I said, "Come on, my nigga, you really think that nigga ain't gonna tell his boys he got robbed?"

He said, "Yeah, I'm sure he is, but he not gonna say it was us!"

Again, I stood there silent feeling disrespected, trying to suck in the whole situation when Jenks said, "Plus, my nigga, I got a four thing for you off the key just because I know you fuck with them niggas like that."

At this point I was upset and said, "Naw, I'm cool; yo, I don't want shit from that, this is some crazy shit, dog, fa real," and while rubbing my head I walked off and got back in my car not even speaking to the rest of my niggas that were on the porch, saying to myself, "this shit ain't over," while heading to my spot.

Barely awake, the next morning I could hear my cell phone ringing back to back at like eight-thirty. At first, I wasn't going to answer it till I was fully awake but then I thought about Cynthia and my son and wanted to make sure it wasn't her with an emergency. Come to find out it was Jenks calling me. Before I could assume anything, he called right back and I answered saying, "What's good, yo!"

He said, "My brother, yo, somebody kidnaped my lil brother!"

Not knowing the story or what happened, I said, "Where you at?"

"Tara's house."

I said, "I'm on my way," then hung up with him, grabbed one of my handguns and shot by Tara's spot. I got there and his mother and father were there, upset while Tara was in the living room with the kids and a few of my niggas sitting on the couch, with "I'm ready to kill someone" faces on. I put my pistol on safety, then put it underneath the couch. While sitting down, I asked, "What happened?"

Jenks said, "Eddy and them went by my mom's and got my lil brother this morning."

Rubbing, and shaking my head I asked, "So what's up now?"

Jenks said, "Here, call Eddy from this phone."

Eddy said, "He wants to holla at you before we meet up to make a swap."

Although I was there to support Jenks and his family, I was still feeling a certain way about Jenks disrespecting what I'd said about not robbing Eddy and now got me dead smack in the middle of it all.

Eddie answered the phone saying, "Who is this?"

I said, "McNeill, what's going on?"

He said, "You tell me, Mizz, how ya people gonna disrespect."

I said, "Yeah, I know that stupid shit wasn't supposed to happen, I'm pissed about it myself, but we here now and need to go ahead and do what we gotta do to fix it!"

He said, "Yeah, I feel you, Mizz, I knew you wouldn't just say fuck me after all we been through."

I said, "Naw, cuz, that's part of the reason I'm here now trying to get this shit right. Where can we meet?"

Eddie said, "We'll count the money, make sure it's twenty thousand and weigh the work up, make sure it's a key, then call me, I'll meet you somewhere down op."

I said, "Ok," then hung up asking Jenks if he still had everything.

He said, "Naw, it's short a half and eight g's that I didn't get back from Monsta."

I said, "You call him for it?"

He said, "Yeah, he ain't answering, but fuck it, just call Eddie back and tell him that it's all here."

I called Eddie back and said, "What's good, it's all here."

He said, "Ok, now go to the basketball court on the Mass Ave side and put the bag in the middle of the court, my people gonna come out and get it, and once I count the money and eyeball the work, I'll have my folks let him go."

I said, "I'm on my way."

He said, "Cool, I'm waiting, I'll be able to see you when y'all come in."

Getting in the projects, me and Jenks agreed that if there was going to be a shootout, there would be no time to pull out our guns, so we better just walk up with them out and cocked already.

Reaching the park, I could see Eddie and like ten dudes on the roof of the project buildings with guns in their hands as well. I yelled out, "Where he at?"

While holding a phone in his other hand, Eddie said, "Throw the bag in the middle of the court. I'm calling right now for him to be released. You sure it's all there, Mizz?"

Now upset myself, I said, "Yeah, but I thought he was here with you?"

He said, "Naw, but he definitely straight and getting released."

Jenks threw the bag in the middle of the court and asked, "How long before I see my fucking brother!"

Some lil dude ran out the building with a scarf covering half his face and got the bag, then Eddie said, "They just let him go, he should be calling you in a minute." Then him and the rest of the dudes on the roof with him disappeared into the building somewhere. Me and Jenks headed back to my car, still unsure on what happened to his brother or where he was at. Jenks looked at his phone once we got back in the car and saw he had five missed calls from Tara. He called her back and she said, "Your brother here!"

Looking confused, Jenks said, "How the hell he get there so fast?"

She said, "He said he escaped like an hour ago but ain't have no phone or money on him to call."

Jenks said, "Ok, cool," and hung up telling me what Tara said and to turn around and ride back through the projects to see if we could catch back up with Eddie and them now that we knew for sure that his brother was ok.

No one was out there, but Eddie called me back within the next twenty minutes saying everything was short. Jenks, knowing it was him on the phone, wanted to speak to him so I handed him the phone and he asked Eddie, "Where you at, let's get up again."

The phone hung up, then I asked Jenks what he said.

He said, "He said don't worry, we'll see each other out here in the street, but it's cool, I'ma kill that nigga when I catch him."

I dropped Jenks back off to Tara's crib, then shot up to my cousin Tony's crib to let my clique know what was going on. Around this time everything other than my music career had seemed to be falling apart, my drug clients were decreasing, I wasn't getting anymore hoe money and I had accumulated beef with like three to four different lil cliques around town which I really didn't give a fuck about, besides the fact that it had me strapped up more often than I had been in the last couple of years. Now that Vidal was back on his feet and moving around, I figured that the nigga Damien should be also and felt like it was time to slide back through there. Strapped up with a new forty-five driving a rental Rodeo, I scooped Vidal up and rode through their block seeing if we could catch the nigga out there sleeping. Damien wasn't out there, but seeing that there were a few restaurants, sub shops and hospitals down there, there were plenty of nurses and doctors walking to and from getting something to eat when Vidal noticed some dude coming out of a store and said, "That's one of his boys right there!"

We were in the middle of traffic, plus had a trolley from the Green Line coming up in the center of the road. Dude looked over and noticed us staring at him, then smirked his lips as to say, "yeah, y'all see me," but doubting we would do anything because of the circumstance we caught him in. I stuck the gun out the window, aimed at his face and shot one time. I knew I missed when he dropped his bag and took off running up the side street. I couldn't get another shot due to the heavy traffic. I took the first left I could while saying to Vidal, "Trust me, I'ma merk one of these niggas over you getting shot!"

Getting back from Houston, I hadn't really seen too many people being that I was dealing with so much drama within days of me touching down, so I figured I'd go by Greenwood to tell Donna about my trip plus tell Big Mike that I got a few keys coming tomorrow. Before I asked for Donna, I spoke to Mike seeing that he was on the porch when I pulled up. I said, "What's up, Big Mike, what you been up to?"

Trying to sound smooth and saying it in a way like he really didn't wanna speak to me he said, "Same old same old, Mizz, just chilling."

Noticing his attitude, I asked, "What wrong with you?"

He said, "Nothing, I'm good."

I said, "Oh ok, well tomorrow I'ma have a few keys of some bomb power, you ready to make some move?"

He said, "Naw, I'm good right now. I just got a key a couple days ago."

I instantly got heated, I had showed this nigga how to whip coke and now he's acting like he didn't want to spend any money with me, plus he's got this lil shitty attitude like he doesn't need me anymore. All I could remember me saying to myself before asking for Donna was, I knew I shouldn't have shown this nigga shit! I knew it and this was what I got for trying to be friendly! Even though I was mad, I wasn't going to let him know and think he was slowing me down from doing shit, so I just said, "Cool, hit me up," and asked him to call Donna downstairs for me.

Donna, being able to tell something was on my mind asked me, "Are you alright?"

I said, "Yeah, just tired. What you doing tonight?"

She said, "Nothing. Why?"

I said, "I'm coming to get you a lil later. I'll call you when I'm on my way."

She said, "Ok," then went back upstairs and I left and went down to Frank's place to chop it up with niggas for a few."

Soon as I came in Ray [Benzino] said, "What's up, Mizz," seeming to be happy about something.

I said, "What up, Digs," while slapping five with everyone that was there.

He said, "I got some good news. I spoke to Russell Simmons earlier about a possible deal for the Wise Guys."

I said, "Def Jam?"

He said, "Yeah, my nigga, Def Jam, but keep it low because it ain't official yet, but it's definitely in the making wit a dot com deal for the source."

That information and a shot of Remy definitely changed the attitude I had from speaking with Big Mike. While sitting in Frank's for a few hours talking about all the lil problems that'd been occurring lately, Belnel Mike and a few niggas from around his way had come in, one being his man Eight that had got shot a few months back in a shootout around the corner. I said, "What's good, man. You straight?"

He said, "Yeah for sure!"

I said, "I had asked Belnel Mike about you to see if y'all needed anything or needed me to do something, but he said y'all straight."

Eight said, "Good looking, fam, but I'm straight," while lifting up his shirt to let me see that he was strapped with a forty Glock.

I said, "Ok, well shit, let me know if you ever need anything."

He said, "Ok cool," as I went on to holler at one of the Belnel dudes that I was more familiar with named Sneek. Me and Sneek went to school together and word was that he was doing pretty good for himself from pimping, so I figured I'd chop some game with him to compare notes even though I didn't have the hoe anymore. I said, "What's good, Sneek. How's the pimping treating you?"

He said, "Alright, I can't complain, I heard you got a bitch out here now, huh?"

I said, "Had one, but the bitch just chose up on a nigga couple weeks ago."

He said, "Yeah, who called you with the serving?"

I giggled a lil bit feeling a lil embarrassed and said, "My man Calvin."

He said, "Naw, the bitch ain't do you like that."

I said, "Yeah, but a nigga still alright out here."

He said, "I know that's right, plus them hoes come and go. Just keep pushing and stay down and come up on a couple more even better than the last one."

I said, "That what's up. I heard you got a green BMW on some gold rims killing him out here."

He said, "It's all right, it's outside if you wanna go check it."

I said, "Ok, I'ma take a peep at it on my way out. I'm getting ready to leave anyways, but it was good talking to you, my nigga."

He said, "Same here, Mizz, anytime you wanna holla or hang out hit me and we get up."

I said, "Ok, cool," while giving him and everyone else dap on the way out the door to get Donna.

I pulled up blowing the horn and Donna came down and got in the car with an overnight bag on her shoulder asking, "What hotel we staying in tonight?"

I said, "Chill, we ain't staying in a hotel tonight."

She said, "Oo," then just stayed quiet till I pulled up at my apartment and got a ticket at the underground garage. Anytime I felt like things weren't going right or I was upset about something and wanted to get away from the street life in a hole, I'd want to be around Donna. It was like she was my portal into a regular life, non-stressful and always gave off an aura like she had my back if I lost it all. And no matter how many chicks I was fucking or how many niggas were ready to move on my call I never felt like any of them had my back like Donna did.

Over the next few weeks my name got involved in several shootings, a few I knew about and a couple that I wasn't even there for, but it was Sheldon and Sco, so fuck it, I might as well been.

One night I left Cynthia's house about 1:30 to go to downtown and see what females come out the club. My first instinct was to get my gun out of her closet but seeing that we were on bad terms getting that would have started an argument with her asking why I needed that if I'm coming right back. So, I figured fuck it, I'll leave it, I'm getting on the highway there and the highway back, I'll be straight. Well, soon as I got off the highway, I saw a blue Honda Odyssey mini-van riding behind me with the hazard lights flashing and the driver waving his hands out the window signaling me to pull over. Looking through my rear view I realized that it was lil Eddie with Ron in the passenger seat. Part of me was thinking, "Mizz, don't pull over for these niggas on these back streets without no strap." Then the other half of me was like, "fuck these hoe ass niggas, let me see what the fuck they talking about!"

I put my hazards on and pulled over and got out with them pulling up right behind me. I walked to the driver's window and said, "What's up, Ed, what's popping?"

Eddie said, "Mizz, you told me that the work and money was straight that day and it wasn't."

I said, "Yeah, well you told me that Jenks' brother was with you and he wasn't."

Ron pulled out what looked like a Glock and pointed it at me saying, "Fuck all that. I should kill you out here right now. I know you know something about my lil nigga getting killed!"

It shocked me, so I paused for a sec and stared at him, that's when Eddie grabbed his arm lowering the gun saying, "Go head, Mizz, go, just get out of here."

While running back up to my car I could hear someone saying, "You fucked up! He already pulled it out, let him do what he need to do."

I jumped in my whip and went to my spot seeing that it was only ten minutes from downtown to get my other pistol and shot back down there hoping they were still out there riding around the clubs. I circled around for like an hour before saying fuck it and left. Before going back to Cynthia's, I rode through one of Ron's kid's mother's spots to see if I saw anything which I didn't, but in the back of my mind I knew he'd be over to this spot one day soon. I said to myself that I was gonna play that spot every day till I caught up with him!

Getting back to Cynthia's house she noticed I had my other pistol out on my side while waiting on her to come down and open the door. She said, "Another gun? What happened now?"

I said, "Nothing, I don't wanna talk about it, let's just go to bed."

The next day Ray [Benzino] got wind of what happened and knew me and my clique was going to be riding around for at least the next few days trying to get some payback, so he called me telling me that he needed me to come out to New York to lay a track, basically wanting to take me out of the action and have me get back focused on my music. After riding around a lil bit and making a couple plays, I headed out to New York around five in the evening getting there at almost nine. Soon as I walked into the studio Ray [Benzino] said, "What's good, McNeill. I'm glad you came."

I said, "Fa sure, I'm with you on trying to make this music thang pop."

He said, "I know, it's just that I just heard about that lil bullshit last night and figured you'd be out trying to find them niggas."

I said, "Yeah, you right but it ain't over though. I'ma get right back on them niggas' ass when we finish this!"

We both laughed a lil bit then he said, "McNeill, you crazy. I got love for you an don't wanna see nothing bad happen to you and keep in mind that we close to getting this paper an getting away from all the bullshit so be smart an be careful!"

This was one of those rare conversations that me and Ray [Benzino] would have where I knew that he was speaking from the heart. These were the types of conversations we would have when I was a kid coming over his house with dreams of being a rapper and being down with RSO. So, when I told him I appreciate that, I truly did on a whole other level. My mind was so set on getting at Ron for pulling out on me that once Ray [Benzino] played the track we were recording to that's all I could think about writing about. The first few lines came to me easier than ever with me starting off saying, "I'm looking at my life through the barrel of a nine wishing that I could reach for mine, but I wasn't strapped this fucking time." My verse came out dope, in my opinion that was the hottest sixteen I'd written to that point. Once Ray [Benzino] finished laying his verse I came up with the idea of calling it, "You Should of Squeezed" and he agreed; after he added samples of Tupac that fitted perfectly as a hook he said, "McNeill, this shit hot, I'ma get someone that's already in the industry to feature on this with us."

I was already feeling good about how well I did on the track in such a spur of the moment situation but now hearing that Ray [Benzino] liked the song well enough to put a guest feature on it boosted my ego even more. But it still couldn't take my mind off Ron pulling a gun out on me. I gave everyone dap and left the studio three in the morning heading home.

Teddy and his girlfriend, Shanell's daughter Sha Sha turned three and they invited me to her birthday party. Shanell was a good cook, so even though it was for the kids I knew that there would be something good to eat and some drinks for the adults to go upstairs and get to while the party's going on in the back yard. Plus, I'm a pretty humorous dude when I wanna be so people would like being around me knowing that I'm going to say a few jokes, and it really set the tone and got the mood right. I knew most of Shanell's family and friends from attending other get togethers but this year it was a couple of new people I'd never seen at any of the functions. One being her girlfriend Tina. From the moment I walked in the yard I noticed Tina aggressively looking at me as if she knew me and was waiting for me to speak. Although she did look familiar I couldn't pinpoint from where, but from how aggressively she was staring at me I figured that she would find the time to create a conversation with me within the next couple of hours that I had planned on being there.

After some food and a few drinks, me and Ted decided we were gonna go sit in my car to smoke one before Sha opened her gifts and cut the cake. Before walking out front Teddy told Shanell, "I'll be right back, I'ma bout to go out front and blow one."

Tina, hearing that, said, "I'm trying to smoke, too. I got some, do y'all mine if I come?"

I said, "Naw, not at all, it's cool." She grabbed her purse, followed me and Ted to my car and got in the back seat wasting no time in asking me if I remembered her.

I said, "You look familiar, but I can't remember from where."

She said, "Last year sometime, you came into my husband's autobody shop to buy a Benz from him."

Then it came back to me and I remembered her and said, "Oh yeah, you was taking care of some paperwork or something that day. I remember you coming out the office."

She said, "Yeah, that was then," saying it in a way to insinuate that she and her husband were having problems now. Still I said, "I haven't seen or heard from Kenyatta in a few. How's he doing?"

She said, "He's fine I guess," trying to sound like she hadn't been keeping up with him. After smoking one joint, Ted was ready to get out and go back to the party.

Tina said, "I got a blunt to smoke if you want to," while getting in the front seat after Teddy got out. After telling Teddy to tell Shanell that she'd be in there in a sec, she lit her blunt up asking me, "How many women you got?"

I said, "A few."

She said, "A few meaning three or four?"

I said, "A few meaning three and sometimes four!"

We laughed about it for a second, then she asked me for my number.

I gave it to her saying, "I don't need ya husband calling me with no bullshit."

She said, "Naw, never that. I got this."

I said, "Ok, make sure," then we put the rest of the blunt out and went back into the cookout.

In my mind I was thinking, damn, this nigga supposed to be a real pimp and he married, as well as what is it that I could possibility get from this bitch. She's an older married black woman, though still attractive I doubted she was still, if ever getting money from the service. What I was looking for if anything at the time was another white girl in her mid-twenties to replace the void that I was feeling from Gretchen leaving. But her being Kenyatta's wife I felt like she was at least deserving of a phone call or two to at least hear what she'd been around, seen or possibly still had access to.

Once Sha Sha cut her cake and opened her gifts I gave her a hundred dollar bill telling her to buy what she wants. I stayed for another half hour, smoking and having a couple more drinks while Tina flirted and tried to entice me to bring her with me that night which wasn't going to happen. I had plans on getting with my squad late night and ride trying to bump back into Ron and them. After chopping it up with Ted and telling everyone goodnight I left. On my way down the stairs Tina came in the hallway yelling down, "Hold up a minute, I'ma bout to come down." She got to the top of the stairs and said, "So, handsome, when can I expect to see you again?"

I said, "I gotta few things to take care of tomorrow in the morning and evening but I'll be free around seven. Just call me around then."

She said, "Ok, I will and be careful out here with your fine ass."

I said, "Thanks, I'm good, hit me up tomorrow."

She said, "Ok, I will then."

I left with my strap already in my car. I called Sco and Sheldon to meet me up Franklin Hill Ave in a few hours so we could take a peek at a couple of spots that I wanted to check out. Knowing I was going over to Tammy's house and hadn't spoken to her in a few, I figured I'd give her a call to see what she was up to before I just popped up over there and could barely speak to her. She answered the phone saying, "Hey, stranger."

I said, "What's up, why you call me that?"

She said, "I haven't been hearing from you lately. I called a couple times an you didn't answer so it's like you're becoming a stranger."

I said, "Naw, don't say that. I just been going through a lil something, so I been a lil busy but I ain't becoming a stranger."

She said, "Yeah, so when you gonna make time for us?"

I said, "The weekend, I should be finished taking care of what I need to take care of by then, then I'll put something together for us to chill and relax."

She asked, "You promise?"

I said, "Yeah, you got that where you at now?"

She said, "At my girlfriend's house."

I asked, "Have you been being good?"

She said, "Of course, only person on my mind is you!"

I said, "That's a good thing."

She said, "I heard that you haven't been seeing Sharee lately."

I said, "Naw, I feel back."

She said, "That's good, make sure you leave it like that!"

We laughed a lil bit then she said, "Now, you need to do the same with Asia and I'll be happy."

I said, "Soon she doing something for me, not right now but real soon."

She said, "Yeah, I'll believe it when I see it or in this case hear about it."

We giggled a lil bit then I said, "I'ma call you a lil later. I got police behind me a few cars an I ain't right."

She said, "Ok, luv you, be careful, call me later."

By this time I confidently knew that Donna, Tammy and Asia were truly in love with me and even though Cynthia was my son's mother we never gained that chemistry or true connection where I felt like she really loved me. Me, being so egotistical and immature, I was basically holding on to what we had because I didn't want her to be with anyone else. Seeing that she had my son, I felt a sense of entitlement and was going to keep us together feeling like that was what I was supposed to do as a man and a father.

I hadn't spoken to or called Calvin in a few days. It wasn't that we had problems, we'd both just been busy doing different things. I was on the way to park at Tammy's crib and jump in the rental car with disco when he called me laughing and playing, not knowing what I went through or was trying to do. I said, "What's good, Cee?"

He said, "What's good, my nigga, what you up to?"

I said, "Chilling, trying to take care of something right quick. What's popping?"

He said, "Cuz, I know you don't give a fuck now, but I den found out from the bitch Gretchen that her and Haburto hooked up New Year's Eve in New York while you was outta town."

I said, "My connect Haburto?"

He said, "Yeah."

I said, "Damn, I wonder how the fuck they hooked up?"

He said, "The bitch said he asked her for her number one day you sent her to see him."

I said, "Damn, that's crazy, Haburto den disrespected."

He said, "Yeah, I knew you'd wanna know about that!"

I said, "Good looking, I'ma hit you a lil later to let you know about what's going on."

He said, "Alright. You straight?"

"Yeah, yeah I'm good. I'll hit you up in a few."

Even though I didn't have Gretchen anymore, I still felt totally disrespected and got upset about it. A part of me went into feelings thinking, damn, as much as I trusted her this is how she was playing me, the other half of me was getting a clear view of how a real hoe could do a nigga when he ain't fully on his pimping. I had fucked Haburto's girl Joanna while he was on vacation and a couple times since then, even once in the ass but I still felt a certain way about him doing that to me while we were supposed to be partners! Getting with Sco and Sheldon, I quickly put what Calvin told me about Gretchen and Burto in the back of my head to deal with the situation at hand. We rode up and down the avenue at least twenty times looking for that light blue minivan and eyeballing every rental car we saw ride by on both sides of the traffic. Around one something close to two we got tailed by a regular blue and white police car for like three minutes obviously running our plates. Once they finally took a right getting off our bumper, I called it a night telling Sco to go back to Tammy seeing that we got tagged plus had been out close to three hours and ain't see them. Granted, I still had a half of key of powder left and things were moving slower. I called Burto the next evening to order a half really wanting to look him in his eyes when we talk and pay closer attention to his actions now that I knew he'd been holding a secret from me.

Having me meet him at his mother's house he came bringing the work as usual. Everything about him seemed the same, it must have been me who had a different posture seeing that while handing me the package he asked me was I ok? The way he smiled, the way he shook my hand and asked me how my son was doing all seemed fake to me now that I knew about him and Gretchen. I said to him, "Yeah, I'm ok, I just got something concerning my son's mother on my mind," really making the decision at that point that I was going to rob him real soon even if it meant killing him in the midst of it all.

Karma had hit me, and I didn't like it, here I was secretly in a relationship with my cousin's girl outright sleeping with Sheldon's ex and now I got a silent attitude with Calvin and now contemplating robbing and killing Haburto over Gretchen. My feelings were all fucked up in a way that I had become mentally and emotionally unstable and no one knew, not even me at the time! Whenever I felt like there was an intense situation in the streets I wouldn't ride with Cynthia and my son in the car.

I had a couple of leather suits custom made by Antonio Ansaldi for my son that I wanted to drop off, plus I had something I wanted to tell Cynthia that I knew would make her happy seeing that she had been complaining about us not spending any time together lately. I grabbed some Chinese food and a bottle of wine before going to her house seeing that I intended on chilling for a few hours spending some quality time with my son. As usual she had an attitude acting like she didn't care for the wine or the food and definitely didn't want me to touch her. I ignored it as if I didn't notice it sitting on the floor playing with my son for about an hour. It wasn't until she had to change his Pampers when we finally indulged in a conversation. I said, "Hi."

She said, "Hi."

I said, "I been here over an hour and you ain't said nothing to me."

She said, "I didn't want to interrupt the overdue time you was spending with your son."

Me, knowing she was right, didn't respond to that in an ignorant way. I just said, "Yeah, you right you right, I have been a lil busy, but I definitely should have been over here more than I have been in the last two weeks."

She looked at me with a smirk on her face and said, "Yeah, you should have!"

I said, "Yeah, well that's why I'ma bout to take y'all to Disney World."

She said, "And when we supposed to be going there?"

I said, "Soon as you take the time off of work and schedule it. I'm paying for it and we out."

She smiled and puckered her lips up signaling me to kiss her and said, "Thank you, that's going to be nice. I'ma start making the calls planning and getting the prices this week."

Her mood instantly changed. She went downstairs and made both of us a plate of food, brought it up, then went back down, then came up with wine, two glasses and a corkscrew telling me to open it up.

I stayed for a couple more hours playing with my son till he went to sleep also laughing, joking and talking with Cynthia like we used to at the beginning of our relationship. Finally, looking at my phone I realized I had four missed calls, three from Tina who I told that I would be free at seven but totally forgot and one from Bum who I was supposed to meet at Frank's at eleven to discuss some things concerning the Wise Guys. It was about quarter past ten when I told Cynthia that I was leaving for a few to take care of something but would be back. She showed a little disappointment in her face but was cool with it seeing that I'd been there four or five hours, plus had promised I'd be back.

While parking my car at Frank's I came across a weird feeling like someone was watching me. That's when I looked over my shoulder towards the traffic and saw Ron now driving the light blue minivan with Eddie in the passenger seat sitting at the red light staring at me. I stared back ready to get my pistol from underneath my seat till the light turned green and he pulled off after nodding his head as if to say yeah I see you, which only made me more furious! By the direction he was heading I figured he wouldn't come this close without going by his kid's mother's house and I wanted to go by there and check immediately! I wanted someone else to drive seeing that they knew my car and by the way I came in, Frank's, dudes automatically knew something was wrong and started asking, "What's up, what's up. You good?"

I said, "Naw, I just saw this nigga Ron going up the avenue and I think I know where he's going. I need a driver."

My man Dee immediately volunteered saying, "Come on, Mizz, I got you."

On the way our greedy Keem said, "I'm strapped too, I'ma ride with y'all."

I said, "Cool," then we rushed to Dee's whip and I directed him to the nigga's baby's mother's house. Pulling up on the street we slowly rode up to the house and passed it while I told them what kind and color minivan we were looking for. The van wasn't on the street nor around the corner, so I figured either he didn't come here, or he did come and ran in and out real fast. I said, "Fuck it, cool, we'll bump into each other again."

I told Dee he could go ahead and head back down to Frank's. With the back window still down, we came to a complete stop at the red light on American Legion Highway. I was laying in the back seat not paying attention, upset that he wasn't there when Greedy said, "Look up, Mizz, is this the minivan you looking for on side of us?"

I quickly sat up, coming eye to eye with Ron and started shooting. From his reaction I knew I hit him with the first shot but probably missed him with the second cause of the angle form which I had to shoot. Seeing that Dee sped off taking that first left, I hit him pretty close with a three-fifty- seven so I figured that if he didn't die he was at least going to be fucked up till the next time I could catch him again. Dee dropped me and Greedy back to Frank's and I told him to get out of the streets for a few. Then I headed back over to Cynthia's house acting as if nothing had happened. Due to everything that went down the night before I never had a chance to speak to Bum about what he needed to speak to me about concerning the group and now that I'd shot Ron I knew Bum wanted to talk to me about both issues so I hit em and told him to come down the spot. Walking in, shaking his head, the first thing he said was, "Damn my nigga, he still living."

I said, "Yeah, I figured that, cuz, this nigga Dee took the left instead of staying on side of them so that I could hit a few more times."

Bum said, "Damn!"

I said, "I know, and I had my .357. If I would have tapped that head once he would have been off this."

He said, "Yeah, I wish you would have just waited for me. I came in Frank's like five minutes after y'all left."

I said, "Yeah, cuz, it was one of those spur- of- the moment go right now type of things."

He said, "Yeah, I feel you but just keep ya eyes open and stay on point."

I said, "Fa sure, but what's up with the group?"

He said, "Well you know that deal that's been in the air with Def Jam?"

I said, "Yeah."

"Well it's going down. Ray [Benzino] wants me to have all the artists at the studio so that we can discuss everything and go over the contracts together."

I said, "Dope, that shit's dope. What time he want us there?"

He said, "At eight."

"Ok, I'll be there."

He said, "Ok cool, and keep your eyes open, my nigga," while on the way out the door.

After calling all my niggas telling them what had happened and to be on point I got showered and dressed, left the house with my Glock nine on me conducting business as usual, speaking with Calvin about the situation. He wasn't happy about it at all, reminiscing on the days when me, him and Ron used to ride around drinking forty ounces, chasing money together out in Brockton. I told him I felt him, but once Ron pulled that gun out on me that night everything went out the window.

Shaking his head, he said, "Damn, this shit crazy."

I said, "Yeah," leaving the conversation alone knowing that it bothered him, seeing that me and Ron were both his main niggas.

CHAPTER SEVEN

Asia had started feeling so strongly about Tammy having feelings for me that she started speaking about me more and exaggerating things between us when she was around her just to get a response out of her. She called me that night while I was on the way to the studio to discuss the contract with Ray [Benzino]. "Babe, it's been awhile. You coming over tonight?"

The way she just out the blue said, "Babe" struck me as weird, but I really didn't pay it any attention and seeing that I hadn't seen her in about a week I was in the mood to fuck her.

So, I just said, "Yeah, I'll call you once I leave the studio."

She said Ok calling me babe again before she hung up. I thought nothing of it, turned the music up and kept pushing to the studio. Getting there late I expected to walk in and see niggas smoking, drinking and celebrating the deal. Instead, all the artists were holding their contracts and looking confused about something. I said, "What's popping? Why all the long faces, we on Def Jam now. Right?"

Ray [Benzino] seemingly upset, handed me my contract and said, "I don't know what's going on right now, they saying they wanna take a day to look over the contract so they can fully understand what they signing to."

I said, "Yeah, give me a pen so I can sign this shit right now. I don't even need to read it, you been holding niggas down this far I don't expect nothing less of you in the future." Then I signed the contract and gave it back to Ray [Benzino] telling him to roll up something while the rest of the group started walking out of the office claiming that they would bring em back signed tomorrow. I could see in Ray's [Benzino] face that he took them niggas acting like they didn't trust him as an insult. No more than ten minutes after they left, we were smoking a blunt when Ray [Benzino] came out and said, "These niggas are going to fuck around and mess this up for everybody."

I said, "Now you see why I never liked none of them niggas, after all the clothes you bought them niggas and the trips you took em on, this how they repay a nigga. Fuck them hoe ass niggas if you ask me!" He said, "Yeah, I feel you but I'ma give em till tomorrow before I jump to conclusions."

I said, "Yeah I feel you, I probably want them niggas to sign it badder than you do, it just that I could see it in their faces when they walked out that they acting funny style."

He said, "Yeah, well we'll see what happens tomorrow."

I said, "Cool," while giving everyone dap on the way out, then calling Asia and heading to her apartment. In my mind I was thinking, *watch these niggas be on some bullshit tomorrow when it comes to those contracts.* I called Asia saying I'm on my way.

She said, "I'm not home. Can you come get me?"

"Damn, where you at?"

"At Tammy's house."

I asked, "When you get there?"

"Earlier."

I asked, "Tony there?"

"No."

I said, "Ok, listen for the horn an come down when I blow."

"Ok."

Now I was thinking, yeah that's what that babe shit was for, she was doing that shit because she was around Tammy. Twenty minutes later I pulled up at Tammy's house and blew the horn. Tammy came to the window and yelled out, "She'll be down in a minute."

I could hear in the way she said it that she had an attitude about me picking Asia up. Before Asia even came out the hallway, I could see that Tammy was calling my phone. Asia was getting in the car so I just put the phone on mute and put it in my inside coat pocket knowing that Tammy would leave a message expressing whatever it was she wanted to say. Asia got in and said, "Hey."

I said, "Hey."

She asked, "You ok?"

"Yeah, why you ask that?"

She said, "The look on your face, you look like something's wrong."

I said, "Naw, I'm good, just relight that blunt in the ashtray."

Once we got to Asia's crib, I started feeling more tired than horny, and while she was in the shower, I checked my messages seeing that I had three knowing they were all from Tammy. They all said basically the same thing: fuck you, you're a liar. I'm getting tired of this. Stay with your bitch and how you gonna pick her up in front of me.

Trying to keep all these females satisfied and separated and a secret started to become exhausting to me and was actually taking a toll on my body and mind. When the reality of the situation was, none of them did anything for me but stroke my ego and fulfill my big appetite for sex! Asia got out of the shower and came into the room in a lil silk nightgown with nothing underneath it obviously wanting to fuck. I was in my boxers laid up high and tired, dozing off. I was under the assumption that I was the only one fucking all these women at the time, so I felt obligated to keep them all sexually satisfied in order to keep them from going elsewhere.

This night I was just too tired, in between having sex with Cynthia a couple days ago, riding around with the drama, plus those stressing messages from Tammy I just wasn't in the mood and she was. When she got in the bed, I told her to go to the other end and open her legs facing me so I could look at her pussy, she made a curious type of expression with her face but still got in the position that I told her to. Now I said, "Play with it yourself for me tonight, I don't wanna rush to get up in you.

I wanna sit back for a few and just really enjoy being in your presence."

She smiled and said, "Yeah," then put her two fingers in her mouth long enough to make sure they were wet, then laid back spreading her legs, then her pussy lips and started slowly rubbing her clit; though I was tired my dick got hard when she really started to really get into it. She started moving faster in a circular motion saying, "Daddy, I'ma bout to cum." I climbed down on top of her and got in the pussy cumming quickly, her performance brought me to a climax like I'd never had before, and I knew this lil act was something that was about to become part of my routine for some time to come!

Calling Ray [Benzino] the next morning I could hear in the way he said, "What's up, McNeill?" that something didn't go well with the rest of the group and their contracts.

I asked, "You hear from them niggas?"

He said, "Yeah, them niggas talking about getting their own lawyer and that the contract only seems to be good for me."

I said, "Yeah."

He said, "Let me hit you back in a minute, McNeill. These niggas on the other line now."

I said, "Ok, hit me, let me know what's good."

About thirty minutes after I was getting off the highway from Asia's, when Ray [Benzino] called me asking, "McNeill, where you?"

I said, "Near Ashmont. What's good?"

He said, "Come over the crib, hurry up."

I said, "Ok, on my way."

I pulled up and I saw Ray [Benzino] and his father standing outside seemingly upset. I got out and asked, "What's up now?"

Ray [Benzino] said, "I just got in an argument with them niggas on the phone."

I said, "Which one?"

He said, "All of them, they all together over one of their cribs, them niggas den called up to Def Jam asking to speak to Russel

Simmons like they the Wu Tang or something trying to make a deal without me!"

I said, "Naw."

He said, "Yeah, I feel like going to find em and pop one them niggas after all I did for them lil bitches."

I said, "I'm strapped now, let's go check by all their cribs."

"Naw, I got a better idea. I'm dropping the whole project and starting a new group with me, Cool Jesus, and they called Made Men, and working on your solo project while featuring you a few times on the album."

I said, "Hell yeah, that sounds better to me. Shit, you know I didn't wanna fuck with them niggas in the first place."

Without having an address or being able to catch a nigga on his block you had to just stay strapped and when you did bump into the person you were trying to see, handle it right then and there. That's how it was with trying to get at Damien. I could never catch him hanging on his corner, but every day I'd be strapped hoping to bump into him, till one day Vidal called me saying that dude was up in Nashua Street on bail that he wouldn't be able to make for getting caught with two guns, and he was facing ten years. I never liked hearing about anyone going to jail, but I definitely looked at it as one less nigga I needed to focus on for the time being.

A couple months had passed since me and Tina had exchanged numbers, even though I hadn't made time to hook up with her yet. At that point we were still starting to get to know each other better through conversation and I must say the fact that she was more than ten years older than me, married and had been through a lot in her life, I saw certain mature characteristics that I hadn't seen in the few women I'd been dealing with for the last couple years and found them appealing. The way she trusted me with certain information concerning her husband, knowing we knew each other made it easy for me to trust her with certain conversations and take some of her advice.

One night after leaving the studio late I rode up to the Rolls Club to sit outside front and watch the crowd let out. I had missed calls on my phone from both Tammy and Asia and here they were getting into Tammy's rental car leaving together. I was in a rental myself parked a lil further down the street so neither one of them saw me. The last time I picked Asia up from Tammy's house, Tammy complained about it so I promised her that as long as I fucked with both of them, I wouldn't do it in her face. So, I definitely wasn't going to get Asia for the night. Being that Tammy had a rental car I was paying for, I knew she wanted to drop Asia home and come meet me somewhere. I wasn't in the mood for it seeing that we had just stayed at the Ramada together a few days ago. I figured fuck them, they both probably think I'm still in the studio recording so I'll just leave em together babysitting one another while I figure out if I'm going over to Cynthia's or picking up Donna.

That's when I saw Teddy's girl Shanell and Tina walking to the parking lot. I blew the horn once and flicked the high beams signaling them to come over, basically just wanting to say hi and stay on the low. Once they got to my car and noticed it was me, Shanell said, "Hey, Mike, my friend was just talking about you."

Then Tina said, "You gonna live a long time. I just said to Shanell that I was going to call you once I got in the car."

I said, "Yeah, that's what's up, did y'all enjoy y'alls selfs tonight?"

Tina said, "It was cool but I'm trying to enjoy myself now."

I said, "You better get home before your husband starts looking for you."

She said, "My husband's outta town for the weekend. What's up with you? You should come over for a few."

"Come where?"

She said, "My house. Shit, you know I trust you!"

Part of me was like, naw, I don't wanna be fucking the nigga's wife up in his house, then the other half of me was saying, hey, man, this is pimping. Then I asked, "How long before you can be there?"

"Ten to fifteen minutes, we heading there now."

I said, "Ok, cool, I'll be there parked up the street a lil bit waiting on you."

She said, "Make sure because I wanna do a few things to you."

I smiled and said, "We'll see," then made a U-turn in the middle of the street so I could go in the opposite direction of where Tammy and Asia were headed. I stopped at the gas station to get a water and some condoms, so when I pulled up, she was just getting out of Shanell's car. Not really wanting to be seen going into ill will house, I locked my door, ran down and rushed into the house. Even though she invited me over we both were kind of nervous about me being there so once I got in the house conversation was minimal. She has some big titties so those were the first thing I went for unstrapping her bra, then sucking her nipples for a few getting my dick hard, then I laid across the bed with my pants half down with my shoes still on saying, "Lay down and give my dick a kiss," really meaning come suck it. I enjoyed that for about ten minutes before telling her to come bend over on the edge of the bed. All the pictures of ill will and paraphernalia almost made my dick soft while I was putting the condom on, but she was so wet and horny that once I got it on and in her I fully got back right and started tearing that ass up spanking her, telling her to say all types of shit till I finally came.

Once I finished, she brought me a wet rag to wipe my dick off and some tissue to put the condom and the wrapper in. After pulling my pants up I headed straight for the door not saying much at all, basically just, "I'll call you tomorrow."

She said, "Ok," while making sure she had the condom and wrapper, seeing that she wanted to be the one to get rid of it so she could feel comfortable knowing that there was no evidence of another man being in the house.

Christmas time had come around and even though I wasn't getting as much money as I used to I was still eating, plus I had over a hundred thousand in my stash still and wanted to show my family and the people I cared about some love. While out shopping I bought my sister a beautiful gold and diamond cluster ring, and my mother and Donna matching fur coats.

I got Asia an older model Honda Accord stick shift that I had to teach her how to drive, Cynthia got a white gold ring with an expensive diamond on top of it, and I told Tammy that I would give her the money to register and insure the car she was planning on financing at the end of the month. In all including my son, my dad, and some aunts I easily spent fifteen thousand on top of giving my squad work for cheap so that they could have extra money to do for their people as well. Even though things were moving slow I was in the spirit, and was confident that shit would get back moving like it was supposed to. Cynthia had finally got the trip together and planned for February vacation. We were leaving the sixteenth and coming back the twenty-fourth and I, personally, was pretty excited seeing that I'd never been to Disney World or Disney Land.

On Christmas Day, I felt good riding around handing out gifts, everyone was happy and that alone put a smile on my face. If there was anything that bothered me at that time it was the fact of me having this secret relationship with Tammy behind Tony's back, as knowing that he would be hurt was part of the reason I couldn't tell him. But on the other hand, I had got so caught up that the way she sexed and respected me became obsessive and I didn't know what to do or when this was going to stop.

New Year's Eve was my day. I went to the Versace store and jacked five thousand on an outfit, belt and shoes. I wanted to really look nice this year for the countdown. I was ego tripping even though things weren't going as well as they used to for me. I wanted to wear something that made a statement saying I'm still that nigga out here and my money is still out of the average nigga's league! While at the bar I bumped into Willie McGinest from the New England Patriots and felt good from the love and recognition he gave me once he noticed me. He introduced me to his cousin Mac and his man Bob saying, "This the dude Mike I was telling you all about."

Bob shook my hand and said, "Willie said ya music hot, he said it's the best shit he heard from a Boston artist."

I said, "Word, that's a dope compliment but I'm trying to be the best artist a nigga ever heard period."

He said, "Yeah," then I ordered two more bottles of Don Perignon, giving Bob one for their table, after shaking Willie's hand telling him it was good to see him. He told me to get his boy Bob's number cause he's running his new record label 55 Entertainment and that he'd like to do something with me once the football season's over.

I said, "That sounds good," exchanged numbers with Bob, then carried my bottle back to my section telling Calvin what had just happened. Overall the night went well with me leaving with Cynthia to go stay and wake up with my son on New Year's. Unconsciously, I knew I was getting ready to rob Haburto, that's why I'd been spending the way I was and really wasn't getting it like that. I called him the day after New Year's wishing him a happy New Year's and telling him that I needed to see him. He said, "Same to you, Mike. What you trying to do?"

I said, "Two if it can happen, I got my man with me but if not, just one will be good."

He said, "Naw, it ain't around like that, my people gone to Santa Domingo for vacation and won't be back till next week; only thing left is a half of one."

I said, "Damn, well that's cool for now. How long?"

"Thirty minutes, go to my mother's house."

I said, "Ok," then hung up, far as Haburto knew, me and him were still on good terms so he had no reason to lie to me about the connect not being around and I wasn't going to fuck up my stick for two birds by taking a punk ass half of a key or risk running up in his mother's crib looking shit when he saying ain't nothing. So, I went to the spot, got the money to pay for the stuff and met him at his mother's house to get it, smiling and playing the same way we usually did, telling him to call me when his people get back as I was pulling off. A whole month had passed since I'd been trying to rob this nigga for two birds; every time I'd call for something he kept saying not yet not yet, acting like he hadn't had any work since that last half I bought. It got to a point where I started to wonder if he got hip to what I was trying to do. Around this time Tammy called me saying she was going to get her car and she was wondering if I was still going to give her the money to register and insure it.

I said, "Yeah, how much is it?"

"Seven hundred."

I said, "Ok. I'll be through there shortly." I went over there, snuck her the money, then sat there and smoked a couple blunts and shot the shit with Tony and Sheldon. A few hours later, Tammy and her mother pulled up in a new black Mitsubishi Galant, blowing the horn and smiling. We all went downstairs to take a closer look at the car, then I said, "This is nice, Tammy, let me take it for a test drive."

She got out of the driver's seat and said, "Go ahead."

I asked Tony and Sheldon did they wanna take a ride real quick. They both said no, so I left by myself to go feel it out real quick. I rode through Mattapan Square and then through my project, on my way back, I dropped my phone and reached down to get it and fucked around not seeing the person in front of me coming to a complete stop. I hit them right in the ass, lucky I was familiar with the nigga I hit, and he let me slide by giving him five hundred for his damages instead of calling the police, seeing that nothing was really wrong with his car. But Tammy's car on the other hand was pretty fucked up considering that she just came home with it. When I pulled back up with it crashed, she covered her mouth and said, "Oh my God."

I said, "Yeah, I know but don't worry I'ma pay for it to get fixed and have it back like new for you."

She said, "Ok."

"Go ahead now and bring it to Kenyatta's shop an get me a price and tell him I said to put a new bumper cover on it."

She said, "Ok," then left to get it done.

Noticing how calm Tammy was about the situation Tony said, "Damn, that went over smooth, if that would have been me that crashed, she would have made a big deal about it."

Then her mother waited till she had a chance to say something to me alone and whispered to me, "You must be sleeping with Tammy."

I said, "Naw, why would you say that?"

She said, "Trust me, I know my daughter and she ain't mad about that y'all must be involved."

I waited till Tammy came back with the price before I left. She came in saying, "Four fifty."

I gave her five hundred then apologized and said, "Get a rental and I'll pay for it for the few days it takes for your car to get fixed," then dipped.

For the last six months everything had seemed to be going on a downward spiral, first off someone killed one of my partners and I didn't know who did it, second I lost my hoe to my nigga, my connect's starting to act funny, my clientele had fallen off dramatically, the deal with Def Jam was now off the table and on top of all that my feelings for these females had gone haywire. In my sick mind I thought I was really in love with all four women, and this trip with Cynthia and my son coming up next week was just what I needed. I was anxious to just get away from it all for a few. The cell phone, the guns, the weed and liquor, the constant sex, I was ready to feel a sense of normalcy, take a couple weeks out of the street to figure out what my reality really was.

A couple of days before we were planning to leave, Cynthia was shopping to get several bikinis and some summertime wear for her and my son. She was really happy and excited about the trip, it'd been a while since she'd been this touchy feely and passionate towards me, seeing that she knew I was sleeping with other women, but for now she seemed to have put all that aside and was fully into me and our relationship like she was in the beginning. Once I dropped Cynthia and Michael Junior off I spent the rest of the day situating all my street shit like making sure the coke and guns were accessible to my clique if they needed 'em, collecting money and fronting out work to the few niggas I had still moving for me. Around eight o'clock that night one of my friends named Ace called me asking was I around and if so, could I meet him and Hurst at Frank's.

I was out eating dinner with Donna spending some time with her before I left for a couple of weeks so I told him yeah but he had to give me like a hour to like an hour and a half. He said, "Cool, just hit me when you on your way down there."

Ace and Hurst had been making moves together lately so when I pulled up, I figured they wanted to holla at me about some work and they did. Ace asked me can they buy four and a half and I front them four and a half until I get back, apparently hearing that I was leaving in a couple of days. I never really cared for Ace much after I got locked up with him for the pistol back in the day seeing how him and my ex-girlfriend Toy got into a full relationship while I was in jail, and him knowing how I felt about her, but Hurst was my man sort of like a big brother to me and I was down to do anything for him that would help him get ahead. So, I said yes. I sat in Frank's for a few kicking the shit with niggas having a couple shots, then told Ace to meet me at Hurst's crib with the half of the money they had in like thirty minutes. Granted, the lil voice in my head was saying don't do it, and I never liked mixing up money and friendship but I was definitely with seeing my niggas do good, so I went and got it and dropped it off to them asking Ace before I left was he gonna definitely have that for me when I get back.

He said, "I give you my word."

I said, "Cool," and left. I went to Cynthia's and laid up talking with her anticipating how fun the trip was going to be and making suggestions on things we should make sure we do and see before we leave, then I went to sleep planning on just staying in all day tomorrow with her and my son which was the day before we were supposed to leave.

The next morning, I woke up around eight-thirty, close to nine hearing my phone vibrating in my jeans; by the time I got to it, it had stopped but I noticed it was Ace and I had two prior missed calls from Hurst. I knew the coke I gave them was good so in my mind I was thinking, what now? I hit him back making sure that no one got shot or that the feds weren't kicking in doors. I said, "What's good?"

Ace said, "Yo, it's an emergency, my nigga, you know I wouldn't be calling you this early if it wasn't."

I said, "Drama?"

"Yeah!"

I said, "Where you?"

He said, "Come by the crib and I'll be outside." I put on my pants starting to get dressed when Cynthia rolled over and asked me where I was going?

I said, "Go check on Ace real quick, he's got some type of emergency."

She said, "Damn, ain't nobody else he can call? Shit, y'all ain't even like that."

I said, "Chill out, baby, I'll be right back," then I walked to her closet and got my Glock nine out the shoebox.

She said, "What the hell you bringing that for if you coming right back?"

"Chill out, bae, I promise I'll be right back," I said, then kissed her on her forehead and left out heading to the crib. Pulling up, I saw Ace's car but he wasn't outside like he said he would be, so I blew the horn for him to come out expecting him to be in the crib; instead he came out the garage of the abandoned house across the street from the crib with an upset look on his face. I asked, "What's going on?"

"I stashed the work you gave me at my cousin's house and her baby's father found it and took it, then she called me when he came home. Then me and Hurst went back an kidnaped the nigga to take him to get the shit but now he acting like it's gone and he can't get it back."

I said, "Where he at?"

"Tied up an blindfolded in the garage."

"So, what you want me to do?"

He said, "Go inside and act like it was your shit and if he don't take you to it you gonna kill em. I go in and pistol whip him twice before saying anything to him, then ask, 'Where my shit?'"

Bleeding from the head and mouth he started crying now, claiming to have half of it and some money at his father's house. I said, "He's lying, that was too easy, if it was really there, he would of told y'all that."

Hurst said, "Yeah, I feel you." Ace wasn't thinking straight seeing that it was his last, he wanted to believe him.

Now being serious I said, "You should just kill this nigga and leave him back here."

Then Ace said, "Naw, let's put him in the trunk and take him to his father's crib. I'm trying to get my shit!"

Right after we put him in the trunk, YG pulled up asking, "What's up?"

Hurst said, "Just follow behind us and I'll tell you what's up when we get to the next spot."

Before going to his father's, I told niggas to follow me up to my cousin's crib right quick which was in the same direction as we were heading. We got there with the nigga still in the trunk and I ran upstairs real quick telling Tony what's up and to hold my pistol for me till I get back seeing that we didn't need two guns for this one person. Tony took the pistol from me then said, "I don't even know why you entertaining that shit, you should just let them niggas take care of it from here."

I said, "I know you right but I'm already in, now I'ma just slide through this last spot with them, then I'm coming back to get that from you."

He said, "Alright, be careful," then I left. I followed them to the address the dude told Ace his father lived at. Soon as we got to the spot everything felt blotched. Ace was taking the dude out of the trunk right in front of the house with his pistol showing, the next door neighbor was peeking but trying to act like they weren't watching, I immediately felt like this was about to go bad but still got out of the car to go in and help Ace. Getting inside we realized his father was home with two other people. Once they noticed Ace walking the dude in at gunpoint they panicked. I left my gun at Tony's house so I reached for my beeper as if it was a gun yelling, "Don't move, don't move!" to help get the situation under control. Within minutes we heard police sirens outside and police on a bullhorn yelling, "Come outside with your hands up, we know y'all in there!"

Me and Ace looked at each other, then simultaneously ran towards the back door and went down in the basement. On the way down, Ace threw the gun in a vent and we could hear it sliding down landing somewhere on the concrete floor. There was a small wooden door that I unlocked hoping to be able to make a run for it but there was no chance to, seeing that the police had the back surrounded like the front, then we got arrested!

Getting to the station the first person I saw chained to a pole was Hurst. YG wasn't there so I assumed he had gotten away. Once we were fingered printed and booked, they put us in separate cells side by side one another. Getting the paperwork with my charges on it, I noticed that they didn't charge me with a gun, then I asked Hurst and Ace were they charged with a gun. When they both said no, it brought me a lil relief, feeling that the situation would be less serious as it would have been if they had found the gun. Still, I was wondering how they didn't find the gun when we definitely had one and I heard it hit the ground after rolling out the vent somewhere. Still, in all I felt a sense of relief! Within the next hour we were visited by Craig. He was a cop who grew up in our neighborhood that never seemed to forget where he came from. On top of that he was one of the few dudes that my sister dated growing up and he had accumulated a good relationship with me and my mother due to how polite and respectable he was. Although Craig knew how we were, I could still see the disappointment on his face to see us in cells; still curious about that gun, I asked him if the police were still over there on the crime scene. He said no, they had left.

I said, "Well, on this paper or none of ours it doesn't say anything about being charged with a gun."

He said, "That's because they didn't find one. Once I saw that it was you guys getting arrested I made it a point to be the first officer in the house to get information and gather evidence." By the expression on his face, the statement he just made and his body language I knew he had found the gun and didn't turn it in. I shook my head and mumbled "good looking" out before he walked out saying good luck!

The next morning was like a concert at the courthouse, news cameras from every station, all the well-known detectives and every seat full of our families, friends and spectators, just wanting to see what's happening. Although Ray [Benzino] didn't come to the courthouse, he took the initiative to send Marty Lepo and a couple of representatives from his law firm to represent us at the arraignment. Looking into the audience, I saw at least ten women that I had slept with in the past not including the four I was currently sleeping with. Donna and Cynthia both had twenty thousand on them, Asia had seventeen thousand on her and my cousin Tony and Tammy came with thirty-four thousand on them. In all I had just over ninety thousand in the courtroom. As gruesome as the DA had tried to paint the picture we weren't indicted on the spot, so once Lepo, his son Carl and Mike Natola who became my lawyer spoke on our behalf, the judge agreed on giving us all bails at only five thousand apiece. Before going back downstairs to the lock-up, I signaled Tony giving him the ok to bail Ace and Hurst out as well. Once I was finally released, I wasn't in the mood to deal with anyone's attitude or dramatics over which female I decided to leave with from the courthouse so I spoke to all of them individually for a moment. All except Tammy then left with Calvin to meet the lawyer at his office to discuss prices and strategies. Although she wasn't with us, Ace's female cousin was also arrested and arraigned for making the phone call that led to the victim being kidnapped and even though that was her kid's father she was now our co-defendant in the case but was let go on a personal. My lawyer Mike Natola told me that as long as the case stayed in district court, he would only charge me five thousand but if we got indicted like he assumed we would, then he'd have to raise the price up to fifteen. I said, "Cool," and gave him three grand right then the first time coming to his office.

Seeing that Ray [Benzino] sent these lawyers up to see us in the first place, I had assumed he was paying Ace and Hurst's fees. Considering how heavy he thought I was still hustling, I didn't expect him to do anything for me, just sending the lawyer to the court on the arraignment was favor enough for me. I've always been big on holding my own and knew what it was I had to do! I spoke to Cynthia but didn't actually go over to her house till the next day which was the day we were supposed to have left for Disney World and the look on her face said it all. I saw disappointment and anger all at the same time. I was there for about twenty minutes and she hadn't said a word to me. It got to the point where I had to leave before I got upset and said something that made the situation worse. I felt that she was upset about not going on the trip when in my mind she should be focusing on the fact that I could be going to jail. At that instant I started having mixed emotions about our relationship.

Two weeks later I was on Galvin Boulevard heading towards Quincy when detectives jumped on my bumper; within minutes they pulled me over putting me in cuffs without asking for my license or registration. I asked, "What's going on?"

He said, "You've been secretly indicted on kidnapping charges," then took me to the police station down Fields Corner. It was a Sunday afternoon so after reading me my rights the police officer locked me in a cell figuring I was just going to sit there till court in the morning.

I yelled for an officer asking him, "What's up with my phone call and a bail bondsman?"

The officer said, "With the charge you're facing the bail's probably going to be ten or twenty thousand trying to leave from here so you might as well lay back and wait till tomorrow."

I said, "Naw, it's early, call and see if there's a bondsman available and let me worry about the money!"

He called one, then said to me, "Yeah, Mr. Payton said he'd come but the bail's going to be ten thousand and forty dollars."

I said, "Cool, call em back, tell him to come after I use the phone and call my people."

I called my cousin Tony and he came down there with in the next forty minutes with eleven thousand on him to get me out. I left from there and went straight to Hurst's crib to tell him and Ace about the indictment. By then the lawyers had already called them to inform them of it, saying go somewhere and lay low till the morning so you can walk into court tomorrow on your own recognizance.

The next morning in court they took all of us into custody, even me that had just bailed out the day before for ten thousand and re-arraigned us in Superior Court which meant we just went from facing a year or two to facing fifteen to twenty. They gave Ace and Hurst fifty-thousand-dollar bail and me twenty-five seeing that the dude said I wasn't with them when they first took him. The judge wouldn't credit the ten thousand that I had just got out on the day before, seeing that I hadn't been officially arraigned, meaning that I had to have twenty-five thousand to get out again which was cool seeing that I brought thirty with me. I left the courtroom within an hour with no choice but to leave Hurst and Ace behind to go to lock-up seeing that I didn't have enough to get both of them out.

Things went from bad to worse overnight now. I got twenty-five thousand tied up in the courts, my lawyer wants fifteen thousand now, granted I lost five thousand on the shit the dude stole from Ace and on top of that I'm facing ten to fifteen years over a nigga I barely even liked. It might have been my stress that was getting to me a lil bit, but I instantly started feeling like Cynthia was acting different. Ever since my arrest and us not going to Disney, our chemistry had been all the way off. She hadn't shown any compassion towards me, nor any interest in our relationship since and I wasn't feeling that. I started feeling that she was only with me because I had money and the moment things seemed to be slipping away so was she! I still hadn't gotten up with Haburto; it had got to a point where he had just stopped answering my calls period till the number I had on him was just off. One day I bumped into Joanna in McDonalds and asked her what's up with Haburto and she said that she wasn't sure because they finally broke up a couple of months ago.

I said, "Damn, you got a different number on him than the one I got because the one I got is off?"

She said, "No, that's the last number I had on him; we got into a big argument and fight over the phone, and then he told me fuck me and that I ain't shit, that's why he's been fucking my cousin. I told him I don't care, fuck both of them; matter of fact, I told him about us!"

Shocked as hell, I said, "Naw, no you didn't."

She said, "Yeah, I did. I could tell that his bitch ass was hurt too."

I said, "Damn, that's probably why he ain't been reaching out to me."

She said, "Fuck him, Mike, he ain't shit anyways, but a middle man a big ol front."

At that point I was tired of hearing her mouth and whatever she had to say so I said, "Alright thanks," then rudely walked off without even ordering some food. I left wondering how long Haburto knew about me and Joanna, thinking, damn, here I am about to rob him for fucking with Gretchen behind my back all while he cut me off for fucking with Joanna. My home boy was doing pretty well for himself going to New York, getting his coke at a good price and coming back and I knew I could hook up with him and make a couple moves and I did.

Within days of me mentioning I'm trying to buy something, we were in New York putting two keys in the trunk of his lil bitch's car to carry back for us for a thousand apiece. The coke was bomb, way better than the work I was getting from Haburto. It was so good that over the next couple months I was able to get back a few of my customers that I lost due to the coke not being so good and it was definitely at a good time seeing everything I was going through with the court case and the losses I had taken.

Around this time Dave Mays and Ray [Benzino] decided that they would put up the fifty thousand to bail Hurst out, so now only Ace was left. A good month after Hurst got out, Ace's mother called me saying that she had forty thousand and wanted to know if I could try to raise the rest from our other friends, and I told her that I'd give it a shot and reach back to her in a few days. It was well known that Ace was a stingy dude and all about Ace, so when trying to collect money on his bond I got the same response from everybody being I ain't got it, not even Ray [Benzino] wanted to put in and he was rich. Seeing that me and Do Wrong had made a few moves and I made the money to pay my lawyer since I'd been out, I figured I'd help him and ask Do Wrong to go half with me on the ten thousand, five apiece. Really not wanting to, he said yes and we put the ten thousand together and brought it to his mother; within hours, Ace was out and it did feel good seeing him come through the door at Frank's and just being out after everything we'd been through over the past few months. Even though the lawyers weren't saying anything too good at the beginning of the case I refused to let it stress me out, so I lived as if I didn't even have a case. Me and Tammy were still staying in hotels, me and Donna still eating at expensive restaurants and I still shopped at the most expensive clothing stores. I still had that older model Benz that I got from Kenyatta we never did any of the insurance jobs we were supposed to do and I came to a point where I felt ready for a new car, even with the court case I wanted to live a little so that if I did do some time I could say I enjoyed myself before I left. Cynthia was upset but our relationship wasn't right, so I really didn't care when I told her to take the plates off the Benz and put them back on her Honda Accord because I was coming to get it to trade it in on a new car for myself. I was definitely becoming tired of dealing with all these females, but out of all of them the one I grew to really trust was Donna, so when I went to the dealer to get a brand new Benz 500 SEL I put it in Donna's mother's name. It was a beautiful car, navy blue and light blue with tan interior. Even my mother said, "Boy, don't you think you should have at least waited to see the outcome of your case before you bought that?"

I smiled then kissed her on her cheek and said, "Naw, Ma, cause if I go to jail, I'd be happy to know that I left it with you!"

Now I was riding around in a sixty-thousand-dollar car paid for, strapped up and still selling drugs and recording music with the Made Men all while facing fifteen years with an attitude like fuck it.

Me, Tony and Sheldon pulled up in front of him and Tammy's apartment and Tammy and two of her girlfriends were leaned up against her car smoking a blunt. She smiled and said, "Nice car, Mike."

I said, "Thanks."

Once Tony got out, he said, "Hey, baby," to Tammy.

"Hey."

Then he bent his neck a lil bit and said, "Give me a kiss," and she did, then he asked, "Is there any food cooked upstairs?"

She said, "Yeah."

Tony said, "Alright, Mizz, I'll get with you later," then went upstairs, while Sheldon jumped in his own car and pulled off. Then I pulled right off not saying bye or blowing the horn. Within the next ten minutes Tammy called me and said, "You could have said bye."

"Yeah, yeah, yeah."

She said, "What's wrong with you? I know you ain't tripping because I kissed Tony?"

I said, "Naw, not at all."

"Because he only did that because you were there."

I said, "Why you say that?"

"Why you think, Mike? Tony ain't stupid."

I said, "Whatever, Tammy, I ain't stupid."

"Whatever, Mike. Well if you're trying to make an excuse to run over to your bitch Asia's house you can't tonight because her friend Turtle there. Haha haha, and that's supposed to be one of your loyal bitches."

By then she hung up. I called Asia's phone and got no response, tried back two more times and got no response, when on the regular she'd answer the phone so fast it would seem like she was waiting on my call. I had gotten so caught up into myself and thinking that I was special that I totally overlooked the fact that these women showed no class by dealing with me in the first place, seeing that I was so close to their exes. Turtle was Eddy's boy and even though he didn't participate in any of the drama, I still took it as total disrespect for her to try and sneak him over knowing I wouldn't agree with it regardless to her telling me way back that Turtle was her daughter's godfather. She showed a sign of disloyalty and I knew from there on I would never be able to fully trust her again!

A few months had passed, and a few positive things had happened in regards to our court case. The dude who got kidnapped had got locked up on a probation violation and started to have a change of heart about pursuing the case seeing that if we went to jail there was a big chance that his baby's mother would go do a lil time as well. Plus, he bumped into a couple dudes I was feeding in there that said a word or two to him that helped him make his new decision. As for my personal life, me and Cynthia had finally broken up, the controlling side of me had me feeling some kind of way seeing that I did enjoy having sex with her but emotionally I knew we'd been done for a long time now and I was holding on for nothing, so I let her go for the time being! Even though I was still dealing with Asia and Tammy, my feelings grew stronger for Donna. The lease on the apartment I had from Bum was up and couldn't be renewed so when looking for a new place I felt it was time for me and Donna to move in together. I gave her a few thousand and told her to get us a place not in town but not too far, and within weeks we moved right at the tip of Randolph, close to the highway which was good for her seeing that she worked at the airport. Most of the time I'd let her drive my Benz to work while I stayed with rentals through the hood still making moves with Do Wrong.

One morning Tony called me asking me if I was in town yet.

I said, "Not yet but I'm on my way. What's good?"

I could hear in his voice something was bothering him. Then he said, "Come through when you do."

"Cool. About thirty minutes." When I pulled up he was sitting in his car on his cell phone but hung up when he saw me, then got out of his car and got in mine. I asked, "What's good?"

"Some crazy shit this morning, me and Tammy was arguing and your name came up so I come out and asked her what the fuck, what, are you fucking Mike or something. She said, 'I ain't been fucking you, what difference does it make.'"

Then Tony told me, "At that point I slapped her, then she grabbed her stuff and left and now won't answer the phone, so I figured I'd ask you. Are you fucking Tammy?"

I could see in Tony's eyes that he was hurting and as much as I cared about Tammy, I loved Tony and felt like he deserved the truth or at least enough of it that I felt he could handle at one time. So, I said, "I wouldn't call it fucking her but yeah, dog, we did have sex a couple times."

"I felt it, but I just thought me and you was better than that."

I said, "Yeah, you right and it's been bothering me that it happened but somehow it did."

Really upset, he said, "Ain't no somehow, y'all both just said fuck Tony and went somewhere and fucked."

Even though we were talking about it, I didn't feel the need to tell him that it'd been going on for over a year and that she was in love with me and considered herself to be one of my girlfriends. I said, "Naw, it wasn't about fuck, Tony."

He said, "Yeah it was, the moment you stuck your dick in her you said fuck Tony!"

Then he got out of my car slamming the door saying, "Fuck you, too, there's no need to reach out to me from now on me and you ain't shit." Then he got in his car and pulled off.

Looking at my phone, I had two missed calls from Tammy. I called her back and she was crying telling me what happened. I told her, "I already know, I just left from meeting up with Tony."

She asked, "Did you tell him about us?"

I said, "I told him that we had sex a couple times."

"That's it? You didn't tell him that you love me? You didn't tell him that were together?"

I said, "He was hurt, it wasn't the time to go into all that."

"Well what about me, Mike, I'm hurt and after all we been through and discussed you gonna make me sound like some lil bitch you just fucked a couple times?"

I said, "Naw, it ain't like that, Tammy, this whole thing just complicated."

She said, "It don't seem complicated when you fucking and cumming up in me, now it's complicated, that's some bullshit to say, Mike."

"This shit crazy."

She said, "No, Mike, you crazy to think you can just play with people's feelings and emotions and take no responsibility for it, you crazy to think this day wasn't ever going to come."

"I need a second to figure this shit out."

While crying, she said, "Figure what out, Mike? Either you love me, or you don't, there's not much to figure out and if you don't know after all this time you'll never know."

I said, "What you expect me to do right now, Tammy?"

"Be a man, be the man that I fell in love with."

I said, "Just give me a minute, I'll work it out."

"No, Mike, forget it, just forget about me, I'll work it out by myself. I feel so stupid right now but I'll be good, just worry about yourself like you been doing and I'll worry about me," then she hung up.

I felt like shit at that point and needed to smoke a couple of joints to get my head right. I called Calvin to see where he was at, he answered the phone laughing hard as hell. I was like, what's good, and he said, "Tony just called me telling me what happened."

I said, "Yeah."

"Yeah, nigga, I told you on the Cape that shit was gonna blow up in ya face."

I said, "Yeah, I know. Where you at?"

"Leaving Jen's crib heading in town, I'll hit you when I touch down."

Within the next ten minutes Asia called me saying, "I knew you was fucking her."

I said, "I ain't in the mood for that bullshit right now. What's up?"

"Nothing, Tony just called me telling me about what's going on."

I said, "I don't give a fuck what he told you! You should have told me that you had Turtle over your crib a few days ago."

"I knew she was gonna go back an tell you, that's why I told that bitch that."

I said, "Whatever, Asia, I'll call you back in a few," then I hung up on her thinking, damn, how many people cuz den told.

Although I stayed in contact with her mother and my father, I hadn't heard from Bobby Brown's sister Carol in a while, so when her number popped up on my phone I knew it was about something out of the ordinary. I answered like, "Hey, Sis, what's going on?"

"Hey, bra, nothing much. Listen, me and my boyfriend was talking, and he said that he knew you and that you was his man."

I said, "Who that?"

"Ceally."

Really not excited to hear it was him, I said, "Yeah, we cool. What's up with him?"

She said, "He's out in Detroit trying to get back to Boston and was wondering if you could help him with some money to catch a flight."

In my mind I was thinking Carol must have told Ceally that I'm on my feet cause I ain't heard from this nigga in years, but I still I asked, "How much?"

"Four hundred."

I said, "Yeah," then told her where to meet me and gave it to her saying, "Tell him to holla at me when he gets in town."

On my way to the studio to record a song with Made Men, Cynthia couldn't resist calling me to talk shit about what she'd heard about me and Tammy a few days ago. Really not wanting to hear what she had to say I just said yeah yeah yeah.

She said, "Yeah, that's why we're not together now. You're a dog and you're ignorant."

"Yeah, whatever."

She said, "Yeah whatever, but you need to come bring some money by for your son, cause I notice that ever since we ain't been together you've been slacking on him."

"You right, I'll be through there later with something for him. Is there anything else?"

She said, "No, just take care of your son and I'm good."

"Ok," I said, then I hung up.

Walking into the studio, Ray [Benzino] had a big smile on his face as if he couldn't wait to see me to tell me something. While taking my jacket off I said, "What's good with you?"

"Chilling, you tell me what's good."

I said, "What's all the funny smiles about?"

"McNeill, I knew you was fucking her. I'm surprised it took so long to come out."

I said, "Yeah."

"Yeah, cuz, so how's the pussy?"

I said, "Man, I don't wanna talk about that dumb shit, let's get to the music."

"We gonna do that, but damn I can't know how good the pussy. She looks like she got some wet."

I said, "Fuck all that."

"Cuz, don't tell me you den fell in love with her."

I said, "Cuz, I came to record music."

"Cool, let me leave you alone about her cause I can see you getting upset, so let's just record."

Later in the week I got a call from Bum early in the morning sounding semi-hysterical, so I said, "What's good, cuz, you all right?"

"Yeah, you see the news?"

I said, "No, why, what's up?"

"Did you speak to Do Wrong?"

I said, "Naw, not yet. Why?"

"The police looking for him, saying that he shot his baby's mother's sister in the chest."

Shocked, I said, "Get the fuck out of here."

He said, "Yeah, it real, cuz."

I said, "Where you at?"

He said, "Hyde Park, come through."

"Ok," I said and then I headed over.

After being there for like a half hour, the whole team came through with nobody hearing from Do Wrong yet. Within the next hour, Do Wrong called Bum's phone saying he was somewhere safe for the time being but he was trying to get his shit and get up out of town by the morning. Bum said, "Ok, whatever. You need me to do something, let me know."

Then I said, "Tell him if he needs something just say it."

He said, "Yeah, tell McNeill, I need to speak to him."

Then, Bum passed me the phone. I said, "What's good, my nigga."

"I'm alright, it is what it is now, but listen, most of my money in coke, seeing that we just re-upped, you think you can take it and give me the cash for it? So I don't have to stress trying to move nothing on the run."

I said, "Fa sure, my nigga, how much is it?"

He said, "Eighteen thousand worth."

I said, "Cool, I'ma put the money in the trunk so that when you call ready to meet, I'll have it on me."

He said, "Thanks, my nigga, I appreciate it."

"Fa sure," then I hung up.

Next morning him and his lil bitch that make the New York runs for us met me, Bum, and Ted at the Hyde Park spot. I gave him the eighteen thousand and took a half of key plus of coke he had already cooked up. Then he left saying he'd call us once he gets somewhere and gets settled in. My clientele was pretty good at the time, so it only took me a couple days to move the work I got from him. But it had been close to three weeks now since he'd left and I hadn't had any powder since and never took the time to get to meet the connect in New York so I would know who to ask for if I went down on my own. I had some money, but I wasn't making any, and once again had started to lose my customers. The lawyers had called us out of the blue saying they wanted to have an emergency meeting at Lepo's office right now to discuss an idea that they'd come up with. I called Ace and Hurst, found out where they were then scooped them up and shot out to the office. The lawyers figured that seeing that the victim was already doing time and didn't want his kid's mother to go to jail that we'd see if he'd recant his story, basically commit perjury by refusing to speak to the DA and that way they would have no choice but to throw the case out and give him ninety days for the charge. Me being the only one with any money out of the three of us, I asked how much should this cost me. Lepo suggested no more than five more thousand. I thought about it for a second and said, "Let's do it." Next, Ace had to go tell his cousin the plan and have her go speak to the victim in person on a visit to see if he was down for it.

All in all, the court date came, and he refused to speak, and the case was dismissed. Between the five g's I lost on the package, the fifteen I paid my lawyer, and the money I paid the other lawyer I was out twenty-five over a nigga I barely even fucked with, just because we from the same crew, and on top of everything he never seemed truly appreciative of everything I'd done for him. I was so mad at the time that I made a mental note to myself saying that if the opportunity ever presents its self, I would kill em! Since Do Wrong left, my money making had seemed to have been on pause and things got even worse when Lepo called me asking to come out to his law office saying it's important. I had paid all my fees from the kidnap case. So, I was curious what it could be that he wanted on my way up there.

Walking into his office sitting down he started shaking his head saying, "Mike, you got some serious problems."

"What you talking about?"

He said, "I got some friends that work for the feds and they knew that I had your last case, and one of them told me that they're doing a major investigation on you right now. They are following you every day and your phone could be tapped. They made you a red light, meaning that when the police run your license plate it states not to stop because the feds wanna see all your moves. I had my nephew who is a cop check if that information about your plate was true and I spoke to him about an hour ago and he said positive on what I asked him about. That's when I called you. Whatever you're into, you need to dead it for a few at least until the heat's off. Trust me, you'll be no good to no one in federal prison."

We shook hands. I thanked him and left, thinking *what the fuck am I about to do now?*

When it comes to drinking, I've always had a lil sip here and there but after Do Wrong left and I got that information from Lepo I saw myself starting to drink more often, I went from only drinking in the bars to actually going to the liquor store and buying a half of pint of Remy for the car.

A few months had passed and the Made Men album was completed and I had a couple features and a preview of some of my solo project on it With Wise Guys no longer together, Ray [Benzino] felt as though he no longer needed the studio out in Canton and decided to shut it down and move everyone that worked for Surrender Records up to New York to work for the source. As an artist, I got paid according to the music I recorded along with occasional gifts I would receive along with the other artists just for being a Ray [Benzino] artist. So, once everyone left, in a sense I was left behind and felt sort of alienated even though at the time I had a lil more than fifty thousand still. My Benz needed a full tune up and oil change, so it was at the dealer for a couple days which left me with the duties of dropping Donna off and picking her up for a couple of days in her car.

That Friday on our way home I noticed we were being followed by a tinted up unmarked vehicle. I took an unnecessary right, then a left to try to shake em off or verify that they were definitely following us and there they were taking the turns with us now on my bumper with their lights on. I pulled over and without asking me for license and registration they told me and Donna to get out, frisked me, then told both of us to sit down on the curb while they went through Donna's purse. Within minutes four more police cars pulled up, two unmarked and two regular police vehicles with one having a female officer that frisked Donna. After a good thirty minutes of them tearing through the rental from the engine to the trunk, they finally wrote our names down and let us go. I'd been pulled over and frisked several times before, but this time had a whole different feel to it. I could tell they were looking for something specific as if someone told them I was dirty, especially when they looked in the engine considering that's we're I would hold guns when I was moving four to five of them to different spots.

It'd been months since everything came out about me and Tammy, and I hadn't spoken to Tony or her after figuring it was best that I just fall back and let time develop everything into whatever it was gonna be. On the way to drop Donna home after being searched, I noticed I had a missed call from Tammy. I wasn't surprised, seeing that I knew she couldn't have fell out of love with me that fast, but seeing that it'd been close to ninety days since we spoke, I didn't know what to expect her to say.

After dropping Donna off, I called Tammy and could immediately hear in her voice she was still hurt and was about to want some answers. I asked, "How you been?"

She said, "I'm cool," saying it with a tone of sarcasm to her voice.

I asked, "What you been up to?"

"I've been like you lately."

I said, "Yeah, how's that?"

She said, "Just trying to figure shit out."

I giggled a lil, then said, "I see you still got your personality."

"Yeah, I got to, but what's going on with you. How come I haven't heard from you in so long? What, you just said fuck me?"

"Naw, it ain't like that. I just don't know what's going on, so I figured it be best if I stayed away for a bit."

She said, "You don't know what's going on because you haven't tried to find out what's going on."

I said, "I heard y'all still together, so I know a lil bit."

She said, "You ain't heard shit, that's just what you're assuming."

I said, "Y'all been fucking since then. Right?"

With an attitude she said, "So, what the fuck does that mean? The whole time I was with you, you was fucking Donna, Asia, Cynthia and who knows who else. And I believed in you and everything you lied to me about, so don't try to say you can base anything on me fucking him a few times in the last three months!"

I said, "I ain't judging you. I was just saying…"

She said, "Yeah. whatever, Mike. with that you was just saying shit. My thing is that everything is out in the open now and instead of us being closer, it seems like we're becoming more distant."

"Yeah, so cause it's out in the open I'm supposed to pick you up and drop you off at the crib while Tony still lives there. Let's be for real about shit, Tammy."

She said, "No, but you could of, at least kept in contact to let me know how you feel, and once I leave the house I'm out. We could have met up like we used to, me and Tony ain't together and he knows that."

I said, "Trust me, you still giving him the pussy time to time. He's trying to get shit back right with you."

"No, he not. We already discussed that he knows, we're just friends and I'm being nice not putting him out."

I said, "Yeah, but when he hitting that pussy from the back, I'm sure he be thinking y'all maken different plans."

She said, "Whatever, Mike! And for your information, I barely even fucked him back those few times we had sex, plus on top of that he knows I'm getting ready to move next month and that he can't come with me."

I said, "Where you moving to?"

"Why, you moving in with me?"

I giggled and said, "You never know."

"Everything's a joke to you. That's the shit I can't stand."

I said, "Damn. You never know, that's not a no."

She said, "Well if you say that when I do finally move, I'ma make the decision for you by changing my number."

"Yeah, so when's that happening?"

She said, "The first. I already put a deposit and started packing."

"Damn!"

She said," Yeah, damn, what you doing now. Can I see you?"

"I'm about to run around for a few but I'll be done in a couple hours."

She said, "Ok, so should I make plans on seeing you tonight?"

I said, "Yeah, I'll call you once I'm done."

"Ok, Mike, we'll see; trust me, one day, all this me chasing you is going to stop and you're going to miss me and it's going to be too late."

"Damn, I just said yeah. Why you saying all that?"

She said, "Because it's the way you say and do shit, Mike."

"For real, I'ma call you in a few," then I hung up.

Although I would say I had business to take care of, it came to a point where I had absolutely nothing to take care of besides riding around, drinking and smoking weed. I had become so used to being a key player in these streets that I truly believed that no matter how long I stayed out of the game I would easily be able to get back in and make a killing when the time was right. That attitude had me lackadaisical, keeping up my image, still spending money all while not making any for months.

As it got late, I got tipsy and high, then called Tammy when actually I hadn't planned on getting up with her when I told her I would. I knew that sleeping with her again was going to restart everything and possibly put me in even deeper when in reality mentally and emotionally I wasn't there. Especially with everything I was going through with not getting any money and the feds on me. Still, I got more liquor and weed, then had her meet me at the Ramada in Quincy and got it in. Within in a couple hours of fucking she told me she loved me at least twenty times. She said it so much it was like she wanted to embed it in my head so I would start being more thoughtful about her feelings and start taking responsibility for the situation again.

Right before checkout time the next morning I left to go get Donna so we could go pick my car up from the dealer; granted, before leaving the hotel I did agree to start keeping in touch with Tammy, basically putting myself back in the same situation I was in before Tony had found out about us. With the studio now being closed down and my group being disassembled, my communications with Ray [Benzino] went from a lil bit to none. It became clear to me that all his focus was on Made Men and my solo project had taken a back seat or just out of play period. In an attempt to promote the album, I heard from Hurst that the group was going on tour with the Ruff Riders and Cash Money. Word was that they were joining the tour in the Midwest and working their way back up to Boston to perform at the Fleet Center where I would then join them to perform a song that I had on the album. Even with that being said, I still felt strung along by the way Ray [Benzino] left information like that out there for me to hear second hand as opposed to calling me himself so I would know it was official, then seriously prepare. I was already regretting my decision to not pursue signing with Tony Draper's Suave House because of my loyalty to Ray [Benzino] and with him now showing his true colors and not honoring anything that we discussed and planned, it was clear to me that I fucked up letting that opportunity pass me by knew from that point on that if I was ever going to be successful in the music biasness I would have to do it without any assistance from Ray [Benzino]. Since having Willie McGinest's boy Bob's number we bumped into each other a few more times in clubs, and in the street but I still hadn't taken the initiative to call him. At this point, not calling so fast turned out to be a good thing seeing that we were able to build an even better relationship on the few times we did see each other. I knew that they knew that I wasn't star struck, nor a dick rider so when I did reach out the phone call was welcomed, and the respect was mutual. Within minutes Bob called Willie on the three way to tell him that I finally called and the love was the same, after a good ten minutes of talking about the music business and Willie's plan for his label, Willie instructed Bob to reach out to a specific producer in California to have him email over six to seven tracks for me to choose a couple from to record over, saying he's anxious to hear how I'd sound over a different producer's music. Before hanging up, Willie gave me his cell number telling me to call him once I received the music and picked three tracks so that he could hear which ones I liked. Although Willie hadn't accomplished anything in the music business, I knew he was connected to some well-known producers and artists like Snoop Dog, they could probably make moves with. So, to see him wanting to be hands on with me doing a few songs gave me the incentive to step my game up. Cash Money and the Ruff Riders were scheduled for a two day show this weekend and it wasn't till the afternoon before the second show when I finally spoke to Ray [Benzino] about me performing. As big as this venue was I would've expected him to be more concerned about me practicing and being on point than he was; instead, his focus was on making sure I'm going to just be there, period. Couple hours before the show I spoke to Belnel Mike and decided I'd link up with him and a few of his dudes from his crew and go together. Pulling off from the meeting spot, I told dudes not to drive too fast because I had my pistol in the car. The nigga Eight started giggling, then reached in his waist while sitting in the passenger seat and pulled out a forty-five. I said, "Ok ok, we right," saying in my mind, damn, these niggas keep guns on them! After getting in and getting a back stage pass, I didn't feel the need or want to sit around Ray [Benzino] or the other thirty to forty people he snuck in by rotating the few VIP passes he had. Once me and Ray [Benzino] saw each other and spoke he didn't mention anything about me performing, so I suggested to Eight that we go upstairs to watch the show and fuck with some hoes and we left. At the end of Cash Money's performance we headed back downstairs, at the intermission when I saw this dude Kevin I knew saying, "Yo, what's up, Mizz. I just saw a big commotion going on downstairs.

Some people were saying that it was Made Men beefen with the Ruff Riders."

I said, "Yeah, good looking," then we raced down to see what was happening, getting to the back stage entrance. Security and police had it blocked off but I could still see Rapper DMX Jada Kiss and Styles standing with a group of their boys seemingly upset. I didn't see anyone from my crew, so I called Bum to see where they were and he said, "We just had a big fight with the Ruff Riders and SCO and Hawk got stabbed so we going to make sure they straight."

I said, "Yeah, well them Ruff Rider niggas are still here, I'ma about to catch them at their tour bus and give it to them."

Bum said, "Ok, be careful," then he hung up.

I told Eight and Kenyatta what had happened and what I planned on doing while running to my car to get strapped. They both said, "Whatever, let's do it," while getting into Kenyatta's car to get the forty-five they had with them. We pulled around the back of the Fleet Center and parked across the street from the parking lot where the tour busses were parked, turned off our headlights with intentions of killing someone once they came out to leave. Within ten minutes of waiting I got a call from Ray [Benzino] asking me where I was.

I said, "Still down at the Fleet."

"Yeah, Bum told me. What's up, naw, McNeill, that ain't a good move right now, the police is already all over this and everything gonna come back on me if you do it that way. Just fall back for now."

Really not feeling what he was saying, I said, "Yeah, alright," then told Eight and Kenyatta about Ray's call, and then we left.

A good month and a half had passed since me and Donna got pulled over in the rental, so I sort of placed the incident in the back of my head till the day Donna called me saying that her supervisor called her into his office saying that they're releasing her because there's proof that she'd been renting cars for someone that was not licensed and suspected to be selling drugs. At the time, I was driving in a rental from her job and they wanted it to be returned immediately. I was so upset that they treated my girl like that and that she was going through shit over me, period, that I drove right up to the door leaving the car running in the parking lot screaming out, "Fuck this job, anyways you didn't need these bitches! They see you coming to work every day in a seventy-thousand-dollar car, with or without them you gonna be straight, fuck them. Let's go!" Then we got in my Benz and went around the corner seeing that we were at the airport and rented her a car from another rental company till I decided what the next move was going to be. Donna wasn't upset about losing the job at all, she knew that she could find more employment. The most important thing to her was that I had her back and at that point in our lives she was sure of that, so once I said everything was straight, she was confident that it would be.

Although me and Eight from Belnel didn't shoot the Ruff Riders' tour bus up that night, the incident in general happened to lead to me, him and Kenyatta to become tighter. We went from bumping into each other on occasion to hitting each other up on the phone and seeing what's good. The beats I got from Willie McGinest's producer were dope, though they all had like a West Coast sound to them which really wasn't my thing. Still, in all I picked three from the six he sent me and wrote some hot joints for them and was ready to record. Speaking with Willie, he definitely sounded committed and anxious to work with me but it was playoff season and the Patriots were in and he felt as though he needed to put all his focus into football telling me to just keep writing and that we'll get together in the off season and make some things happen. Willie's a real dude, so hearing him tell me that instilled me with hope for my rap career that I hadn't had since the Wise Guys' Def Jam deal and I was confident that he'd hold his word.

It had been at least six months since I gave Bobby Brown's sister Carol the money for Seally to get back to Boston and I hadn't heard from him once to say thank you or anything. One day out of the blue he called me sounding untrustworthy, asking was I around and if so, could I meet him in the back of Madison Park High School because he needed to speak with me about something important. I told him give me an hour and I'd call him back. I had been hearing that since Sealy had been in town he'd been spotted hanging around Eddie and his crew, which made me even more skeptical about this phone call to meet. My lil shooter Moe Black was running around with a Tech nine at that time, so I picked him up before calling Sealy back to meet me within the hour. I headed down to Madison Park to check the scene before calling Ceally to tell him I was around. Sealy answered but now he was saying he won't be back around for another hour, so out of curiosity I said, "What's good, what's going on?"

"I don't wanna talk on the phone, I'll tell you when I see you."

I said, "Cool," then hung up. Me and Moe went to my spot and chilled for a couple hours instead of riding around, with a Tech and a Glock on us waiting on his call. Close to two o'clock I said, "Fuck it, Moe," then dropped him back off. Ceally not calling back left a bad taste in my mouth, and from there I knew I could never trust him again.

By the weekend of that week I saw on the news that he had been killed sitting in the passenger seat of Whitney Houston's Rolls Royce while riding with Bobby Brown. I had mixed emotions concerning his death; half of me felt bad for him considering all the years we'd known each other, but the other half of me was still suspicious of what he wanted with me that night. This led me not to make plans to go to his funeral. My cousin Tony called me asking me did I hear about what happened to Sealy and saying it's only right that he forgive me over the Tammy situation seeing that he'd already forgiven Tammy and it was both of our faults that it happened. I was glad to speak with Tony again and by this time Tammy had moved into her new spot down Madison and he was staying elsewhere.

The first couple days of Tammy living in her new spot I came through and spent the night, me messing with Tammy had become more of me being addicted to controlling her as opposed to me having feelings for her. Once Tammy moved into her new place, she became more difficult to deal with; it was like when she moved, she gained a new attitude. Her mouth got more slick, and her demands for me to make a decision on what I was going to do concerning being in a relationship with her became stronger. Since dealing with her, my relationship with Donna was always a topic that wasn't up for discussion. So, once she started identifying Donna as my girlfriend and speaking of her more frequently, I knew Tammy was changing. Asia was still around, but she was so content with whatever time I spent with her that I never felt a challenge which led me to adopting a whatever whenever type of attitude about her.

One night I was over Tammy's house and we got into a heated argument to where I slapped her and left. In the past, I'd raised my voice at her and left but this was the first time I put my hands on her and I knew I was losing control of the situation. With Donna not working for a few months, by my choice I had been taking care of all the bills plus paying for a rental for her to be able to get around. On top of me still doing things for all my women and living the way I was when I wasn't getting money, over the course of ninety days I had run through close to twenty thousand, and money was officially getting low. I had the title to my car so I felt that no matter what if needed to I would be able to get rid of that and get roughly sixty thousand to get back on my feet, but before things got to that point I figured it was time to start making some moves again, with the feds on me and all.

Every time I went to New York to re-up with Do Wrong he'd go into this building and take care of all the business, so although I knew his name, I never actually saw what the connect looked like. One day I decided I'd have Donna drive me up to the city with twenty-five thousand on me so that I could find Swavea, Do Wrong's connect and do some business. Getting to the city and finding the block we used to go to was the easy part, but now I had to find Swavea! I knew he was Spanish and spoke good enough English but that's all I knew. While leaving the money in the car, I had Donna park down the street with the doors locked while I walked up the street and asked questions. The first two dudes I asked did they know Swavea said no, but in a way like they did but just didn't know who I was. The third person I asked was a short, dark haired Dominican wearing a few gold chains and a nice watch. He said to me, "Maybe I do. Why you looking for Swavea?" I was thinking that this could probably be him, explaining to him that I was from Boston and that he's a friend of my friend and that I wanted to have a word with him for a minute. He asked me if I was I police.

I said, "Fuck no, I'ma real nigga."

"Where your car then?"

I pointed down the street. He looked and asked, "The one with Massachusetts plates. Right?"

I said, "Yeah," sort of getting upset myself. Then I asked again, "Do you know Swavea?"

"Yes, yeah, Swavea no around right now, he go back to my country for a month. Is there anything I can help you with?'"

In the back of my mind I'm thinking either this nigga don't know Swavea or he's just cutting Swavea's throat for the play, but either way I was here and ready to make moves so I said, "Yeah, I'm trying to get a whole one but I want a sample first."

"Yeah, you sniff."

I said, "No, but I can look at it and tell if it's what I want."

"You got the money now?"

My arrogance led me to let my guard down. I had a pocket knife on me and figured that if he tried to pull some funny shit I'd just stab him up and hit the highway. So, I said, "Yeah, not on me. It's in the car."

"Ok, come wait in the hallway and I'll bring you out a sample. If you like it, we do business right now simple and fast."

I followed him into the hallway, then he said, "Wait right here," then ran upstairs a couple flights but I was still close enough that I could hear his keys rattling and him unlocking the door. He went in and came right back down within no more than two or three minutes which helped me feel even more comfortable on making the move. He brought a whole key down in a plastic bag, opening it up just enough for me to smell and see that it was some bomb ass fish scale. Satisfied, I said I'd take it.

"Ok, go get the money, let's count it out real quick."

Getting back to the rental, Donna asked, "Did you find him?"

"Naw, but I got someone else though."

She said, "You sure that's safe, Mike?"

"Yeah, I'm good."

With an unsure look on her face she said, "Ok, be careful," before I got the money out of the back seat and headed back to the hallway. Once I got back in the hallway, I expected to go into the house to count the money but instead he said, "Let's do it right here," which was in the center of the stairway, only blocking people from outside from seeing us. But if someone came in or down they could, which made me start to feel a lil uncomfortable, but still I thought, fuck it, let me do this right quick and get the fuck out of here. After counting out like three thousand in hundreds, I heard a door upstairs open then close with whoever came out heading down. I stuffed the money in my pocket then put the bag with the rest in it inside my jacket, as two younger Spanish looking dudes were coming down the stairs. The person I was buying the coke from moved to the side of the wall then spoke to one of them in Spanish. Right then I got a bad feeling about what I was doing. I moved to the side of the wall as well to give the two dudes space to walk by. That's when one of them pulled out what looked like a three fifty-seven revolver and the other one a ten to twenty inch machete, telling me to hand over the money. I stared at him for a second shaking my head feeling more like a fool than I was scared before going in my jacket to hand him the bag. The dude with the knife came closer to me putting it close to my neck telling me to empty my pockets. While I was taking the three g's out, the fake connect searched my waist taking the knife I had clipped to my belt. Once they had the money, the person with the gun pointed it at my head and told me to leave. Walking towards that door without my money or the work was the most shameful moment of my life. Once the door locked behind me

I turned and looked through the glass door seeing the three of them running upstairs probably to a different floor than the one I expected that they came from.

Getting back in the car, Donna could tell something was wrong before I said a word. Looking curious, concerned, and nervous all at the same time, she asked, "What's wrong, are you ok?"

"Yeah, I'm cool," then I started telling her what just happened while she was driving around waiting on me to tell her exactly where to go. Though the depressing side of things was short lived, now I was upset and wanted to kill them. I called Ray [Benzino] to see if him or any of my niggas that worked for the Source were in New York at the time hoping to get a pistol and a ride, so I could let Donna leave and straighten shit. Coincidently, this was one of those weekends where everyone from the office went back to Boston, and only having Donna with me and no strap I was left in a helpless situation. The only option I had was to take the loss and leave. Things had gone from bad to worse. I was down to five thousand dollars after that loss. My baby's mother Cynthia put child support on me and all of a sudden random people along with the women I was sleeping with started to tell me I was looking like I lost weight and was fatigued.

By this time, drinking Remy had become a necessity. I was quietly on a pint a day on top of smoking weed and could easily see myself spiraling down, but figured as long as I get my money back up everything else would fall back in place as well. As much as I loved my Benz and how it felt riding around in it, I knew it was time to make a move and get rid of it. Even with the miles I put on it, the book value was still in between fifty-seven to fifty-eight thousand which should have been enough money for me to get back in the game and get shit right. Back in those days, Mercedes made their big bodies out of all metal and steel so just crashing a stolen car into it might have not done the job. I didn't wanna risk just getting a check and getting the car fixed, I needed it totaled so that I could get all the money from it. I decided to let my people in Rhode Island do a number job on it and paint it another color so that way once I reported it stolen it could never be found and the insurance company would have no choice but to pay me…. so I thought!

With the car now reported stolen and me in a rental that the insurance company was paying for, I felt a sense of relief thinking that I was going to receive my check within a month or so. With a lil less than five thousand cash to my name, I figured all I had to do now was just chill and have patience and I'd soon have enough money to regain everything I once had.

Although me and Tony were speaking again, it was easy to tell that things were different between us. Every time we saw each other he'd smile and speak, but I could see a troubled look behind the smile.

Picking Donna up from Greenwood one day, I bumped into Tony out on the front porch talking to Big Mike. The look on both their faces when I pulled over let me know that in some way, I was part of their conversation. I nodded my head. "What's up," I said, but didn't bother going over to speak so that they could continue their conversation. Instead, I blew the horn for Donna to come on so that we could leave. After talking with Mike, Tony came to my window and said, "What's up, Mizz," before he got into his car and pulled off. Once Donna got in the car, she asked me did I just see Haburto.

I said, "Naw. Where?"

"That's who was just in the car with Tony underneath the tint, they just served Big Mike."

I just said, "Naw," downplaying it but was really feeling some type of way about it. I hadn't heard from Haburto or Big Mike in months, I regretted showing Mike how to whip coke so much that killing him had crossed my mind, as for Tony and Haburto I knew in conversation they spoke of me fucking both their girls and had said fuck me which led me to no longer feel resentful about what happened between me and Tammy and not giving a fuck about how he felt like any regular nigga.

After slapping Tammy I hadn't spoke to her until one night we were both inside Club Back Stage. At first, she acted as if she wanted to keep the conversation limited but by the end of the night we spoke more intensely, which led to me going over her house after the club.

Next morning before she even woke up, I got dressed, then tapped her to tell her that I was leaving. She rolled over, upset saying, "Whatever, Mike, fuck you, you got what you wanted, now you gone. You couldn't even wait till I got up and cooked breakfast. It ain't even nine o'clock and you're leaving. Fine, just leave and please never ask to come back because you not gonna!"

"I have to take care of something early. Chill out, I'll be back this afternoon."

"No you won't, go ahead and lock my door on your way out, I'm done trying with you. Just go home, and leave me alone."

Before closing the door to leave I said, "I'll be back a lil later, I promise."

She yelled out, "Fuck you!" as I was closing the door.

After starting the rental, I checked my phone while the car heated up and noticed that I had four missed calls from Donna at about seven o'clock that morning. I pulled off and right as I got ready to call her back, I looked in the rear view and saw Donna in the car behind me with Tony. I pulled over shaking my head mad as a motherfucker and told her to get in. Me and Tony stared at each other but didn't speak. I was so selfish at that time that in my mind I was saying, damn, this nigga still chasing this bitch! I knew in Tony's mind he expected me and Donna to go through some shit, but we didn't, we spoke one or two words about it, then it was over.

Donna was so in love with me at that time that something as small as me fucking someone else couldn't have separated us. Bringing her down there was a waste of time and gas.

Over the next month Donna and her mother had been interviewed by a couple of special investigators sent by the insurance company to record their statements on what happened to my Benz, seeing that it was in Donna's mother's name. On both occasions they were asked if there was a male that drove the car on a regular basis to which they both said no. They had gone as far as to say to Donna's mother that they asked neighbors in her community if they had ever seen the car and all of them said no, which led them to believe that the car was never parked in front of her house because she never drove it.

The first thirty days had passed, and I didn't get paid yet and the insurance company was not giving us any information other than it's still under investigation. On top of that they told us that they're no longer going to pay for the rental and in order for us to keep it we'd have to pay for it but once and if the claim gets paid, they'd reimburse us. So now, instead of waiting for my check to come I was hoping and wondering if it was going to come. Everything was fucked up and it felt like the bottom had fallen from underneath me. I was down to only a couple thousand and rent was due plus car insurance, which they still expected me to pay even though they hadn't honored my claim nor were any longer paying my rental. It got to a point where I couldn't afford the apartment me and Donna lived in anymore. In order to keep us together, I asked my boy YG if we could move in with him for a couple months till the insurance company paid me or I figured out my next move. YG lived on the first floor of his uncle's three family by himself and had plenty of room so when he said sure, he didn't mind, I knew he was speaking from the heart and I appreciated him for that.

After me having Donna call the insurance company at least twice a week for the next month they finally told us that they'd come to the conclusion that they had reason to believe that insurance fraud had taken place. That was it. After me having close to three hundred thousand cash, and a rap career, I was officially broke, not recording or even writing music!

Over the last two years, I'd given several people money when they were in need. I bailed homies out when they got arrested. I bought some people expensive gifts on top of giving out plenty of drugs to put dudes on their feet when they were down and out and here I am fucked up and there's no one I can turn to for help. My cheerful, always uplifting attitude, immediately changed from the moment I got that information. I became miserable and hateful and the fact that I was drinking more often didn't help the situation one bit.

The first month of staying with YG I gave him five hundred dollars for rent and nothing on the second month, mainly because I didn't have it. Riding rentals became way too expensive, so in order to stay mobile I pawned my gold chain with the diamond encrusted Wise Guys piece for just enough to be able to finance a Ford Tempo in Donna's name and put a G and change in my pocket because in the back of my mind I was gonna get things right, then go back and get my shit!

Donna had got another job working at a hotel downtown which was pretty far from where we were staying in Brockton. For the first month I would get up and bring her to work and come get her once she got off. But with me being stressed out and off my feet trying to figure out how I'ma get back on, being responsible for getting her back and forth was just too much on me at the time. We came to the decision that it was best for her to move back to Greenwood for a few, basically just until I got back right.

Asia had recently moved from out near the airport to an apartment building on Blue Hill Ave. Even though I wasn't into her like that and, really only contacted her when I wanted sex, I still considered her my bitch and knew she was down to do whatever it was that I needed her to. So, instead of me continuing to live with YG and letting him pay all the rent, I decided to move in with Asia. That way I could be closer to Donna and lessen my living expenses seeing that she had Section Eight housing. It could have all just been in my head, but when I bumped into certain people, I could sense that they were glad I was going through some hard times. Hoes that used to see me and couldn't help but to flirt with me started to just wave and keep moving. Niggas that were getting money that used to hit me up just being on my dick, stopped calling like they assumed that since I was down and out, I was going to ask for help. Between me being angry and drinking Remy all day, I started to see everybody in a different light. My Benz gone, my money, and connect gone and so were all the fake friends that were around just to benefit from me.

Pimping had proven to be a good move for Calvin, and between Jennifer and Gretchen he was getting well over a thousand dollars a night, and it was obvious that he was doing pretty good for himself. Me and Calvin's communication had slowed down which was understandable, and I must admit that in the early stages of me being off my feet he looked out for me on a few hundred here and there, but me feeling like he was purposely keeping his distance had begun to slowly take a toll on our friendship. When we were both broke, we were tight, when I got paid, we were even tighter but now that I was fucked up, we didn't link. I loved him so much that I would put a wool over my eyes to how shit was, but the reality of the matter was that I felt that he was turning his back on me as well, when I was part of the reason he was in the position he was in.

As my thirst for alcohol got stronger so did my bond with the dudes from Belnel. It got to a point where me, Eight and Kenyatta were inseparable. If you saw one, you saw the other two. The thing about it was that they were at their peak in the game; they were making thousands and I was broke and fucked up, yet that didn't seem to matter because as long as they had it, I had it. I'd been in a gang damn near my entire life but never experienced the love and loyalty that they started to show me in such a short amount of time, and I appreciated it and became willing to die or go to jail over our bond.

One evening we saw some dude that they wanted to kill before he got comfortable with being out of jail. At this point we hadn't put in any work together, but we were aware that we all were shooters. That night Kenyatta suggested that him and Eight needed to get strapped and go get at dude asap saying,

"Mizz, I'ma drop you off first seeing that this ain't got nothing to do with you."

"Fuck no, cuz. I ain't going nowhere, if it got something to do with y'all it got something to do with me. I'm riding!"

Eight started laughing and said, "You know nezzy ain't trying to get dropped off."

Then Kenyatta started laughing too and said, "I know, my nigga, I'm just fucking with you."

Within the next twenty minutes I was parked around the corner from where they knew the homie to live at while they hopped a couple fences across to the next street to see if any of the cars looked familiar. Two minutes later I heard shots going off while I'm in the car waiting for them to come back. I was looking at the fence they hopped but instead they both came running around the corner and got in and we were off. After getting pretty far from the shooting I asked, "Y'all get him?"

Eight said, "Naw, that bitch got away."

Then I said, "That nigga lucky than a muther fucker."

Then we went back to the spot to lay low for a few, even though no one got merked. That night it was certified that we were riding for each other on whatever with whoever.

I was living with Asia now, but still kept close contact with Donna. I hadn't heard from Tammy since Tony brought Donna down to her house. I called a couple times, but she didn't answer. I had spoken to Ill Will wife several times after I slept with her but really didn't have time or the inclination to hook up with her again till one day she asked me if I was all right. I said, "No, I need some money."

She asked how much. "Just to throw a number out there."

I said, "Three hundred."

"I got you; come by my girlfriend's house."

I got the address and slid right through there. I came over and had a seat in the living room figuring it's only right that I chill for a second since she was looking out for a nigga. Then I asked, "Where's your friend that lives here?"

"She went out for a few," she said, then she reached into her bra and handed me the three hundred. She asked me would I like a beer.

I said, "Yeah, why not?"

She went and got it, came back, then had a seat right next to me. Without saying anything I zipped my pants down and stood up in front of her indicating that I wanted my dick sucked. With one hand I was drinking my beer and with the other I was rubbing her head while she was going ham on my dick. I let her suck it just long enough for me to finish my beer, then I nutted. After cleaning my dick off, I told her I'd call her later, then left. I had appreciated that money way more than my actions had shown, and even though I didn't show her any respect, I had respect for her and knew at that moment that we were heading in the direction of building a friendship that would last for some years to come.

CHAPTER EIGHT

I hadn't seen my son in some months at this time; half the reason was that I was upset with Cynthia and the other half was that I was ashamed of the condition I was in and the fact that I was broke and didn't have anything for him.

My mother called me one day notifying me of an upcoming court date that I had saying Cynthia asked her to call me because she didn't have any numbers on me anymore and didn't know where I was staying. The way she was pressing me for money after all the nice things I did for her and gave her and my son when I had it, hurt me; the night before we had court, I called Cynthia and told her that I wanted the jewelry back that I bought her, asking her to bring it to court with her in the morning.

She paused, getting real quiet for a few seconds then said, "Fine," then hung up!

The next morning, I got there late, and she was in the lobby waiting with an angry look on her face.

The first thing I said was, "Did you bring my jewelry?"

Her facial expression changed to a more subtle look, like she was about to do something that she really didn't want to, then she said, "Yeah, I got it." I reached my hand out for it without even sitting down and she went into her bag, got it, then handed it to me.

I said, "Thank you, and as for the judge, make sure you tell him about all the things I used to do for you and my son when I had it," then I turned around and walked off.

She asked, "So, you leaving?"

I just kept walking not even answering, never seeing the judge that day. My mother called me that night upset with me telling me that since I left the courthouse the judge granted her the most money he could give her without me having a job. So now on top of me being broke, I owed Cynthia four hundred and eighty dollars a month that I had no intentions on paying.

Over the next few months all the drinking I was doing finally took over, although I was still functional, I knew I had become an alcoholic and was displaying no swagger or self-esteem, and I was miserable. The people that used to see me and express their love for my music and commended me for how well I was doing would see me and not know what to say to me, but I could see in their faces that they were thinking damn!

While living with Asia we had started to become closer. I respected that even though I wasn't getting any money and had a drinking problem she seemed to still be attracted to me the same way she was when I was on top. She knew Donna was still by my side, and wanted to see me get back on my feet as much as she did, so instead of trying to create any problems over our relationship she befriended Donna, making things comfortable for me. I appreciated that there were times I would hear Asia on the phone addressing Donna as her wife in law, and with how everything fell apart for me, that gave me that slight feeling of control that a man needs at times to feel like a man. My life was full of coincidences. I was always finding someone or something that would connect my past to my present. For example, in the beginning stages of dealing with Asia it came to light that her and my ex-girlfriend Toy were cousins and that Asia used to be in a relationship with Keith Peterson, who used to go out with my sister. She was also good friends with Cory West who was Toy's baby's father. And, also, the person who took Toy from me when I was younger.

One early morning at about eight o'clock I was up drinking the rest of a pint of Remy I had when someone pulled up blowing their horn. I looked outside and it was Toy with the window down asking, "Is Asia home?"

I said, "Yeah," then went and told Asia that Toy had pulled over and got out like she was coming upstairs. Asia got up and went into the bathroom while I buzzed and unlocked the door, then sat back down. I hadn't seen Toy in at least two years, so once she came in I got up and gave her a friendly hug while Asia was still in the bathroom at the time. She sat down across from me while asking how was I doing and how have I been. I didn't know what to say being pretty sure that she had heard that I wasn't doing so hot, on top of that I was sitting there looking a mess, drinking Remy and it wasn't even nine o'clock. I said, "Ok," but from how she was staring at me and the bottle of Remy I knew she thought otherwise. The look on her face told it all, it was one of disappointment and concern. I could tell she wanted to say something else to me but felt it wasn't appropriate at the time. Once Asia came out of the bathroom, I took the bottle of Remy and the glass of water I was using as a chaser into the bedroom after saying bye.

A good hour passed, and I could hear Tony getting ready to leave. On the way out she yelled out, "Bye, Mike, take care."

"Ok, you too," but in the back of my mind I knew that she meant it sincerely, considering the condition she just saw me in.

Kenyatta was in a serious relationship back then, so he would hang out with me and Eight in the daytime but for the most part at night he'd be home, where me and Eight would wind up being in some club every night. The Rolls Club was our main spot, everybody involved in that establishment knew me from the owner to the secretary to the promoters, so we never paid or waited in line to get in. Even being off my feet, they respected me and paid homage to the days I was doing good and would spend hundreds in there a night. Between me and Eight there was never a time you would catch us without a gun. The staff at the club knew me so well that they started letting me stash pistols in the office feeling that, that was safer than me walking around drinking with it on me all night.

Once Tammy considered herself completely done with dealing with me, I had started to see her in the clubs more often. On several occasions I'd try to engage in a conversation, and she'd wave me off, most of the time by saying go home to Asia or Donna. I found myself trying to start arguments and looking for some pity by saying, "Yeah, you acting like that because my paper's fucked up, but it cool."

A couple of times to save face she said, "It ain't got nothing to do with your money," but for the most part she'd try to act like I wasn't even around and kept pushing. Losing control over her definitely bothered me. It was one of the things on my list of reasons why I was drinking. I had already felt like a piece of shit for doing that to Tony, but with her now acting like I ain't shit while I'm down and out made me feel stupid, realizing that she never cared about me. It was the money and the lifestyle I lived all the time. There were several people that owed me two or three hundred from coke that I fronted out that I didn't look for at the time I was making thousands. But now that I was hurting, anytime I saw someone that owed me anything I wanted it and I wanted it right then and there!

One night in the Rolls Club I bumped into Chris Murray, a nigga that'd been owing me three hundred for close to two years now and I was ready to get paid. Me and Chris were talking, and I was being pretty aggressive with him seeing that I had called him a few times back then and he hadn't answered. While we were talking some dude a couple feet taller than me weighing about two forty, walked over and asked Chris if he was alright.

I said, "Why, if not, what you gonna do?"

Chris said, "Yeah I'm cool, go ahead, I got this."

"Yeah, you better go ahead before you get yourself in something you can't get yourself out of."

Before walking off he said, "Just holla if not, cause you know I don't give a fuck about nothing."

"Yeah, stick around, I'ma see you when the club is over."

He said, "I'll be here, ask Chris."

"Who the fuck is he?"

Chris said, "a young dude that don't know what time it is."

I said, "Yeah, well I'ma bout to show em, and how much money you got on that right now?"

He reached in his pocket and gave me a hundred and forty dollars telling me to call him in the morning for the rest. Then I walked off looking for Eight. I found him and told him about what just happened. First thing he said was, "Well let's go wait for him outside." Then we left, got in the car, I strapped up then pulled the car down the street a lil bit just enough so that we could see the parking lot without anybody seeing us. A good fifteen minutes later the club started to let out and we got out of the car and started walking up the street slowly trying not to be seen till I spotted him. Looking in the middle of the parking lot, I finally saw him leaning against a car smiling looking as if he was flirting with some chick. My plan was that as soon as I saw him get in his car, I was gonna run up to the exit and start shooting before he pulled off. It so happened that while we were across the street waiting on him to get in his car my cousin Tony pulled up in a rental car kinda tipsy asking us what we were up to. I told him I was trying to kill this nigga that's in the parking lot for coming out his mouth.

He said, "Yeah, fuck waiting on him to come out. Get in, let's pull up on him."

Eight jumped in the back, I got in the front with the pistol, and Tony pulled in passing a couple cars going out while I was letting down the window. Tony pulled right next to him and I started shooting. I knew I hit him with the first shot but still let off three more when he fell, and tried to hide in between a couple cars.

Mia, who I used to mess with back in the day and a couple more people that knew me, were out there so that's why I didn't get out and make sure I killed him, but considering that the situation was just over him running his mouth I felt as though one body shot was significant and I was cool with it. After stashing the gun and giving police some time to clear out, Tony dropped me and Eight back to my car telling me to call him in the morning so that we could get up and chop it up.

Getting up with Tony the next day I thought he was going to ask me more questions about what happened between me and Tammy, but instead he did most of the talking, telling me about another situation that occurred while he was trying to regain trust and respect for her. He told me that one night he went over Tammy's house and started banging on the door because he knew she was there and not answering the phone for him and must have had company when he just stayed over there a couple of days ago fucking. When she finally opened the door for him, Ray [Benzino] was sitting in the living room talking on his cell phone smoking a blunt. I instantly got mad, in my mind I was saying, "this mother fucker Ray [Benzino] a snake," overlooking Tammy's role in the whole thing. Also, the fact that I had been being a snake ass nigga myself, karma had gotten me back. By the time Tony dropped me off, I sensed that he just wanted me to know what happened so I would feel more stupid than I already did. And if that was his intention it worked, now she possibly fucked one of my so-called niggas and I was getting a taste of my own medicine, knowing that she couldn't care less about how I would feel about it. Even though I felt that she wouldn't give a fuck, I still left her a message on her phone telling her that I knew about her and Ray [Benzino], hoping to touch any lil piece of conscience that she might still have, telling her that she was a hoe for that and saying, "I bet nothing come out of him fucking you beside him being able to say that he fucked you!"

I still had a white gold chain, with a diamond encrusted piece, and a stainless steel Rolex, with a diamond bezel that I got as a gift from Ray [Benzino], and my initial thought was that this was a gift, so, I refused to pawn it, but after hearing about him messing with Tammy I felt like a peon wearing it, knowing that he was buying females gifts of more value just for fucking them, so I was ready to get rid of it. I sold Kenyatta the Rolex for a Gee and Teddy the chain and piece for fifteen hundred.

The alcohol and my arrogance had me so blinded that I didn't even think about trying to flip that lil bit of money. I had run through hundreds of thousands selling weight and in my sick mind at the time, to attempt to do anything small was beneath me and not even an option. So instead I bought boots, sneakers and clothes and used the rest to fund my day to day weed and liquor habit until it was gone.

One weekend me, Eight and Rosco from Greenwood, and his female cousin Keisha went to Club Cosmo in two separate cars. While at the door, Rosco got into an argument with the bouncer for trying to deny us entry due to what we were wearing when every time we'd come there with Ray [Benzino] we walked right in. While we were having problems getting in, three dudes wearing sweatpants and basically the same thing we had on were standing behind us waiting to be escorted in. At the time, none of us knew who they were, and we were wondering why would they be getting special treatment, especially before us. The security got deeper while telling us to exit the hallway while letting the three men in who weren't wearing what was considered the dress code either. Before the last of the three men went in, him and Rosco had a brief stare down that turned into some words with Rosco being more aggressive asking him, "What the fuck you looking at?" and adding, "I'll fuck you up." By the guy's height, and the way the security was acting, I figured the guy Rosco had words with was a basketball player or something. But me not being into sports wouldn't have been able to identify him as anyone, but I did have the feeling. Once we were back outside, we split up with Rosco and Keisha going one way and me and Eight going another but had made plans before we split up to go to a hair show that was coming up the next day.

The next day I didn't hear from Rosco through the day but we all ended up meeting up at the club for the after party to the hair show. I hadn't seen Ray [Benzino] in a while, so I took the opportunity to holla at him about a few things since he was here, mostly about what's going on with the things we discussed about me making music. While we were talking, I noticed Rosco's cousin Keisha at the end of the bar looking upset talking to one of the same tall guys that we saw the night before at the club. Rosco must have seen the same thing I saw, then put his drink down and headed in that direction. I finished the rest of my drink and started to walk behind him. Before I walked off Ray [Benzino] grabbed my arm saying, "Fuck that shit, McNeill. Chill, let Sco do that shit," seeing that we could see Sco moving his hands like there was a problem. Still, I went over there and soon as Rosco threw a punch stealing on the dude, a fight broke out from there, and even though we were jumping the dude, he was swinging back definitely holding his own. There was a brief moment where me and the dude were exchanging blows one on one and he was getting the best of me. That's when one of the younger boys from my hood pulled out a knife and started stabbing the dude, then we all broke out heading to the cars to leave.

Me and Eight both had our guns outside in Calvin's car, which was too blocked in for us to just get in and pull off. Luckily, I looked over and saw Ray [Benzino] in his car across the street getting ready to pull off by himself and flagged him down telling him to wait a minute for me. Soon as me and Eight got in, Ray [Benzino] with a worried look on his face said, "This shit fucked up."

"Yeah, why you say that?"

"The dude that got stabbed is a Celtics ball player named Paul Pierce."

"Yeah? I thought he was a ball player or something from how tall he was."

Ray [Benzino] said, "Yeah, he ain't just like an average player, that's the Celtic's star, they brought him here expecting him to be like Jordan or something."

I said, "Damn, but you should slow down so we don't get pulled over cause me and Eight both got guns on us." Then I pulled the forty-five out my waistline and sat it on my lap to get more comfortable. He looked at the pistol seeming to have gotten more uncomfortable asking, "Where y'all going?"

"To Kenyatta's crib down Ashmont."

He said, "Ok, I know where, but trust me, McNeill, this thing is far from over. Watch, by the morning." I could see his relief once he finally got me and Eight to Kenyatta's crib by how fast he said, "I'm out," and pulled off. Me and Eight handed Kenyatta both guns on the back balcony, then jumped in my whip that I left parked there and left.

The next morning, I was awakened by a phone call from my mother saying, "Michael, your face is on the news as a person they wanna question in connection to a stabbing that happened last night at a club."

After hanging up with Moms all the calls started pouring in, even Asia's mother called saying that she just saw me on the news. The first person I called was Ray [Benzino], ready to pack up and leave town. Ray [Benzino] claimed that he had left for New York after dropping me and Eight off last night, so I said we were ready to head that way too. Although he didn't say no, I could tell by his tone and the long pause that he didn't want anything to do with me considering how hot I was. He said, "You think that's a good move, all they're gonna do is use that as an excuse to run up in the Source."

Feeling him trying to separate himself from me aggravated me to where I said, "I'm cool," then I just hung up. After that I called Attorney Lepo asking him what he thinks. He said he saw it on the news and as long as they didn't say that there's a warrant out for my arrest, I should be good.

"Yeah, but they saying that they want me for questioning."

"Fuck em, you do have to answer to that, they only want you for questioning. Well, you're not around for questioning and if they happen to pick you up, just say you want a lawyer and they'll release you; as long as you don't have a warrant, you don't have a problem."

I said, "Cool," then just fell back in the crib with Asia. I had heard from Rosco a couple of times basically joking about the situation till a couple days later him, Hurst, and Trev's faces were on the news with warrants wanted for the stabbing of Paul Pierce, a member of the Boston Celtics.

When I was eighteen, I had been arrested for stabbing a bouncer at the same club. As part of my punishment I was told to never come back to that establishment. But seeing that the name was changed from what it was when I caught the case, I was under the impression that the club now had new owners and it would be cool for me to go there. But getting to the club that night I came face to face with the same owner who had pointed me out to the police and came to every one of my court dates all the way up to my trial and sentencing. Even though I was in my thirties at the time and years had passed, we easily recognized each other, and I casually spoke with him, even making a small joke about how we were both now bold. After a brief conversation, I paid him and he welcomed me in, but not without saying "have fun and be good," which I took as a reference to the case I had caught years ago. Word was that after we left the club that night Paul Pierce got stabbed, at least twenty police were out there asking questions and investigating the situation. I assumed that the owner was going to at least tell them I was there, seeing that I had did time for stabbing someone there before. So, it was no surprise to me when I heard that the police wanted to question me, but I never talked to anyone about anything! Even though I didn't get locked up in the Paul Pierce stabbing case, a couple weeks later I ended up getting arrested for driving without a license and already had a warrant out for my arrest for the same thing. The next morning, Eight came and bailed me out from Dorchester court for fifteen hundred, knowing that once I got out, I was going to run again but not giving a fuck because we were brothers like that.

Within the next few months, the white-collar crime game had slowed down and although Eight still had a few dollars it wasn't anything like he had six months prior, and it was time to make other type moves. Next door to Kenyatta's crib were a couple Spanish dudes, Moe and Jean, that were getting a couple of bricks and were cool with Eight. I told Eight to see if they'd front us something so that we could try to make a couple moves in the coke game together and he did. Jean hit me and Eight with four and a half apiece in powder for a fairly good price considering what it was going for at the time. I wiped mine and Eight's up, bringing back an extra six deuce on each one. Doing business with Jean went cool at the beginning. Me and Eight would wait for one another to finish before going to see Jean to get more. That went on for a good month to where even though I owed Jean, I had accumulated a lil something of my own and was feeling a lot better about myself even though I was still drinking like a fish.

An acquaintance of mine named White from Franklin Hill had been doing really good for himself at one point but like me had fell off. His boy, Dave June from Franklin Hill was a good friend of mine and at the time he had just came home from doing some time, so when I bumped into him, I gave him my number and address and told him to holler at me so that we could see what we might be able to put together.

A couple of days later Dave, White, and another good friend of mine named Mice stopped by Asia's to check on me. White told me that even though he hadn't been getting any money lately he still had his clientele and could move some shit. This nigga was moving pretty heavy at one point so it wasn't hard to believe what he was saying, plus having Dave with him whom I wanted to lookout for, It was easy for me to make the decision to hit him with something. I gave him four and a half, figuring that this was also a good move for me to have someone experienced and hungry on the team, so I was pretty excited about the moves myself. That night this nigga Brubby that lived in Asia's building must have seen White and them leaving my building and figured it was about business. On my way down the stairs he came out of his niece Keisha's apartment, and out of the blue asked me if I had an eight ball for sale. Everything about him said snitch to me, we rarely ever spoke, and all of a sudden he was asking for drugs? I said, "Naw, I don't sell drugs," then kept walking downstairs.

Within that week I had got the word that the feds came and got White for snatching a wiretap machine off Brubby. The first thing came to mind was I knew that nigga Brubby was trying to set me up. Even though it was only three G's that I lost, being that I was just getting back on my feet that paper hurt me. I still owed Jean money and the rest of the work I had was all in the street and was coming back too slow to stack. When I spoke with Eight about everything, he told me he was having some complications on his side with the coke as well, to the point where we decided to just say fuck Jean and not pay him for the work.

Asia and Tammy no longer were hanging out together, Asia was now kicking it with Dameka who is Donna's cousin Big Mike's baby's mother, which didn't do anything for me but put my business more out there than it already was. Even worse, Dameka lived one street over from Greenwood on Rockston and Asia started going over to her house every day which led to her and Donna seeing each other damn near every day.

Nothing was going good for me. I was completely broke again, I wasn't doing any music, and I took my drinking to the next level and I lost my lil whip. All the people I had done shit for were looking down on me and whispering lil sucker shit about me instead of trying to help a nigga and pull me up. The only two people outside of Asia and Donna that I felt had my back were Kenyatta and Eight, and that came to a stop the day Homicide picked both of them up on a cold case. I was devastated. It seemed like the world just stopped. Seeing them being arraigned the next day took me to an all-time low. I was so hurt to see my friends like that, I cried as soon as I walked out of the courthouse. Donna had been working for some time now and had saved up enough money to get an apartment, and coincidentally she moved into a building right across the street from Tammy's grandmother's house. Me knowing Donna, she had rushed to get an apartment mainly so that we could live together again.

I must have stayed with her close to two months straight before I started to stay back and forth between her and Asia's houses. With Eight and Kenyatta locked up, I became ten times more miserable. Me and Vidal were still close, but he loved me so much that he couldn't bear being around me watching me drink like I was, and for some strange reason I couldn't stand drinking around him. I knew he believed in me and I always felt like I was letting him down.

Me and my cousin Tony started speaking more often and getting up off and on, but on a daily basis, me and Teddy started running together. I appreciated Ted, he was someone I did things for when I was up who seemed not to have forgotten, and was returning the favor when I most needed him.

One night me and Ted were riding around smoking weed and drinking and decided to go downtown to fuck with some hoes at the let out of the club. While Ted was parking, I happened to see the Patriot's corner back Lawyer Milloy standing next to a brand new Expedition seeming like he was looking for someone; when I got out I went right over to him to say what's up. He was tipsy which was understandable, but he was still displaying that same shitty attitude he had when I met him at the studio with Willie McGinest. After he spoke and barely shook my hand like he would probably do a groupie, I looked in the truck seeing that he had the back door open, and saw my ex-girlfriend Toy. I immediately got salty. I spoke to her and she spoke back, asking me if was I all right. Before I could even answer, Lawyer closed the door telling me to move on.

I said, "Fuck you, nigga, make me move on."

"Yo, nigga, you better go on, you don't know me like you think you do."

I said, "Well show me, nigga, show me I don't know you like I think I do."

Before he could say another word, the police pulled up telling whoever was driving the truck that Lawyer Milloy was in to pull off because he was illegally parked. It was a one-way street, so the driver had no choice but to go around in a complete circle and come back while leaving Milloy there, not knowing that we were arguing. I saw an opportunity, so I calmed down saying, "Listen, man, we friends with some of the same people. This is all just a misunderstanding. Come get in my car an I'll take you around the corner to your people."

He said, "Cool," and started walking to my car with me and Ted and I noticed a correctional officer from one of the jails I did time in named Jones following, so I said to myself, fuck it, he's coming too!

We got in and Ted asked me where we were going. That's when I locked the door and said, "to the bricks" and made a motion like I reached under the seat and got something saying, "Y'all den fucked up."

It was obvious that both had quickly sobered up. Once Ted got on the highway, now with fear in his voice, Lawyer asked, "Where we going, cuz?"

I said, "Shut up, bitch, and don't call me cuz. You didn't call me cuz when you was out there trying to impress them hoes. Don't worry about where we going."

C.O. Jones asked me, "Can I get out?"

I said, "Fuck no, you wanted to be a dick rider, well keep riding his dick now."

He said, "I just came to make sure y'all was good. You know I always looked out for you when you was locked up."

I said, "No you didn't, you was acting like a hoe when I was up there, now you acting like a lil bitch; shut the fuck up back there."

"Cuz, I apologize."

I said, "Shut up, hoe, and if you call me cuz again I'ma buss you in the mouth."

Jones said, "Mike, this shit crazy."

"It ain't get crazy yet, shit bout to get crazy in a minute. Yo bitch ass shouldn't even be in my car right now. You here because of dick riding, matter fact, Lawyer, tell him you didn't need him to be dick riding and call him cuz."

Lawyer said, "I didn't need you to be dick riding, cuz."

We pulled up in the bricks and I told both to get out, then I told Lawyer to walk with me so we can talk, then he apologized again. I said, "Ain't no need for that. I just wanna holla at you, put you up on some game." I grabbed his knee and asked him, "What would happen if I shot you in your knee?"

"Naw, please, cuz, I'll be shot."

I said, "Fuck just being shot, I'll be fucking up your career; everybody that's depending on you, you would've let down just for being ignorant. I wish I was in your shoes. I'd be more thoughtful of the people that made sacrifices for me to be in that position. Feel me?"

He said, "Yeah, I definitely do."

Even though he was scared, I could tell he was paying me close attention and learning something from this situation that would have helped him later when he finally got his millions, seeing that at the time he was still under a rookie's contract.

I told him and Jones to get back in the car so I could drop them off, seeing a sigh of relief on both of their faces. Jones said he was going to Four Corners and Lawyer said he was going to Marina Bay in Quincy. On the way to drop Jones off, I decided he deserved to walk for dick riding, then told Teddy to pull over a good fifteen minutes from where he was going, telling him to get his dick riding ass out and walk the rest of the way. Even though I felt that Lawyer learned a lesson and was truly remorseful, I wasn't completely done with him yet. Once we got to Quincy, I told him to get the fuck out and walk so that he could have time to reflect on everything that'd just happened and realize how lucky he was tonight.

Ray [Benzino] got an ear of what had happened and decided to reach out to me to have me come out to Miami to record after me not hearing from him in close to six months. I hadn't even been writing or thinking about music but felt like I needed to get away for a minute, and as for music, I'd just wing it with some old verses I wrote that no one had heard.

Getting to Miami the first thing I wanted was a drink which was easy to make happen seeing that there was a liquor store across the street from the hotel that Ray [Benzino] set me up in. I must say that once me and Ray got together and started talking, I realized that him bringing me down there was more about my well-being as opposed to me doing music and I had no choice but to appreciate that.

While getting some food on the beach we bumped into one of the dudes Ray [Benzino] bought weed from named Problem and Ray [Benzino] told him to come through my hotel spot in twenty minutes with a couple ounces. Problem came through and Ray [Benzino] paid him then broke me off like a half saying that, that should hold me down for a couple days. Me and Problem smoked a couple and chopped it up, realizing that we had some things in common which was that we both loved drinking Remy, then we decided to take a ride to get some. Ray [Benzino] told Problem what studio he'd be at later, telling him to bring me through there at about eight o'clock, then left.

First night was cool, granted I was tipsy and high, when it was my turn to get in the booth, I did my thing. Me and Ray [Benzino] completed a song over a track that he got from one of the producers Ja Rule records with. Problem loved the song, telling me I ripped it, saying he believed I should have a deal with my style and delivery. On the way back to the hotel, Problem told me that Ray [Benzino] told him that Ja Rule and Murder Inc were in town, and that he had planned on trying to get Ja Rule on a track while he was there. I said, "Yeah, that's what's up, dope."

Problem said, "Yeah, but I don't like being around them Murder Inc niggas, they be acting funny style."

I said, "How?"

"I can't explain it, they just got a funny way about them. You'll see, trust me. I don't even like fucking with Ray [Benzino] when he around them because he starts tripping a lil bit."

I said, "Trust me, my nigga, I'm in town too and my niggas don't want me to see nothing else but them being a hundred, ain't gonna be no tripping. Trust me!"

He said, "Alright, just remember I told you, I'll come through to check you tomorrow once I finish with my baby's mother," while dropping me back to the hotel.

Saturday morning, I woke up, smoked one, and finished off the rest of a half pint of Remy I had before getting in the shower and getting dressed. Twelve o'clock came and I called Jenks and Dog and got no answer, before going across the street to get me another half pint of Remy. I wound up dozing off for a few hours expecting to have missed calls from Ray [Benzino] or Jenks once I woke up, which I didn't. It was eight o'clock now and I was still not getting an answer from either one of them and I was tipsy all over again and now pissed off. Problem called me at a lil after nine to see where I was at, so that we could get up and smoke one. I told him at the hotel. He said, "Come downstairs," because he was right around the corner. Getting in his car he could tell I was pissed, asking me, "What's good with you?"

I said, "This nigga Ray [Benzino] nor Jenks is answering for me all day, just left a nigga stuck up in the hotel room."

Problem said, "Damn! That's crazy, I'm about to ride out to my crib on the other side of town. You rolling?"

"Yeah, hell yeah. I ain't got shit else to do."

Pulling up at Problem's spot, I was impressed. It was a tall building full of condos with security at the front desk. Getting upstairs his shit wasn't plush but it was decently furnished, definitely a nice spot. After being in his bedroom for like ten minutes he came out showing me an AK 47. I held it for a second, taking a peek through the scope saying, "Yeah, this is nice."

He said "Yeah, that's my murder weapon," then he lifted up his shirt and showed me a thirty-eight revolver and said, "This my going out or handling business joint."

I said, "Ok, I hear you. I see you ain't for the bullshit."

"Naw, fuck naw." His cell phone started ringing, he looked at it then said, "This Ray [Benzino] right here probably wanting some weed."

I then looked at my phone to see if I had a missed call, which I didn't, then said, "Yeah, well don't tell him I'm with you unless he asks."

Ray [Benzino] and Problem chopped it up for a second, then Problem hung up saying, "That's why they ain't answering for you, they hanging with them Murder Inc niggas over at Glass House Studio, but he did ask me if I could stop by your hotel and get you on my way up there."

I said, "Yeah, well what'd happen if you couldn't do it, then I was just stuck all night."

Then I showed Problem my phone saying, "Look, Ray [Benzino] still ain't called me his self."

Problem said, "I told you them niggas get funny as shit when they around Ja Rule and them niggas."

I said, "It's cool, I'ma holla at him."

On the way to the studio, me and Problem stopped and got a pint and started swigging back to back till it was done, throwing the bottle right out when we reached the parking lot of the studio.

Getting to the intercom, Problem suggested we say that it's Mike for Ray figuring that way we shouldn't have any problems or funny looks once we got in. Once we got buzzed in and upstairs, I could see Jenks through a set of glass doors talking to Ja Rule, so, seemingly upset I went through the first set of doors heading in that direction. All the while I didn't see Erv Gotti and one of his bodyguards Big Fred sitting on the couch on the side of the wall that wasn't made of glass. Soon as the door closed behind me, Fred jumped up and snatched me from the back locking my arm in a position that I couldn't move, asking me what I wanted.

Mad as shit I said, "I'm here with Ray [Benzino]."

Then he pushed me forward saying, "Yeah, well this ain't Ray [Benzino]'s studio session. Don't come in here like that."

While he was talking, Jenks, seeing what was happening came out saying, "Hold up, Fred."

"Naw, that's my people. Dog, you can't disrespect like that."

Now Ray [Benzino] and Ja Rule came up front trying to calm everything down after hearing all the commotion. Ray [Benzino] listened to the story then paid Problem for the weed and told him to just bring me back to the hotel without asking me how I felt about the situation. So, I just left not saying shit to him. Soon as me and Problem got back in the car he reached in the ashtray and handed me a blunt saying, "Light this, cuz. I didn't like that shit. I told you bout how funny these niggas be acting, my nigga."

I said, "Yeah, I'm heated, dog, this big nigga put his hands on me. Trust me, if I was home, I'd stank that nigga. I got bodies, I don't play that shit."

Problem said, "Listen, my nigga, I like you, you a cool ass nigga. If you really wanna straighten that shit I'm with you. We can go get the three eight right now."

"Good looking, let's go get it. I'ma peel that nigga when he comes out the studio."

We got to Problem's house. I went upstairs with him, got the revolver, wiped it down good, put it in my waistband, then left heading back up to the studio. Getting back up there we noticed that all the cars were gone, so I called Jenks to see where they were and if they were still around Ja Rule and them.

He said, "What's up, McNeill. You cool?"

"Yeah, I'm good," while hearing music in the background like they were in a club or something.

Jenks said, "Yo, Big Fred said his bag on grabbing you, but you gotta understand that, that's Ervan Ja's bodyguard, and with them not knowing you or the reason you walked in like that. He was just doing his job." I down played the situation by saying, it's cool, I'm not even sweating it, you all still together?

"Yeah, but once we leave this lil spot we heading back that way then I'ma call you, then come get you."

I said, "Cool," then hung up asking Problem what club or bar does he think they all might be at.

He thought for a second then pulled off saying, "I bet I know where them niggas is at."

Getting over to this small club that he assumed they were in, sure enough, all their cars were there parked in the lot. It was only eleven something, close to twelve which was early for Miami, so Problem suggested that we pull over, smoke one, and wait an hour, and if they don't come out by then, we'll just leave and come back right before the club ends.

I said, "Cool," while he was parking up the street at an angle where we could still see the front door of the club. Before we could finish the blunt, I saw Jenks and Dog come out, then Ja Rule, Erv then Fred. I got out and started walking down the street, while Problem started the car making sure he could easily get out of the parking space. Jenks saw me, then tapped Dog, then pointed in my direction saying, "Here come McNeill."

They were all in a group and I didn't wanna make a mistake and shoot Jenks or Ray [Benzino], so I walked all the way up to the front where they were standing. Once I got close enough to shoot Fred, I could see a policeman in the hallway of the club standing next to a metal detector. Me and Fred ended up catching eye contact staring at each other while I'm saying to myself, *This is a lucky motherfucker*. Jenks put his arm around me, then walked me off saying, "Chill, McNeill, that shit squashed, cuz, you can't let that lil bullshit come in between the business moves niggas got set up, that's a small thing to the bigger picture."

I said, "Yeah, fuck that nigga," then I showed Jenks the pistol saying, "If the police wasn't out here I would kill this nigga."

Jenks asked, "Where you get that!"

"I'm good, cuz. I'll hit you in a few," then I jogged back up the street and jumped back in the car with Problem, then we pulled off.

Before I could say anything, Problem pointed to the left of me showing me a police officer sitting in his car with his lights off saying, "I'm glad you didn't shoot."

I said, "Yeah, there was police in the hallway of the club, too, that's why I fell back."

He said, "Fuck it, my nigga, it ain't worth going to jail over. Let's go put the pistol up and smoke a couple, get our heads right. Fuck them niggas."

I said, "Yeah, you right. I'm done with it."

After putting the gun back at Problem's crib, we rode around smoking blunt after blunt like we knew this was probably going to be the last time we got up.

The next morning Ray [Benzino] called me claiming that everybody was leaving and saying that my flight was at eleven o'clock and that he was sending a car to come get me and bring me to the airport within the next thirty minutes. I knew he was bullshitting about everybody leaving, but I didn't give a fuck cause I was ready to go anyways, so I said, "whatever," then hung up, packed my shit and waited downstairs for the car to come.

CHAPTER NINE

Asia had been acting real funny lately, not wanting to do lil shit when I'd tell her to, barely speaking when I was over there, and all of a sudden having these random attitudes for nothing. That was the first time I ever suspected her of messing around with someone else. Come to find out I was right. Keith Peterson had come home from doing over ten years in the feds and started fucking her on the low while I was laid up drunk in her house. On top of that, when I found out and confronted her about it that's when she decided to tell me that she was moving out and didn't want me to know where her new place was, saying she needed some space for a few. I still had a place to stay, seeing that Donna had her own place, but Asia cheating on me was a sign of how bad things really were starting to get seeing that this was a woman that would bend over backwards to make sure I'm straight. There was a time she worshiped the ground I walked on, and to see her now look down on me, touched me! Even though I loved Donna, I was so used to having both of them to run to that once we stopped speaking for a couple months, something felt missing.

A few months later I assumed once Keith Peterson was finished with her, Asia would reach out wanting to see me. I never considered myself to be in a relationship with Asia, but once I finally stepped foot in her new apartment, I will say I was glad to have my situation back even though I knew I could never trust her and would always quietly resent her. One good thing that came out of her fucking with Keith was that he gave her a decent Ford Taurus that I immediately started driving.

Within weeks I was pulled over and arrested for my old warrants and a new DUI charge. Being that I didn't have the money for bail, I had Donna call Calvin to see if he could come get me out. Once I got back on the phone, she told me he said yeah but he was gonna leave me there for a night so I could learn a lesson. I was hurt, feeling like after all I'd done for him, he's gonna leave me in jail. I wasn't a kid, so to hear all that lesson bullshit let me know how distant we'd really become. I was mad at myself for even having Donna ask him for anything.

After spending a couple of days riding to all the courts that I had default warrants in, the last judge gave me a two hundred dollar bail which Donna was able to post for me. Seeing that I had two open charges for the same crime, I knew I was facing some jail time, and with the judge scheduling my court date sixty days later I had plenty of time to get into more trouble.

One night me and Greedy's brother Kari went up to the bricks after leaving the bar, and while I was talking with Booda a couple of dudes that moved in a couple of houses from Vidal's sister Ebony came out drunk and talking reckless. One of my homies named Lamar stole on one of the dudes and started beating his ass, that's when his man pulled out a small caliber pistol and fired a couple of shots in the air. Without even getting out of the car, I shot the dude once at close range with a .44 caliber Deringer that I was carrying at the time. Then Kari pulled off. Within a couple of days some females were seen loading items into a U Haul truck moving, knowing that those dudes suffered the chance of getting killed if they came back around.

That weekend me and my cousin Tony got together and went to a party that my boy Beefy was throwing at Prince Hall. After a couple of drinks, I bumped into DJ, who was a younger dude from Belnel that I was pretty cool with considering that he grew up getting the game and being about that trigger play from me and Eight before Eight got locked up on his life bid.

Over the last year, DJ started hanging around all types of different people and getting involved in some of our Corbet Street in house problems that we were having that didn't concern him, so I took the opportunity to check him on it. Once I started talking to him, I could tell by his posture that he wasn't feeling me talking down to him even though he didn't say anything. That's when Tall Curt took it upon himself to speak up for him saying, "Yo, Mizz, watch how you talking, ain't no hoes over here."

I said, "Mind your business, I ain't talking to you."

Then Curt said, "Well I'm talking to you."

That's when I pulled out the same .44 Deringer that I just shot the dude with up in the bricks a few days ago. Only having one bullet in it at the time, they both backed up, then headed for the door saying, "Ok, you wanna pull out guns, huh, ok, you wanna pull out guns?" apparently going to get a strap.

Me and my cousin Tony left and rode for a second, then headed up to the bricks, within about five minutes I saw my nigga Eight's cousin Jam's tinted up Honda Accord speeding down the street with someone shooting out the passenger window. They were shooting from so far that they actually hit two houses that were nowhere near where and I was standing. I pulled out the Deringer but didn't shoot seeing that I only had one bullet, and figured it was best to save it just in case they made a U-turn, but they didn't, instead they took a right down Standard and left. Me and Tony were in Asia's car that she got from Keith, so I dropped Tony off telling him, "Don't worry, I'ma straighten them niggas out asap."

I had drama now, so I couldn't keep running around here with that Deringer. I called Ted and told him what was going on, and within hours he picked me up and hit me with a decent Jennings nine. We rode around basically smoking and drinking, strapped up talking about all different types of shit, granted I expected them niggas to lay low for a few days after shooting at me. I was cool though, as long as I had something proper now to get off with when I did see them again. For the moment I could have patience.

Later that night I had Teddy drop me off to my cousin Tony's crib so I could smoke a couple with Tony and tell him about what was going on. Right while Teddy was pulling off, Sheldon's brother Will happened to be pulling up parking. He was in the car with his girl seeming to be arguing or disagreeing about something, and by the look on his face he had an attitude. When he got out to go see Tony, I spoke to him and he barely spoke back. Walking to the porch to ring the bell, Tony opened the door just realizing that I was outside as well and said, "What's up, Mizz, come in."

I wanted to finish a lil piece of blunt that I had, so I said, Alright, I'll be in in a minute." Before I rang the bell to come in, Will came back out walking by me to leave not saying bye or see you later. I got instantly pissed off and said, "Fuck you, too."

Will turned around and said, "Fuck you too, Mizz, I'm not in the mood for your bullshit."

That's when I walked off Tony's porch asking, "Why, what is you in the mood for, nigga?"

Now at the time, Will was like six feet two, and about two hundred and seventy pounds, where I'm like five six, a hundred and forty pounds. His demeanor was like he was trying to get aggressive, so I pulled the pistol out saying, "You better go on before I make it to where you can't go nowhere."

He stared at me for a second then ran and jumped in his car with his girl and took off. Tony didn't see what just happened, but came to the door seeming upset. I said, "What's up? Will just called you?"

He said, "Yeah, I'll be out in a second, I'ma bout to drop you off."

On the way to drop me off, I could tell Tony had an attitude by how he just listened and didn't say anything but, "alright, I'll holla at you," when I was getting out of his car at Donna's crib.

A couple of weeks passed and one night coming out of Donna's apartment I saw Tammy mother Darleen coming out of her mother's house. I told her to come here for a second, then asked her how she'd been and what she'd been up to.

She said, "Same 'ol same, trying to make some money." I could tell she was back to getting high, but at the time she still had a lil weight on her and was still looking pretty good so I suggested to her that we go downtown and hit the track, she said she was with it but didn't have anything decent to wear.

I called Donna telling her what I was about to do, asking her what was in her closet that she didn't really wear anymore. Once Donna gave me a description of what items I could choose from, I had Darleen come in and take a shower and get dressed. While she was doing her hair, I put on one of my two thousand dollar suits that I hadn't worn in a couple of years, so that I could look the part while I'm pimping. I didn't have a ride, so I called a friend of mine named Big Moe who lived right next door to my cousin Tony's crib telling him that I was about to catch a cab to his crib to drink a lil Remy and smoke a few blunts with intentions on having him drop me and Darleen off downtown a lil later.

He said, "Cool," then I jumped in a cab over there. I had Darleen with me with me looking pretty good dressed nicely. I was in an expensive suit looking sharp, and I had Teddy's nine-millimeter on me figuring that I should bring it with me just in case someone tried me while I was out on the track. Soon as we pulled up in the cab, I saw Sheldon's brother Will in front of Tony's house sitting on his car staring at me while me and Darleen were getting out of the cab at Big Moe's crib. After I paid the cab driver I got out and asked Will, "What's up? You got some business over here?"

He said, "Maybe."

I could tell by his persona and posture that he had his gun on him, but the thing was that I was sure that he didn't expect me to have mine on me by the way I was dressed. I pointed to Moe's porch while telling Darleen to go up there, then I started walking towards Will. He stood up off his car, then started reaching letting me see the handle to what looked like a revolver, so I dipped behind the closest car, then leaned out and shot at him. I missed and could see him behind another car shooting at me. That's when I let off around five or six more shots at him. My luck, the police had happened to be sitting up the street at the same time we were shooting it out and I didn't see them.

After the exchange, I ran through Moe's house and into his basement trying to stash the pistol once I heard sirens, but it was too late seeing that that cop sitting in his car had seen exactly where I went. Within minutes, several police officers came down into the basement with their guns drawn telling me to come out with my hands up, then they tackled me, cuffed me up and took me to the station on firearms and shooting charges. As for Will, he was cool because once they got on me, he went into Tony's house till the coast was clear. Seeing that I was already out on bail, the judge revoked the bail I had, sending me to Concord without one for sixty days.

CHAPTER TEN

Within a month or so of being in Concord, I was coming out of the chow hall and I bumped into Teddy telling me that somehow the police got a warrant to search his mother's house and found some money and dope. Getting back to my unit, we found out that he happened to have been put in the cell right next to mine which was good so I could share the couple of lil things I had from canteen with him until he went himself.

After I got indicted and my case sent to Superior Court, I knew I was going to jail, it was just a matter of for how long. The D.A. gave me and offer of a year mandatory for the gun and a year for the assault saying that she'd run them concurrently, and I took it. I still had two years that I was facing in the county for DUI, but once I finally got sentenced the court just ran everything together with no probation. It sucked that I was locked up, but overall I got a good deal. Before I got arrested, Donna had told me that she had missed her period a couple of months, but we never discussed whether or not she was pregnant.

Then a couple of weeks after me being sentenced she told me that her doctor confirmed that we were having a baby. Although I was happy about it, the fact that I'd be in jail through the process fucked me up. Once Asia got word of the pregnancy, she expressed some anger seeing that when she was pregnant, I took her to get an abortion, but after that it was either stay down with me or leave me because God willing the baby's coming. By the letters, pictures, cards and money Asia sent me, I assumed she was still down with me, and for the most part just accepted the fact that Donna was about to have my child.

Six months later, Donna gave birth to my daughter, Maya McNeil, taking on my last name just like my son Michael by my first baby's mother Cynthia. The whole time I was locked up I hadn't heard from Cynthia nor did I get to see my son.

A month after my daughter was born, Donna started bringing her up to see me letting her get familiar with me seeing that I was being released in ninety days. Asia was still writing and sending money when she could and claiming to have kept her legs closed while I was down. Granted I had doubts, I had to give her the benefit of the doubt seeing that she did everything I asked of her up to that point.

By the time I got out, Asia and Donna had both moved into new places. Donna just having my daughter moved into more affordable subsidized housing in the Ruggles projects, while Asia took her Section Eight out to a housing complex in Canton, Mass.

It wasn't long at all before I had gotten back into my old habits, the first day I came home I had sex with Donna, then the very next day I had sex with Asia and was already back drinking! Even though I was truly over Cynthia by this time, I still felt a certain way when I went to see my son for the first time in a year and found out that Cynthia was seven months pregnant, coincidently by an older guy named Mike. To see her pregnant disgusted me. I felt like she hadn't known her new man long enough to be having unprotected sex yet along with having a new baby, for some reason I foresaw my son getting deprived of the attention he deserved, seeing that she was now having a new child.

Within the next few days I got a cell phone and numbers on Disco and reached out to him to see how he was doing. No more than an hour after speaking to Sco, Tammy called me saying that Sco told her that I was home, and that she got my number from him, so that she could call and say hi and see how I was doing. The phone call was definitely unexpected seeing that we hadn't spoken since I texted her that message about her and Ray [Benzino]. And with her mother being with me the night I got arrested, I figured she'd heard about it and would have had even less to say to me but that wasn't the case. By the tone in her voice I could tell that she was happy to be speaking to me. It reminded me of the days when I knew she was into me. After a good ten minutes of conversation she asked me if she could see me later, telling me that her and Sco were roommates in a one family house of the highway. I said, "Yeah, why not?"

Even though this spontaneous phone call came as a surprise, I did expect for Tammy to want to see me once word got out that I was home. If even only for a second, I knew she'd wanna see my face but by the way she said "see you" I knew more than a hi and bye was coming!

Later that day while me and Donna were out picking me up a couple outfits and some sneakers seeing that I had gained fifty pounds and couldn't fit into anything I had, I happened to bump into Belnel Mike in the store. Later that day, Mike came to get me so I could ride through the hood and see everybody for the first time. Getting to the block it felt good to see all my niggas again, especially with me being in good health. After having a few drinks on Morton, we slid through the bricks so that I could see Vidal and his sister Ebony whom I'd always looked at as my lil sister. Ebony had a couple of girlfriends over at the time that were checking me out and flirting and it actually felt good to be looked at as being attractive, seeing that I was looking really thin and fucked up before I left. While we were still at Ebony's, Belnel Mike asked me if I had spoken to Calvin yet.

I said, "Naw. It wasn't that I didn't have intentions on calling him or had an attitude with him, but damn, I just did a year, and not once did he send me a dollar or ask Donna or Asia was I straight. And if I expected anybody to look out for me, it was him, seeing that I looked out for him when he was in jail and on the streets." The reality of the matter was that I felt like I didn't even know Calvin anymore, and I wasn't in any rush to see where his head was at. I've always held my own, that's a quality about me, I refused to let myself be compromised, so it was important to me that no one felt like I needed them or expected anything from them. So, unconsciously, it was like we'll see each other when we do. Belnel Mike ended up calling him and handed me the phone, getting on the phone; the love was the same as it always is when we speak.

My pride kept me from speaking on anything that I might have had a problem with, feeling like it would be a sign of weakness to complain about shit another man's doing, friend or not. Throughout the conversation he ended up giving me the address to where he was staying at the time, telling me to come through. So, me and Belnel Mike rode out there, we chilled for a few hours, laughing at old stories just chopping it up. It felt good. It was like when we were in high school before the drug selling, the hoe pimping, and the violence -- just us being us throwing back a few brews. My alcohol tolerance was low, so by now I was high and tipsy when I received a call from Tammy asking what time did I plan on meeting her. I told her within the next couple hours, then hung up. I told Calvin that that was her; he put his hand over his eyes, then busted out laughing saying this nigga's trying to put his old team back together. "Did you see Asia yet?"

"Yeah," I replied, then all three of us started laughing. Considering everything that had happened in the past, and granted I didn't come with any expectations, Calvin still gave me seven hundred dollars on my way out, which I really appreciated. It wasn't the money, it was the fact that if the shoe were on the other foot, I would have held him down the same way, even more, but like I said it was definitely appreciated!

Once me and Belnel Mike got back to Boston, I had him drop me to meet Tammy at her grandmother's house, and from there we got right on the highway and headed to her place off the highway. Between the ride from her grandmother's to her house she must have told me I looked good at least eight times, and although I liked the attention, it was also a reflection of how bad I must have looked to her before I left.

Her place was nice, unlike I could have imagined, it was fully furnished in all rooms with a big screen TV in both the living room and bedroom. It was so nice to me that in my mind I was saying either she was with some nigga that was getting money that got locked up, or they broke up. Either way I didn't give a fuck. I was there and she was horny and happy to be with me.

Conversation was limited, and after a couple of shots and a joint we were fucking. The sex talk was the same, with her telling me she never stopped loving me and will always love me. Granted, I did enjoy myself, at the moment, me assuming that she slept with Ray [Benzino] was in my head and was an extreme turn off, her being Tony's ex and all I went through with him over the situation. It was important that she showed lady-like characteristics with me from now on. Her messing with Ray was a blatant fuck me and I knew I couldn't accept her back in my life even as a side piece. So, I knew that morning when she dropped me off that, that was probably the last time we'd ever sleep together.

I wasted no time getting myself back in the same situation that I was in before I left. I was broke, doing nothing about it as if I was waiting for a connect to just come drop out of the sky and hit me with some bricks. Getting no money had me stressed and miserable to where I lost all the weight I'd gained in jail over a course of ninety days. Worst of all, I was back drinking, but this time even worse seeing that at least at one point I had a preference which was Remy, but at this point I was drinking white liquor, brandy, rum, gin, just anything I could get my hands on or afford. I wasn't doing anything to help Donna with my daughter; once again my life was at a standstill, and the few people that had faith in me getting it back together when I first got out had now disappeared wanting nothing to do with me. I was drinking all day, and even my own son wanted nothing to do with me anymore. One day I went to one of his Pop Warner jamborees to support him; the whole time I was there he stayed away from me, intentionally ignoring and not speaking to me once the whole time. Still, I didn't try to do anything to fix things, instead I just drank more feeling sorry for myself and reminiscing on the life I used to have.

As for me and Donna, our relationship started to disintegrate, and my misery began to overwhelm the apartment. It got to a point where I would go out and drink all day, then come home and start fights with her and say real mean things to her with no regards to the fact that she'd just had my child. I hated living in the Ruggles projects and would say it to her every day after a few drinks, and instead of being man enough to do something to get her and my daughter out of there, I selfishly left without any regards to their safety.

One night after taking the disrespect to the highest level that I ever did with Donna she called the police and I left before they came. While walking, not knowing exactly where I was going, I called Asia to come get me telling her that I was coming to live with her and to come pick me up from the train station I was waiting at. Asia was happy about me coming to live with her.

Over the first couple of months I could tell she felt completed as if she'd finally got something she'd been wanting on for a while, even with me being an alcoholic and broke, she had this attitude like she won. Even though I still didn't consider Asia my girlfriend nor fully trusted her since her fucking with Keith, we did become closer than we ever had been over the next year. For the most part I was somewhere drunk every night and she would wait on my phone call to come pick me up before hitting the highway to the crib. A couple of times I was in Packies, drunk and someone else would call her and she'd just pop up on me saying, "Mike, let's go!"

I cared about Asia but she didn't love me so there was no way that I could have felt that I loved her. I, more or less, saw it as being highly appreciative of her being in my corner. Asia worked jobs from time to time and would do her best to see to it that I dressed decently on top of doing lil things for my daughter on top of taking care of her own daughter on her own. I was no type of father figure for Danasha seeing that all she ever saw me do was drink and come in drunk, and it was easy to see that she had started to lose if not had already lost respect for me.

The Fourth of July we went to Asia's sister Mit's house for a cookout, and Toy's mother Miss Pat happened to live right next door. For the most part, the day went well, drinks, food, smokes, and everyone just having a good time. That is until I got drunk and decided to flirt with Toy; we were talking in the kitchen when Asia walked in getting noticeably upset saying, "I'm leaving, y'all can take care of his drunk ass," then walked out and left.

When I called Asia trying to talk to her she said, "You still in love with Toy so stay there with her," then hung up. I had nowhere to go nor anyone to call, so Toy's mother let me stay on her couch till the morning.

Waking up there had to be one of my most embarrassing moments in my life up to that point. By ten o'clock, Asia came and got me talking shit the whole ride to her house saying that it was time for me leave so that she could start doing her own thing. Me and Ray [Benzino] hadn't spoken at all since my incident with Ja Rule's bodyguard, so it came as a surprise when I got word that he was inviting me to come to Miami for the Memorial Day weekend. I needed to get away for a second with all I was going through, so I was ready to put the past in the past and go enjoy myself.

Calvin had an apartment down there at the time, so when I called him telling him I was coming down he said, "Let's make plans to link up when you touch down."

Getting to Miami I felt relieved, but as usual, as soon as I got situated in my room, I wanted a drink. Being that I knew I was only there for a few days I said to myself I'ma make sure that I'm on my best behavior so I could get through without any problems on this trip. First night we just chilled walking the beach getting high, enjoying being deep like we used to back in the day. The next night we went to the club and I was tipsy before we even went in, seeing that I didn't have my own money

I was ready for Ray [Benzino] to put his credit card up so I could drink all I wanted to for the night.

On the way upstairs Ray [Benzino] stopped to speak to a high yellow Spanish looking dude wearing a white tee shirt and blue jeans. My first impression was that this was a groupie holding us up while I was trying to get to the bar, so I made a motion towards him getting ready to say, "Yo, not now tonight, we chilling," when Ray [Benzino] peeped my whole play and stopped me with a sense of importance to whisper in my ear saying, "Naw, McNeil, chill, none of that tonight, save all that for back home, we'll lose in here and I mean lose bad."

Me, still not fully comprehending, said, "Yeah, man, I'm trying to get a drink."

The Spanish looking dude heard me, then handed me a big bottle of Cristal and said, "Go ahead, to the VIP, and tell them Meech said you can have anything you want to drink up there."

Me and Calvin walked up while Ray [Benzino] and the nigga chopped it up, then Ray [Benzino] came upstairs telling me that the dude just offered to give him a million dollars cash tonight to help him and Dave out with some money issues. Looking around I noticed that there were over twenty dudes in there with high priced jewelry on, most of them had diamond encrusted pieces that had the letters BMF on them. The dude Meech that gave me the bottle of Cristal moments ago finally took his chain out from underneath his shirt and he had one too, all iced out. The rapper game, and Jim Jones, had a song freshly out called "Certified Gangsters" that they stood on the bar and performed, in the middle of game dancing and throwing gang signs. Jim Jones pulled him to the side and whispered something in his ear that led the game to stop throwing gang signs and say a shout out to Big Meech and the whole BMF family. At that point I knew this dude Meech was a serious dude and I was witnessing something that I had never seen before. Once I heard that those niggas were drugs dealers, I was impressed. I saw young niggas in there probably not even twenty-one yet wearing a couple hundred thousand worth of jewelry.

I felt like a peon, every time I'd get drunk, I'd whine about the couple hundred thousand I used to have and there were a few niggas in the club wearing jewels worth that. It helped me realize that, yeah, I lived good for a second, but in reality, I hadn't accomplished anything, in a sense seeing all these niggas that were getting real money were therapeutic for me.

Once I got back home from that trip, I was ready to chase me some paper in some type of way. I said fuck it and bought a quarter for three hundred and broke it down into twenties and fifties. Asia, although still a lil upset about what happened at the cookout, started letting me drop her off at Dameka's house while I used her car to hustle for a couple of hours.

Me and Donna had started speaking again; by this time, she had moved out of the projects and into the new housing development in back of the bricks where I'm from. We even had sex a few times which had basically reminded me of our bond and the years we'd spent together.

CHAPTER ELEVEN

My attempt to start from the bottom never took off; within weeks I had fucked that money up and was riding around in Asia's car drunk asking her for money for gas. Things between me and her had gone from bad to worse. I started to notice her having the same attitude and behavior she'd had when she started cheating on with me with Keith. A couple of months had passed and even though we slept in the same bed, we weren't having sex nor touching one another.

One Friday night after the Slade bar, I decided to have Dre Davis bring me by Donna's apartment with intentions on having sex. Even though we had been apart for some time, my arrogance had me expecting everything to be as it was before we split. After getting to her place and knocking on the door, she opened it but left the screen door locked. Before I could even ask her what she was doing or say I'm here to stay the night, I looked and saw some dude sitting on the couch watching TV. I started pulling on the screen door while saying, "Who the fuck is he? Send him out."

She said, "Mike, if you don't wanna go to jail tonight, leave my house." Knowing that she would call the police, I just got back in Dre's car, then had him drop me to Asia's house. I was hurt and as selfish as it may sound, I felt betrayed and disrespected being that I couldn't imagine Donna sleeping with someone else no matter what I did or how long I was gone.

The next day speaking with Donna about the situation she tried to convince me that, that was one of her family members, saying that I was just too drunk to realize it and that she was just making me think it was someone else as payback. Knowing for sure that she was lying, I acted as if I believed her just to clear the air so I could still come by and see my daughter without any hostility in the environment.

I hadn't seen Donna's cousin Big Mike in a while till one day I happened to bump into him while I was dropping Asia off over his baby's mother Dameka's house. We spoke briefly but long enough for him to tell me about the bomb coke he had and telling me some prices. By the way he was talking it felt like he was trying to feel me out and trying to see what my money was like, so instead of me asking any specifics I just said, "Aight, I'll holler if need be," then shook his hand before I left.

This was a far cry from the person I used to front coke to, his conversation wasn't anything like back when I was helping him get up. By the way I was dressed and looked you could tell I wasn't doing well, besides that I was pretty sure he had overheard that in the streets, so I took his conversation as a sucker's way of being sarcastic.

A few weeks later after dropping Asia off to Dameka's I bumped into my cousin Tony's boy Keith while I was pulling up at Donna's place. He had just recently got out from doing seven years and told me that he lived up there in the same complex with his new girl and was wondering how I was doing. I used to front Keith coke before he went off to do his own thing. I taught him how to stretch coke as well, and like Big Mike he also, sort of acted like he forgot where he came from once he reached a certain level, but by now I was over that and was genuinely glad to see him. Throughout a ten-minute conversation he told me that he'd bumped into Asia a couple of months ago up at the pre-release that he was at seeing Keith Peterson. By the look on my face he could tell something was wrong, so he asked, "Are y'all still messing around?"

I said, "Yeah, I still live with her."

"Damn, I didn't mean to start no shit."

"Naw, it's cool, we been on bad terms lately, I knew something was going on."

He said, "Yeah, I seen her up there like four times."

I said, "Good looking," then we exchanged numbers after me telling him about my daughter with Donna and showing him where she lived. My intentions were to call her and confront her about it once I left from spending time with my daughter, but after thinking strongly about it I came to the conclusion that confronting her was just going to start a fight that I couldn't afford to have seeing that I was living in her apartment and driving her car. A lot of things I'd done to people in the past were coming back on me in full circle. I showed Sheldon disloyalty by messing with his ex and now here she is being disloyal to me when I need her the most. Although I was upset and somewhat hurt over it, I kept it to myself in order to buy myself some more time to get on my feet.

Within that same month Asia woke up one morning asking me out of the blue if I had any intentions on marrying her. Assuming that she was fucking Keith Peterson again and asking me this for some strategic reason, I bluntly said, "Fuck no, what the fuck made you ask me that?"

A big argument ensued and raged on for at least a half an hour with me still not mentioning what I'd heard about her going up to the pre-release. The last time I said, "Fuck you."

She said, "Well if it's 'fuck me,' I want you out my house."

The whole time we were arguing I knew that this was what it was all for, she was dealing with Keith Peterson again and needed me out in order to try to pursue things further with him. On her way out to go to work that morning she said she'd appreciate it if I'd packed all my shit up and be gone by the time she got off.

I said, "Yeah, you got that," but really not knowing where I was going, I knew I had to make some calls. None of my niggas had their own apartments, so my calls were limited. The first person I hit was Calvin and even though I could tell he felt bad for a nigga, he wasn't willing to have the burden of me staying at his hoe's crib. Even though I still felt a way about Donna lying to me about her having company, I had no choice but to ask her if I could come stay with her for a few days. After questioning me how long, as if she really didn't want to let me, she said yes, then I packed my shit up and called Vidal to come get me. Moving into Donna's crib was hectic off the rip, it seemed like we couldn't have a conversation without it turning into a beef with her always asking me how much longer before I'd be moving out.

Within the first ninety days she had called the police twice to have me removed after an argument, once she even told the police that I hit her when I didn't, leading me to be arrested and having to take the case all the way to trial only beating it because she didn't show up.

With my mother living outta town and me and my sister no longer speaking I had no choice but to put up with her bullshit seeing that I didn't have anywhere else to live. It was either there or a shelter and I knew trying to get on my feet from a shelter would be much more of a challenge. With Donna living so close to my neighborhood I was able to get around a lot better than I did when I lived in Roxbury or Canton without a car. A couple of my home boys like Pableto and Dave Pike would come pick me up to chill for a few or at least till I got too drunk and belligerent to bear, then they'd drop me off not contacting me or answering the phone for me for a few days. Often, I'd ride with Donna ending up on Greenwood Street for at least a few hours every day where I quickly got the vibe that I wasn't wanted. Being over there I realized that her cousin Big Mike had really taken things to another level since he got that check from refinancing his house. Instead of getting just one key, he was now getting five or six and had a hell of a clientele selling everything from weight down to twenties, running the apartment like a trap spot down South. At the time Donna's brother Ducky was doing pretty good for himself, it wasn't that he had stacked a lot of money, but he was making enough to drink, buy food and keep a few dollars in his pocket, all while putting me up on to all that Big

Mike had been up to over the past year I hadn't been coming around. It was evident that Big Mike had brought things to a level that I hadn't reached. It was even said that he showed a couple hoes a million dollars cash and had become way more flamboyant than I'd known him to be.

A few things that Asia said to me the last time we argued stuck in my head, whether they were real or not. First, when she said that she should have listened to Tony and not have let me know where she lived because I wasn't going to do anything but pull her down further, second when she said that my friend Bum told her that she needed to leave me because someone was going to end up killing me in these streets, and for her well-being it would be best if she stopped being around me. These were my so-called friends and family saying fuck me, it became known in the streets that I was broke and alone, meaning that none of my homies were willing to ride for me, so, basically, I was solo.

I started getting into arguments with dudes that in my prime wouldn't have even looked my way in fear of getting fucked up or killed, but now with my team talking bad about me behind my back it gave off a sense of vulnerability that the streets feed off and judge you by. Big Mike had helped a few people get on their feet over the last year but by the attitude he seemed to get every time he'd see me around his house with Donna it was obvious I wasn't getting on that list. I was personally responsible for him being where he was at and could tell he didn't wanna see me back up. Ray [Benzino] had changed his rap name to Benzino by this time and had been booked to do a show at the Middle East night club in Cambridge. Once he got in town, he reached out to me to see if I was up for performing with him that night and I said yes thinking that it would feel good to be back on stage with him just like the old days.

Earlier that evening I had practiced my craft, basically just went over my old songs a few times making sure I remembered the words seeing that I hadn't heard nor sung those songs in a few years to that point, but I felt confident once I arrived at the show. While sitting back stage at the show waiting for my turn to perform I raced down four shots of Hennessy which re booted the drunkenness I had let wear off before I arrived.

By the time it was time for me to perform I was ripped. Vidal and Belnel Mike came on stage with me and ended up having to sing the words to my song seeing that I couldn't remember anything after the first line, I was so drunk that night that I didn't give a fuck about what had happened, the reality of the matter was that this was another embarrassing situation on my portfolio that proved that I'd truly hit rock bottom.

As time passed and it really seemed as if it was truly over between me and Asia, I realized I had feelings for her that I never knew I had. With what me and Donna were going through damn near every day, I actually found myself missing Asia at times even though I was still seeing her in the streets often.

At the top of Greenwood was a lil variety store that you could see from Big Mike's back porch and it had seemed like Asia was stopping by there every day as if she was trying to be seen. Me and Big Mike had become somewhat cordial at that time. Even though I knew he really didn't like me I'd find myself giving him game about life and the game that was so real that he had no choice but to respect it and listen.

Over the years me and Asia's niece Shavon had become pretty close, close to where she would call me uncle. Once me and Asia split up, Shavon reached out to me one day to let me know that regardless to me and Asia not being together any more she still viewed me as family.

After a brief conversation I invited her to meet me at the VFW post to have a couple drinks and basically catch up, seeing that I hadn't seen her in a while and appreciated her reaching out. Even though nothing intimate was said during us have a couple drinks, it did fuel my intuition of her having feelings for me but all said and done we drank then left in separate cars going in different directions.

Big Mike had a couple problems come his way, he left a kilo inside one of his trucks in his yard that ended up getting broke into and the coke stolen; that didn't hurt his pockets in any way, but did hurt his heart seeing that he knew that the only people that knew that it was in there was family. He came to Donna's house specifically to talk to me seeing that he was sure that I didn't have anything to do with it and needed someone to talk to. After I listened to him vent for about an hour, he came out and said, "Mizz, I'ma hit you with something to help you get back on your feet." In my mind I was saying this fuck nigga wanna put me on now because he needs a friend, but on the other hand I was happy to have the opportunity to be connected to all them bricks he was getting. Next day I met him on Greenwood Street and picked up a six deuce.

Over the next couple weeks, I had built up a nice clientele and was moving a lil bit for the first time in years, but instead of saving money I was spending buying clothes, drinks and smoking weed and hanging at the clubs and bars. In my mind I was thinking as long as I pay him what I owed him I can get more, and for the first time in a while I had my swagger back and felt confident like a nigga on his come up.

Me and Asia's niece Shavon had spoken a couple times more on the phone over the last month and had happened to make plans for me to come over and have drinks and smoke one night after I finished hustling. That night I paid Big Mike some money I owed him, then had him take me to the liquor store then drop me off over Shavon's crib. Us getting a lil money together led me to be more conversational with him than I should have been, with me telling him that I thought I could fuck Shavon if I wanted to. I was so tipsy and high and moving fast that I totally forgot about him and Asia being in contact. No more than twenty minutes of me being over Shavon's house, Asia came over with an attitude about me being over there. Asia wanted to play it like she just happened to come by and busted us, but her curiosity and anger wouldn't let her hold her composure long enough, walking in huffing and puffing like she was looking for someone. The first thing that came to my mind was this nigga mike ain't changed feeling that he had called Asia an told her where I was and what I just said to him.

While Asia and Shavon exchanged words about me being over there, I downplayed it as something innocent while calling me a cab and going outside to wait for it. A few minutes later Asia came out saying, "You don't have to leave cause I'm here," while getting in her car. Once I got in my cab, I called Shavon to see if she was alright, she said yeah, but she'll call me back because she was talking with her mother. That was the last time I spoke to Shavon on that level again. Ever since it's just been hi and bye when we see each other in the streets.

Of course, when I accused Mike of running his mouth he acted as if he hadn't spoken to Asia like I'm some type of idiot, but seeing that I still needed him to get paper I didn't make anything out of it. He didn't have any coke and said that there wouldn't be any for the next couple days, so I just laid low waiting on a call. Couple of days had passed and I still hadn't heard from Big Mike so I stopped through to holla at him. As soon as I saw him, I could tell from his body language that some fucking shit was going on. I asked him about the work, and he claimed that he was only able to get his hands on something small, just enough for him to make a couple moves. I knew that was bullshit and that he was just acting funny and caught feeling over me confronting him about telling Asia that I was over Shavon's. He wasn't gonna say anything to me about it, but his way of getting me back was going to be by playing games with the coke. Still, all this was partially my fault because I just moved damn near a half a key and didn't save any money. Upset as I was, I did my best not to show any sign of it as I just shook his hand and said, "Alright cool, hit me up when you get right before leaving."

I had about twelve hundred that I was just spending every day eating, smoking and drinking while I waited to see if he was going to hit me with another package.

One night me and Donna's brother Ducky was sitting down the street from Big Mike's house drinking some Remy when a conversation came up about Big Mike re-upping. Ducky told me that Big Mike just got five keys a few days ago which was actually the day before I spoke to him and he told me he only got a lil something. Ducky made a joke about Big Mike cutting me off which instantly upset me. Several times doing something to Big Mike came to mind for the lil shit he had been doing, but being that he was Donna's family I would always find myself refraining from it, but this time I felt as though a warning was in need to remind him of who I still am regardless if I'm broke and drunk.

I left Greenwood and went by Vidal's brother Eric's crib and got my pistol, then went back and let the clip off. Granted, I didn't have any intentions on hitting anyone, I knew that gunshots would draw the police and basically shut the block down for the night plus remind him that those shots could have easily been put through the driver's side of his whip when he pulls in at the top of the street! Apparently, someone saw me shooting and told the police it was me. Without knowing that I'd been fingered I went straight to Packies bar after to have me a drink still strapped with the pistol. After the shooting I got a call from Belnel Mike saying that detectives just left the tavern bar and grill in Mattapan asking the bartenders if they had seen me tonight. I left Packies and went back to Eric's crib to put the pistol back up then went to Donna's to get a quick shower to wash off any gunpowder that might have been on my hands, then changed clothes. Coming out of Donna's house I didn't see anybody but soon as I got in my car detectives pulled up in the parking lot with their guns drawn, yelling, "Get out!" and asking where's the gun. I didn't say anything and was taken into custody for the night.

Next morning in court the judge released me on a personal recognizance seeing that the police didn't find a gun, and the person that called saying that it was me shooting called from a pay phone not leaving their name to be questioned later. Due to a lack of evidence the case was ultimately dismissed on my next court date.

After that situation, I knew I wasn't getting any more work from Big Mike for sure, so there was nothing left for us to discuss. I was spending that lil money I had up every day without plans on how I was going to keep up the little clientele I had rebuilt. Things had gotten even worse when one rainy night I crashed my car speeding home after leaving the bar. Granted I didn't hurt myself, I totaled the car and only had option three on it which meant I wasn't getting anything from the insurance company for the crash. That fast with one mistake I was back to being without a car. Loyde from my hood had recently come home from some federal gun charges and granted we were pretty tight before he fell, with me drinking it was evident from the couple times we were around each other that our chemistry had changed. The second time I saw him I was pretty wasted and had started talking to him in a trying way, and even though he didn't respond I could tell that he was irritated and probably wanted to.

One day me and Duck had been out riding around with his cousin Jonnie drinking for hours, we had beers, wine coolers, on top of mixing white liquor and brown, and hadn't eaten all day. Duck got to the point where he was ready to go home while I was turned up wanting to drink more. All my niggas were on Nelson Street grilling and drinking, so I had Johnny and Duck drop me off over there before they dropped Duck home, While having a couple of shots of Crown Royal with Bum, I saw Loyde pulling up and figured I'd have him drop me off seeing that I was tipsy now myself and ready to go lay down; as soon as Loyde got on the porch I said, "Come on, drop me off."

"Naw, I can't right now. I just stopped by for a second before I go pick up my daughter."

I got upset because he said no and said, "Man, fuck this nigga."

Without saying anything Loyde stole me, the punch fucked me up. He hit me so hard that I got light headed and dizzy, though I didn't fall or get knocked out I wasn't in any condition to shoot a fair one, and it must have been visually noticeable by the way our boy DP jumped in between us saying, "Y'all chill, y'all chill." Loyde got in his car and took off while DP dropped me to the crib. Before dozing off I told myself that I was gonna kill him for putting his hands on me. I ain't never been disrespected like that and wasn't going to be whether I was an alcoholic or not.

After waking up later that night and sleeping some of that alcohol off I came to the realization that getting a gun in a situation like this would be some punk shit. Then I called an OG from my hood named Seawood to have him get in touch with Loyde to let him know that I wanted a fair one;

No more than twenty minutes later, Seawood called back saying, "Y'all niggas too cool for all this bullshit, but if it's a must y'all fight, then y'all can get it done in the morning, get that shit over with so y'all can go back to being homies."

I said, "Cool let's link first thing in the a.m."

He said, "Aight, make sure no weapons come out cause my name is on this."

"For sure it ain't going there, we just gotta get one in now."

He said, "Cool, I respect that; I'll holla in the a.m.," then hung up.

Next morning at close to ten o'clock I heard a horn and went to the window and saw Loyde sitting in his car on his cell phone. I threw on sweat pants and old sneakers preparing to fight, then came outside and got in his car and said, "What's up, let's do it."

Before saying anything to me he handed me his phone, and it was Seawood on there saying, "Y'all need to just chill but if y'all gonna fight, come get me so I can make sure it's just that."

I said, "Yeah, we bout to get it but we don't even need you, we grown men, we can just go somewhere, get it in, then shake hands after and be done with it."

He asked for Loyde and I handed him back his phone, they spoke for a second then he hung up, then I said, "We ain't gotta go far, go right here at the bottom of my street, so that way I can walk back if you don't wanna drop me off after."

Loyde paused for a second then said, "I didn't come here to fight with you, I rather us just talk about this shit. I apologize about swinging on you but I felt like you been coming at me ever since I've been home when me and you are supposed to be tighter than that; once I told you that I had to get my daughter and you said fuck this nigga I lost it."

Listening to him talk touched me knowing that in my straight mind I would have never said fuck that to someone saying that they gotta get their daughter as much as I love my own. I said, "Yeah, I feel you but swinging on me while I'm drunk was crazy."

He pulled over and said, "Hit me back and we'll be over it."

"Naw, I'm good," I said, the whole while thinking about everything, not just this situation but my whole life in general. It was like something came over me at that moment. I was hearing that lil voice in my head saying enough is enough, it's time to put that liquor down. I shook his hand knowing that me punching him back wasn't going to fix what I was internally going through, it was just time for change and I was convinced by the time he dropped me off that I was going to use this situation as a stepping stone because being disrespected is just something I never took lightly.

That night before going to sleep I poured out a lil more than a quarter pint of Remy which I would usually keep as a wake up, I had finally reached the point where I had enough. Having money wasn't even on my mind anymore I had dug myself so far in a hole that I knew in order for me to accomplish anything I had to focus on getting mentally and physically healthy again.

Waking up the next morning my mind was still convinced that I was done drinking, but my body hadn't yet got the memo seeing how nauseous I was from not having my usual sip I always did at that time. I had heard stories of how hard it was to kick a habit, but damn over the next few days my body and mind were going through things I couldn't have imagined. For one, I couldn't eat nor drink any fluids which made me dehydrated. The part of me that still wanted to drink had me moody, being upset at everyone I came across. Within the first week, I must have thought about quitting at least thirty times but looking at my daughter through a clear mind gave me the will to go on.

The first two weeks I just stayed in the house concerned that the temptation would be too much for me at first, but mentally and physically I immediately felt different. One day looking at myself in the mirror I noticed things about my looks that I hadn't noticed before. It was like I had been in an accident and now finally for the first time getting a chance to assess the damage. My face was skinny looking, with dark rims underneath my eyes looking like I hadn't slept in years. I was weighing around one fifty when normally I'm a lil over one seventy, I went from thoughts of killing Loyde for the disrespect to almost wanting to thank him for the kick start to regaining my life. I hadn't spoken to or told anybody about what I was attempting to do just in case I failed. Seeing Duck for the first in a couple weeks, he commented on how I looked instantly noticing a change in my appearance. Once I told him that I was done drinking he commended me on it, shaking my hand and hugging me like he was truly proud of me even though he had no intentions on stopping any time soon.

The first couple of weeks of hanging around my friends sober, felt slightly awkward, the temptation to drink was so strong that I would sit or stand around quiet to where you could easily tell that I had something on my mind. I would constantly say to myself in my mind, "you got this, Mike, you got this," reassuring myself of my own will power and mental strength. The more people that would say, "congrats, Mike, I'm glad for you, I heard about you not drinking anymore," the more obligated I felt to stay dedicated to staying sober. For the last few years I had lived angry under the assumption that people were glad that I fell off, now it was as if the same people that I thought liked seeing me down were the ones saying the kind of up uplifting words that I needed to hear while I was transitioning.

I had been sober for about eight weeks when Donna got a phone call from her aunt saying that the feds were at both of Big Mike's houses on Greenwood searching, she said they told her that they had already arrested Mike and a few other people but were still looking for her brother Duck. Before she hung up with her aunt, Duck called on the other line saying that his uncle called him saying that the feds had Big Mike and that there's a body warrant out for his arrest. After about three to five minutes of conversation Donna hung up looking sad and concerned, asking me to watch our daughter while she got Duck to bring him back here till he figured out what he was going to do. Getting back to our apartment, Duck was pretty distraught which was understandable due to the situation at hand. After talking for a few, and me giving him the best advice I could, he decided that he was ready to turn himself in. Donna called the police station saying that her brother was at her house and he believes that the feds are looking for him. Within minutes Boston Police and DA were at the front and back door knocking. Once they got there, he downed the rest of a fifth of Remy that he was sitting at the table drinking. Seeing that he was turning himself in, the police were rather calm and somewhat polite. Upon arrival, the sergeant in charge asked if he wanted to smoke one more cigarette before they arrested him, then actually waited for him to finish before cuffing him and taking him away.

Donna, Duck and Big Mike grew up tight so me knowing Donna was going through it emotionally stayed in for the rest of the night to watch our daughter and give whatever compassion I could. Granted, me and Mike weren't on good terms, but the real nigga in me still had me willing to do whatever it was I could to help him and Duck out. I had introduced Mike to Attorney Lepo a few years back when he got caught up for some drugs, so when Donna told me that that's who he wanted to hire to represent him I took it upon myself to go to Lepo's office to broker the deal and give Lepo any information I could that might be helpful.

Getting out to Lepo's office I found out that I was close to being arrested as well in the raid seeing that the feds had their eyes on me as one of the main targets. What kept me from being arrested was the various phone calls that were recorded of Big

Mike talking bad about me and expressing how he wished that I would just stay away from him and his house. On several occasions, he was recorded and quoted telling different females including my ex Asia that I was begging him to put me back on my feet, but it wasn't happening! Statements like that kept me for being indicted, seeing that I couldn't be in a conspiracy if the main man was constantly saying that he didn't like me and ain't giving me shit, so in a way his spiteful actions saved me an arrest.

Over the next two years, Duck and Big Mike were sentenced, Mike got fifteen years and Duck got five all while I was still sober and starting to have an appetite for some money. I was hustling, moving like a half of an ounce a month in fifties which really wasn't much, but enough to look decent and contribute to the bills and my weed habit, but coming from where I was a couple years ago being an alcoholic it definitely was an enhancement to my lifestyle. Every time I ran into someone who I hadn't seen in a few years they couldn't help themselves from telling me that I looked good, men and women. It wasn't that I would be wearing anything special, it was that I had put on some weight and started to care about my appearance again and it was evident that I had made some changes. Although I appreciated the compliments, I knew, in reality, that people saying that I looked good was really a testament to how bad I was looking when I was drinking. Being sober had also ignited my thrill to do music again. I put out two songs just to see how the streets were feeling it considering how long it' been since I recorded and how the era had changed. My old listeners and some new ones felt it, which led to me to completing a whole mix tape that I called "The Return: Volume One. "The streets loved it, it wasn't till then that I got on Facebook mainly to promote my music, but I also happened to start rebuilding some relationships with some people that I had fucked off or just blatantly disrespected when I was drunk.

The Boston rap scene embraced my comeback. I started meeting a lot of the new up and coming talent which sparked the idea of starting my own independent label, shortly after putting out a couple of videos on You Tube from my CD volume one. I followed up dropping volume two featuring a few of the artists I'd recently met, from my opinion and what the streets were saying volume two was as hard as volume one if not harder. I felt more like me than ever, even when I was recording with Ray [Benzino] I didn't feel this enthusiastic about my music as I did in these past six months. Barbara Williams, a local show promoter, got ear to the buzz I had recreated and reached out to me asking if I'd like to perform at a venue she had control of saying that it would be good promotion and that she'd definitely make it comfortable for me and my team. I agreed and spent the next couple weeks preparing for my first performance since I was drunk on stage with Ray [Benzino] six years ago.

Pulling up at the club called Sammies that night is a moment that I'll never forget -- seeing my name on the lit up billboard and a packed crowd inside ready to see me perform really touched me. I was truly proud of myself for putting that liquor down knowing that if it wasn't for that none of this would be happening. The night went well. It was a mixed crowd, the younger kids came to hear me perform songs from both of my latest mix tapes while my peers came to hear me perform the songs that they grew up listening to and were familiar with. Once I started to rock my most familiar song, "Treason," it was as if everyone knew it from how the crowd sang along with me, word for word, from top to bottom. That night turned out to be more inspirational than I could have ever imagined it being, that once it was over I was truly convinced that my life hadn't yet passed me by.

Things were looking up for me somewhat, my name was ringing bells again on the music scene, I'd been sober for over three years plus I reconnected with a couple of people like Big Chuck from Four Corners and Bob Francis that were pretty well connected in the music industry and were willing to partner up with me on whatever musical endeavors I had in mind. The way I just up and stopped drinking showed a certain strength that people wanted to be around and I learned early that as long as you're connected and working the money and accolades will come; the fact that financially I was basically just maintaining didn't seem to bother me seeing that I had a legitimate plan, till the day Donna came home from the clinic telling me that she's pregnant again. From that conversation I knew that it was time for me to go full speed in these streets again, between trying to build a label and having a nine-year old daughter growing up wanting things and now a newborn on the way just maintaining was no longer going to cut it.

Over the years I've tried several times to communicate and build a relationship with my first born son Michael but his anger from my absence always got in the way. It so happened that him and his friends considered themselves to be the new Junior Corbets, he also had a friend they called Lil Snoop that rapped and was anxious to meet me after hearing about the label I was starting and my legacy in the hood in general. Whether I liked Snoop's music or not, I knew this would be a good opportunity to start communicating with my son so I reached back out to him asap. After speaking with Lil Snoop, I told him to go get Michael and meet me on Corbet and he did. On the way to drop Michael home after dropping Snoop off we started to talk more intensely about my past and our relationship. Although I'm his father I had to respect that a lot of time had passed and he had grown up, so opposed to trying to dictate things I listened to him trying to get to really know him and see where his mind was at. I took the blame for everything and expressed to him how much respect I have for his mother and his grandfather for doing the best they could without my help for the years I was drinking. He told me that his mother had told him that I was sober, and that he respected me for being able to bounce back. Once he got out of the car, I lit my joint up and cried, partially because I was so happy about the chemistry we had knowing that better days were on the way.

On the other side, looking at him and hearing him talk like a grown man reminded me of all the time I missed and how that liquor destroyed me, but still in all I was at a point in my life that I've prayed for several times and I made sure I thanked God for it that night.

The next day I picked my son up to bring him by my house to see Donna and his sister. My daughter Maya is a very loving person. So, knowing that her brother was coming over made her extremely happy to the point that once he walked in the house, she ran over to him and hugged him as if she knew him for years. We spent a couple hours at my house just talking and eating Chinese food and of course Maya stayed by his side the whole time, happy to have her older brother with her.

Part of my dream of building my own record label was to be able to provide opportunities for these young kids to get out of the streets, on top of us becoming successful, so involving them in anything illegal was never my intention but after speaking with all eight of them, with exception to my female artists, they told me that in some sort of fashion they were all selling low quantities of drugs which strayed me away from my initial plan. On top of everything that was going on, my partners Eight and Kenyatta from Belnel had been fighting to overturn their natural life convictions. When the incident was supposed to have taken place Eight was a juvenile and under a new law that President Obama passed that made him automatically eligible for an appeal. Donna, being pregnant, had already made my decision to get back on official but the thought of my niggas coming home after thirteen years and I not be able to hold them down until they got back on their feet was something that I couldn't fathom, so I started reaching out to some niggas doing pretty good for themselves in the game to see what I could make happen.

Over the next few months Donna had my third child, a handsome lil boy that looked just like my oldest son Michael, so when it was time to name him nothing else came to mind beside Michael McNeil the Third. Everybody that knew me knew I was sober now for close to four years and had just had another child which signified that I was living a more laid back lifestyle, as opposed to how fast paced and wild I used to be. It was no secret that I could get money seeing that it was rumored that I started a lot of the trends that were going on at that point in time like stretching coke for one. I had a few dudes wanting to be responsible for putting me back on, and feeling as though I'd owe them one and would be by their side if it so happened that some drama came about, seeing that it was well known that I'd kill if the situation called for it. This nigga I grew up with named Dirty Mike's lil brother Dave was someone that watched me get money and thugging when he was younger and had plenty of respect for me. Dave was riding around here in foreign cars and was said to be getting bricks. So, once we bumped into each other one day at a gas station I struck a conversation up with him that would eventually lead to us to doing some business together, and within an hour of our first conversation he was at my house dropping off a package. The work was good, by the end of that night I had cooked it up and handed it out to all of the artists I was working with telling them that we were in this short-term and that these are just measures I gotta go through in order to finance the company.

Within days everyone got back to me with the correct amount of money they owed for the work, and from there I knew that this was the start of something prosperous. Meanwhile, the verdict had been pronounced and it was official, Eight and Kenyatta were coming home within a couple months, their charges were lessened to second degree murder charges which meant that the thirteen years they'd spent locked up would be a wrap and they'd be released with time served. I was ecstatic. I just had a new child, me and my oldest son were becoming one. I was back on my feet making thousands of dollars barely doing anything, plus starting my own label and I had a couple of mix tapes out; on top of being sober I couldn't wait for them to get out. Kenyatta came home first with Eight coming shortly after him. We were immediately inseparable, it was just like the good old days, we were together so much that homies in the hood came up with a nickname for us calling us the Big Three.

Both of them wasted no time getting to the money, within a month Kenyatta bought a convertible BMW 645 and shortly after me and Eight bought matching blue five thirty-five BMWs. Things between me and Dave were short lived seeing that once I had enough money to buy whatever coke I needed to run my business I cut him off. Dave was young and was into an immature way of living that I knew would one day get me into some type of trouble if I dealt with him long enough. I knew it was essential that if I sold drugs again at this pace I do it very low key which was the total opposite of what was going on, seeing that I had heard from a few people over that short amount of time that me and Dave were making moves together.

The last time me and Dave spoke was in the beginning of March, the night I gave him the last of a couple dollars I owed him knowing that, that was the last time I intended on dealing with him. He was cool and I appreciated him helping me get to the point where I was currently at having a couple cars now and thousands of dollars stacked. But I could feel by how much he talked that he was going to jail soon and I knew that in order for me not to take that ride with him it was time for me to shift. Now that I had paper to buy work it was easy for me to find another connect with some good shit. I hooked up with an old school player that had it but was real low key about his business, the way he moved fitted me well.

Over the next two months me and my artists ran through several keys quickly, making me his number one customer. Music was being recorded, and my artists had a newfound confidence about themselves. Things were happy in my household. Me and Donna were at a point in our relationship that we'd never been, me and my oldest son were tight like father and son are supposed to be, and Eight and Kenyatta were home from prison. Everyone was eating and things were looking up.

Then that morning came when the feds came knocking at my door with a body warrant for my arrest. The look in my daughter's eyes while they were cuffing me hit me like a car crash. My son was too young to understand what was happening, but

I could tell he could sense that something bad was happening. Donna knows the game and happened to see one of the cops snooping around while I slipped on my shoes and said, "I'd appreciate if you don't look through my things without having a search warrant." Before leaving out handcuffed I asked a female agent if I could kiss my daughter once before I leave knowing that it would be a long before I'd have the opportunity to again. Seeing that they didn't search my house I still had all my money which made me feel good considering the situation. At least I knew that my family had enough to be alright till things got figured out. On the way to the station I asked the fed agent driving if I was the only one picked up on this indictment, then he giggled and said, "No, it's close to fifty of you guys."

My first thought was *damn, my low key connect wasn't as low key as I thought* figuring this was concerning him, but getting to the station, I only saw a bunch of gang bangers that I'd seen in the streets before but didn't know personally. So, I still couldn't figure out what or who linked me to this indictment. A good thirty minutes passed, then the feds arrived with Dave and put him in my cell. All I could do was put my head down and say to myself damn! This nigga! Now being sure that the indictment concerned him, I had no choice but to try to think of some positives like for one I never spoke to him about drugs on the phone and two, I hadn't dealt with this dude in months so it's going to be interesting to see what evidence they have against me and if it's strong enough to hold up in court.

As if things weren't bad enough, two weeks after my arrest, I called home and Donna crushed me… telling me that my oldest son Michael had just been picked up and charged with murder!

To be continued!